Cover Design by:
Elaine McCarthy and Anne Parisi

Cover Art by:
Anne Parisi

MONAGCO PUBLISHERS

ISBN:09709372-1-0

Morbid Curiosity:
Celebrity Tombstones Across America
Volume 1

Photographs and Stories by:
Elaine McCarthy

To my loving children Jackie, Maddie and Meaghan, who can now go to the zoo, beach, park and anywhere else they want me to take them, because the book IS DONE! Most of all I hope they have realized that I have not renamed them SHHHH! Thanks for putting up with me.

Table of Contents

Introduction

As time goes by, things obviously change. Especially when it comes to Hollywood. Today's movie stars have substituted gowns and coiffed hair for a baseball cap and sweats. And the same apparently goes for their final place of burial.

At one time movie stars lived lavishly and guarded their promiscuous lifestyles. Yet they left behind monumental grave sites to remember them by. Today the trends have changed and most celebrities air their dirty laundry shamelessly, while closely guarding their remains. More and more are now opting for unmarked private graves or they bequeath their cremated remains to loved ones, leaving no location for a fan to mourn their dearly departed idol.

Perhaps the celebrities of the past were so egotistical that the very thought of dying without eternal fame would haunt them forever. So in an attempt to become an eternal icon they erected these beautiful tributes to themselves, so fans could mourn them in the style they deserve. My photographs have documented the many tombstones erected by these stars and their families nationwide. Some opting for a traditional lavish Hollywood burial, while other felt the obligation to return home.

Another purpose of this book is to recreate the final moments of their lives as they died. Answering the questions: Is so and so dead? How did they die and when? Most of these celebrities have come from meager beginnings only to be thrust into fame and excessive fortune. Some weathered this change gracefully, while others did a tailspin into an early death.

My book answers these questions and more. Details about their abuses, illnesses, deaths, exhumations, corpse thefts, hearse-jackings, funerals, reported hauntings, controversies, and last words have been told. In Morbid Curiosity, Volume 1, you will read the latest on over 150 humans, a couple of famous animals and one unforgetable puppet. My sources have been from death certificates, accident reports, obituaries, authorized biographies and anything else I can get my hands on.

My travels have taken me over 30,000 miles throughout every nook and cranny of our beautiful country, documenting each and every tombstone listed in this book. Along the way I have met great people who have accommodated me in my quest for the sometimes elusive grave. During my travels I was fortunate to sometimes meet people who had interacted with these stars prior to their fame. For example, I met some older men in their sixties/seventies who claimed to have gone to high school with Jayne Mansfield. As they were regaling me with tales of "Jaynie" I couldn't help but think that if she were still around, she too would be their age. Death has turned her into an icon, frozen in time, forever young and beautiful.

Hopefully you will find this book an invaluable tool in which you too can begin your own adventure in finding these graves. I have tried to keep things simple and easy to follow, because despite my extensive travel, I have problems finding my way out of a paper bag. Seeing these graves are perhaps the closest you will ever come to your favorite stars. It is quite an experience to see the waterfalled grave of Al Jolson or a mega star like Frank Sinatra, in the "cheap seats."

There are some do's and don't's when visiting these graves. Some cemeteries, like Forest Lawn Memorial Park in southern California, discourages people from looking for celebrity graves. But as long as you are respectful and discrete you shouldn't have any problems. For each grave I have written pretty clear instructions on where you will be welcomed in your grave hunting quest. Some cemeteries don't mind; in fact they encourage people with celebrity maps.

Although the majority of celebrity graves are located in either California and New York, don't be surprised if you have a famous person in your town. I lived in Las Vegas for two years before I realized that Redd Foxx was buried in a cemetery just two blocks away from my house.

Sit back, enjoy the gossip, and admire the tombstones of your favorite star. I had a lot of fun putting this together, I hope you will enjoy reading my book.

JOAN CRAWFORD

1908 — 1977

STEELE

ALFRED M

1901 — 1959

Ferncliff Cemetery, Hartsdale, New York

Chapter 1: Glamour Girls
Joan Crawford
March 23, 1903 - May 10, 1977

Lucille Fay LeSueur who later changed her name because it sounded too much like 'La sewer,' was born in Waco, Texas. There is much discrepancy as to her real date of birth due to the fact that Texas did not require people to record birth certificates until 1908.

The family lived, according to Joan, "in a little drab rented house on the wrong side of the tracks." Her father who was a contractor, found the pressures of family life too much; so he abandoned the family. Joan would not see her father again until after she attained fame. By then they awkwardly attempted to have a relationship that really existed in name only.

He spent his last day visiting Joan while she was on the set making a movie. Having only a few minutes to spend with him, she was called to do a scene. As she was leaving she looked across the stage and saw that his eyes were filled with tears. Perhaps he realized that he threw away something priceless, a relationship with his daughter. He waved goodbye, blew a kiss, and left. She never saw him again.

Joan did not start her career in show business via acting. She was first a dancer in a chorus line where she danced her way across the mid-west to New York. Once in New York she was spotted by a big shot from MGM who was looking for girls to sign for the studio. He wanted to test the reluctant Joan for a picture contract. At first she was not interested because she only wanted to be a dancer. But her then stage manager, Nils T. Granlund, convinced her to go. She tested twice and forgot about it thinking nothing would come of it. It was around Christmas time and the unsuspecting Joan left to go to Kansas City to visit her mother.

While visiting her mother the unenthusiastic Joan received a telegram:

"YOU ARE PUT UNDER A FIVE-YEAR CONTRACT STARTING AT SEVENTY-FIVE DOLLARS A WEEK. LEAVE IMMEDIATELY FOR CULVER CITY, CALIFORNIA CONTACT MGM KANSAS CITY OFFICE FOR TRAVEL EXPENSES."

On New Year's Day, 1925, Joan boarded the Sunset Limited for California and reluctantly embarked on a movie career. Her reign at MGM lasted until 1943. As with the other actresses, she was put in movies that *they* thought would be marketable. For Joan, this left her frustrated because she was denied roles that better suited her. Finally fed up with bad pictures, she pleaded with Louis B. Mayer to be cast in *"Madame Curie"* and *"Random Harvest."* But by now, Mayer had a new favorite, Greer Garson and was no long giving Joan the roles she deserved. After refusing Joan's request, she demanded to be let out of her contract. Mayer was at first shocked, and pleaded for her to stay. But Joan argued that the studio's producers and the public had grown tired of her, and that she needed a fresh start to jump start her career. After some thought he agreed and let her out of her contract. She was leaving the studio the same way she had arrived eighteen years before -alone. The final insult was that no one came to wish her well or to thank her for the years of service to MGM. Until the mid-fifties, she remained a free agent, doing films that she hoped would help resurrect her career.

Meanwhile at a party, she was introduced by friend Earl Blackwell to Pepsi-Cola president, Alfred Steele. After much dating they married in the penthouse of the Flamingo Hotel in Las Vegas. Having three failed marriages in her past, perhaps due to her fame, she did not want to add another to her record. She insisted on being referred to as *Mrs. Alfred Steele,* instead of Joan or Miss Crawford. Despite all her efforts, the four year marriage did end, by his sudden death of a heart attack.

Broke and alone she had no alternative but to return to work. She was however, able to co-star in such great roles as *"What Ever Happened to Baby Jane?"* The film grossed nine million dollars and brought new a vitality to her career and also to the career of Bette Davis who starred with her and was in the same boat professionally. To perpetuate the success from the first picture, the two were re-teamed in *"Hush....Hush, Sweet Charlotte."* Unfortunately this would prove to be a missed opportunity for Joan as she was admitted to the hospital for stress. While there, they hastily re-cast Olivia de Havilland in her role. Thankfully for Joan and her fans she would star in the next blockbuster, *"Mildred Pierce."*

By the 1970's roles were hard to come by and she decided to wind down what little that was left of her career. She telephoned Stan Kamen, at the William Morris Agency and told him that she just wanted to "cool it" for a while.

With her semi-retirement came the rekindling of the faith she had adopted in the 1930's, Christian Science. Soon Joan began to seek private counsel from a Christian Science practitioner, Mrs. Markham. Her new found dedication to her religion brought on new disciplines in her life, she quit smoking and drinking. And as time went on Joan spent more and more time alone spending her last days in the company of her CS practitioner and a fan who installed herself in Joan's home.

Near the end of her life, Joan had become ill with great pain. All her life she had refused to burden others with her problems and this time was going to be no different. She now stopped visiting people and allowed no one visited her. When people did call, she always tried to maintain a cheerful attitude.

Her 73rd birthday arrived and with it an outpouring of flowers and greetings. Unfortunately her health was rapidly deteriorating. A hospital bed was delivered to her home to make her more comfortable. It allowed her to sit up and watch television with less pain. As her illness progressed her back hurt and she lost weight. No one knew what was afflicting her, because she would not see a doctor nor take any medicine per her CS beliefs. It was most likely that she was dying of cancer of the liver or pancreas.

By April, 1977, Joan weighed a mere eighty-five pounds and her strength had waned considerably. On the rare occasion that a close friend might visit, they would plead with Joan to see a doctor. Joan's reply was, "I'll be damned if I'll let myself end up in a cold hospital room with a tube up my nose and another up my ass!"

By the end of the month, Mrs Markham was coming to Joan's apartment everyday. Joan told her not to tell anyone how sick she was. Mrs. Markham begged her to check into a Christian Science nursing home. Stubborn Joan just wanted to stay home.

On the morning of May 10, 1977, it is rumored that Joan got out of bed and insisted on making breakfast for her housekeeper and the fan. After she was done she returned to bed, to watch her soap operas. Joan called out to make sure everyone was eating the breakfast that she had prepared. Soon after was dead of an apparent heart attack brought on by the rigors of cancer.

A medical examiner said that her death was attributed to acute coronary occlusion, a heart attack. She was cremated and her urn placed next to her husband Alfred Steele at Ferncliff Cemetery in Hartsdale, NY. Her funeral, which was suppose to be private, had two hundred people who arrived at the funeral home to the stars, Frank E. Campbell, to send off their Joan.

Ferncliff Cemetery
Secor Road
Hartsdale, New York
Directions: Take the N.Y.S. Thruway north to Central Ave. Go about five miles or so until you see a sign for the City of Hartsdale on your right. Now look for W. Hartsdale Ave (100A) and make a left. Go to Secor Road and make another left the cemetery is about a mile on your right. Once inside the cemetery ask for a celebrity map. The office is attached to the main mausoleum so go to the lobby. With your back to the main entrance make a left and go to the end of the hall. Then right, then left, then left again and then one more right. Straight ahead you should see an elevator. She is in the 1st room on your right as you enter. She's in the middle of the left wall. While I was there someone left a lovely framed photo of Joan.

Bette Davis
April 5, 1908 - October 6, 1989
Like her colleague Joan Crawford, Bette's first interest was dancing. It was not until she reached high school that the acting bug bit. From there she developed into one of Hollywood's greatest actresses. Considered "Hollywood Royalty," she remained accessible to her fans and the media.

DAVIS

RUTH FAVOR DAVIS
SEPTEMBER 16 1885 – JULY 1 1961

BARBARA DAVIS BERRY
OCTOBER 25 1929 – JULY 18 1979

BETTE DAVIS
APRIL 5 1908 – OCTOBER 6 1989

"She did it the hard way"

Forest Lawn Memorial Park, Hollywood Hills

Long after her film career had ebbed, Bette did everything possible to maintain her public persona. One venue she frequented was the late night talk shows. Seemingly oblivious she ignored the new social order of guarded speech and on air smoking. Bette will be remembered for speaking her mind about anything and anyone while encircling her poor host in a cloud of second hand smoke.

As her health began to fail her, she fought hard to maintain what was left of her life. Not by giving up her bad habits, but through her sheer stubbornness to die. She had overcome a stroke, a broken hip, and a bout with cancer all in 1983. Finally, on October 6, 1989, cancer that spread throughout her body, ending her life.

Bette had once said that she wanted a funeral befitting a star of her magnitude: "I think I would like it to be a terrible shock. I would hate to pass on after a long, lingering illness. It should be something sudden. And I don't want anyone sending money to any little charity, instead of flowers. I want flowers at the service. I want millions of flowers. I want it to be ludicrous with flowers. I have chosen a song I want played. It was one of my favorites, 'I Wish You Love.' Hopefully, it will make everyone who loves me, weep. I want everyone to weep. Cop-i-ous-ly."

Instead she had a small private service. She was buried in a black evening gown with pearls. Her casket was inscribed with, "The Empress." and placed in a white marble sarcophagus adorned with a beautiful statue of a young woman, (whom Bette felt resembled her daughter). Bette is buried along side her mother, and sister. A sister whom had other ideas for burial, for which Bette abruptly changed. Bette got her way with her sister's burial and the last word, her epitaph reads: "She did it the hard way."

Forest Lawn Memorial Park - Hollywood Hills
6300 Forest Lawn Drive
Los Angeles, California

Directions: Take the 101 to the 134 go east until you see Forest Lawn Dr. Get off and follow the road to the cemetery entrance. Ask for a map at the gate, but don't ask for any celebrity directions or they will throw you out. Follow the main road, Memorial Drive to Evergreen Drive make a left. Then at Ascension Road make a right. Follow this to Vista Lane, left. You will be in front of the Court of Remembrance, her sarcophagus is in front to your left.

Ava Gardner
December 24, 1922 - January 25, 1990

In the little southern town of Grabtown, North Carolina, a not yet sultry Ava Gardner appeared on the scene on Christmas eve, 1922. Her parents were tobacco farmers who were dirt poor due to the economic situation that existed for most in the 20's and 30's. The last born of seven children, Ava enjoyed going barefoot and being a tomboy as a young girl.

By age 18, her stunning beauty was more than apparent. Her brother-in-law who ran a photography studio in New York, put a photo of the young Ava in the window of his studio. As the story goes, someone affiliated with MGM saw it, and made inquiries as to who the beauty was. Ava's brother-in-law put him in touch with Ava and soon she was signed to a movie contract.

Her first 17 roles were only bit parts. Her first starring role didn't come until 1946 where she was cast in a B western, *"Whistle Stop."* While on a loan to Universal Studios she made her first big hit *"The Killers,"* which officially launched her career that same year.

Although successful Ava grew tired with the Hollywood scene and lifestyle. She was given only bit parts or bad roles. It was the same old song for her as for any other sexy actress, she was put in roles that she couldn't display her real acting abilities. The last thing on the studios head's minds was whether or not she was satisfied professionally. Their only concern was whether or not a film would sell and who they could get to make it marketable.

Frustrations with the studios, and three failed marriages to Mickey Rooney, Artie Shaw and Frank Sinatra where enough to make Ava leave Hollywood for Spain. There she made a few more films and later moved to London.

AVA LAVINIA
GARDNER
DEC. 24. 1922
JAN. 25. 1990

Sunset Memorial Gardens, Smithfield, North Carolina

JANET GAYNOR GREGORY

1906 — 1984

Hollywood Forever Cemetery, Hollywood, California

Her last film was *"Karem,"* which she made in 1981. Soon her health started to decline and she suffered a couple strokes which did slow her down. As she recuperated she worked on her autobiography in London entitled *"Ava, My Story."* Although she finished it just prior to her death, she never saw the book in print.

She died of pneumonia at the age of 67. Miss Gardner's body was flown back to Smithfield, North Carolina where she was buried in the family plot.

When I visited Ava's grave I camped out with my kids in a Smihfield campground. It was one of those towns where you feel very safe because everyone was so nice. At the campground, the hosts who were an elderly couple had a bon fire for all the guests. I attempted to get some stories about Ava from them. One of the things they did tell me was that on her visits home, she was unchanged by Hollywood and appeared to be the same hometown girl that left years ago. And although extremely elegant, she was always friendly to fans and the local residents.

Her grave is located about two exits back from where we stayed in the town of Smithfield. Also the town has a museum devoted to her successful career in Hollywood. After I visited her grave which was clearly marked with signs pointing to it's location, I made my way to the museum.

It is very deceptive how such a small building could hold so much. There was a collection of over 100,000 items, including original scripts, photos, costumes and other personal things belonging to Ava.

I was told by the museum curator that in December the town has a big birthday celebration for her. Although the town has dedicated this time to pay tribute to their famous daughter, it is also an opportunity to attract other fans worldwide to share in the down home festivities.

Sunset Memorial Gardens
Hwy 70
Smithfield, North Carolina
Directions: Take I-95 to the Smithfield exit (Hwy 70 Bus.). You will see a billboard prior to the exit with Ava info. Go north on Hwy 70 (Market Street) take that until you come to a fork in the road. The Cemetery is in the center just follow the signs. The museum is 3 miles away on 205 South 3rd Street.

Janet Gaynor
October 6, 1906 - September 14, 1984
Laura Gainor was born in Philadelphia, Pennsylvania. While still a child her parents left the East Coast for San Francisco, California where she graduated in 1923. After high school she moved to Los Angeles where she enrolled in secretarial school and later she worked in a shoe store for a mere $18 per week. One thing good about working at the shoe store was that it was located in an area filled with studios. So being in the right venue for acting she thought she would give it a try.

For two years she landed bit parts so small that she wasn't even given credit for her efforts. This never bothered her because she believed in the philosophy, 'that all good things come to those who wait.' With a slight variation in the spelling of her name "Gaynor", Janet didn't have to wait long before she would be cast as leading lady in the 1926 film, *The Johnstown Flood*." The 20 year old did such a superb performance as the character of "Anne Burger" that the studio heads soon realized that they had a star on their hands and put her in four more films with the lead role.

When silent films made the transition to 'talkies,' she was one of the few actresses of that time to survive the change. Not only did she go on to a prosperous acting career, she became a top draw at the theaters throughout the early 1930's. But soon that would end for her, as another saying goes, "All good things must end." In 1938, Janet didn't appear in another film until 1957's "*Bernardine*." As her career waned, she left gracefully before hitting bottom. After all she did have a stellar career while it lasted and was the first actress to win an Oscar for *Best Actress*.

JEAN HARLOW

Forest Lawn Memorial Park, Glendale, California

Like most actresses of her time she made the transition to television. In early fall, 1982, Janet, and her husband Paul traveled to San Francisco to appear on best friend, Mary Martin's show, "Over Easy." On September 5th, Mary, Janet, Paul and Ben Washer (Mary's Manager) headed for Chinatown for dinner. While en route, their taxi was broad sided by a DWI repeat offender. Washer was killed at the scene. Mary suffered a shattered pelvis, two broken ribs, and a punctured lung. Paul sustained a bruised kidney, broken ribs and whiplash. Next to Ben, Janet's injuries seemed to be most life threatening. She had been pinned between Ben and Mary during impact and broke all but one of her ribs, ruptured her bladder, broke her collar bone, ruptured a kidney and sustained multiple fractures in her pelvis. Upon arrival at San Francisco General's Trauma Center, she underwent five hours of surgery and was later listed in critical condition.

For the next four months she had undergone six additional operations and then was finally released. Paul and Janet returned to Singing Trees Ranch in early 1983 to recuperate. Still she needed additional surgeries that would take place for the next year and a half. She was strong in spirit but physically weak and in constant pain.

In early September, 1984 she was admitted to Palm Springs' Desert Hospital for the last time. With her husband and son, Robert at her side she quietly passed away on September 14th. The cause of death was listed as pneumonia and renal failure.

Hollywood Forever Cemetery
6000 Santa Monica Blvd.
Hollywood, California

Directions: Take the 134 west to 101 south to Santa Monica Blvd. (Between Gower Street and Van Hess Avenue) Once in the cemetery if you want, get a map, (they cost $5.00). If not follow my directions and you should be able to find her. Make a left at the first road outside the office. Keep going until you see Cecil B. DeMille's white crypt, park. This is section 8 the only section with a lake in it. If you bought the map she's #71. Continue to walk towards the Douras mausoleum, staying close to the lake. To your left you'll see a clump of tall (spruces, I think) trees and some tall grass. She is right around there.

Jean Harlow
March 3, 1911 - June 7, 1937

Known for her platinum blond hair, she took Hollywood by storm in the 1930's. Her movie persona was that of a tough girl in such films as *"The Public Enemy"* and *"Red Headed Woman."* Later she made the transformation from "tough girl" to "dumb blond." Little did she know that she would become a trail blazer for future blond sex kittens like Marilyn Monroe, and Jayne Mansfield.

Born Harlean Carpenter in Kansas City, Missouri, she eloped to Hollywood at the age of sixteen with a businessman. Restless, she sought bit parts in films. After separating from her husband she wormed her way into an early 'talkie,' *"Hells Angels."* The public instantly fell in love with her and a star was born.

Unfortunately she did not have much time on earth to enjoy her new stardom. Her young life was cut short at age 26, from uremic poisoning. Jean had been in declining health a year prior to her death, which some speculate was attributed to her honeymoon night beating that she received from her husband, Paul Bern. His inability to have sex with his young bride, frequently threw him into rages that were directed at Jean.

Her problems were compounded by a mother who wanted full control of her life and career. She used her Christian Scientist religion to prevent any medical intervention and stymied Louis B. Mayer's attempt to have his private physician examine Jean. Finally, as her health took a sudden turn for the worse, she was rushed to the Good Samaritan Hospital where she died at 11:38 am from acute nephritis and uremia, kidney failure. One doctor who had seen Jean just prior to her death, felt that with earlier treatment he might have been able to save her with a newly discovered sulphur drug,. But that is poor speculation, because being that there were no dialysis machines or perfected kidney transplants at that time, she most likely would have died anyway.

SUSAN HAYWARD CHALKLEY

She is entombed in a very beautiful crypt in Forest Lawn that was purchased by fiancé William Powell. The Sanctuary where she is buried is marked with HARLOW, but her crypt merely says *"baby."* There were three spaces purchased, one for Jean, her mother, and him. His crypt remains vacant due to his later decision to be buried with his wife, Mousie, in Palm Springs, California.

Forest Lawn Memorial Park
1712 S. Glendale Ave
Glendale, California
Great Mausoleum, Sanctuary of Benediction

Directions: From the Golden State Fwy., to Los Feliz Blvd (east), off ramp. Go east on Los Feliz Blvd. To Glendale Avenue make a right. The main gate is on your left. Jean is located in the Great Mausoleum which is not open to the general public. If you are invited in by a property owner go to the Sanctuary of Benediction. She is in a beautiful room at the end on the left.

Susan Hayward
June 30, 1917 - March 14, 1975

Edythe Marrenner was born in Brooklyn, New York to an impoverished environment. Growing up poor plus a car accident that left her with a permanent handicap only hardened Susan. Instead of melting under pressure, she grew to have great inner strength that would later help her conquer the wolves of Hollywood.

Throughout her life she dreamed of escaping the poverty of Brooklyn for the brightlight of Hollywood. She wanted to be an actress more than anything else. To succeed in this would make her a "somebody." The only person who had faith in her talents was her father. Her introduction into show business was a tough one though. According to her first agent, Ben Medford, her Selznick tests were terrible. Selznick felt that she couldn't act and that she wasn't likeable. Susan's shyness was her biggest detriment. Her nervousness of people, caused her to shut down and appear to be unfriendly. This was another obstacle she needed to conquer before she could succeed in Hollywood.

It was thankful for her that Ben saw the potential to stick with her. In order to succeed they needed a plan. The first thing they had to do was to find her a new name, and Susan Hayward was now reborn. A name change and a new test launched her career almost immediately. Later she would go on to make many successful movies. Even after enduring four losing tries for an Oscar that she desperately wanted, she finally earned it for her role in *"I Want to Live."*

Her biggest contribution to Hollywood was her stance against how actresses were cast. No more would an actress have to succumb to the indignities of the "casting couch" to get a part. Susan fought hard against it and proved to other actresses that one could make it based on their talents.

Her personal life was not so steady and continued to be a series of ups and downs: she survived a suicide attempt, a scandalous affair that made headlines almost ruining her career, the death of her second husband, and a narrow escape from a fire in her apartment. The only she couldn't beat was the cancer that killed her.

In December, 1972, while visiting some friends in Georgetown, Washington, D.C., she suffered a convulsive seizure. After much persuasion she went to Georgetown University Hospital for extensive testing. The tests revealed that Susan was suffering from multiple inoperable brain tumors. The doctor's prognosis was not good; they said that she only had months to live. Little did they know who they were dealing with. Susan had an incredible will to live and she was not going without a fight. Her doctor, Lee Siegel, said that her two and a half year struggle to keep herself alive was absolutely extraordinary. It was amazing that she stayed alive as long as she did with this kind of illness. There is no other case like it in medical history.

Susan was a devout Catholic and requested that Father Thomas Brew, a friend of her second husband Eaton, visit her and give her communion prior to her returning to Emory for a brain scan. On October 17, 1974 she took a turn for the worse and slipped into a coma. Everyone thought that this was the end for her. Instead four days later, she emerged from the coma as if nothing happened. A nurse admitted that her survival was nothing short of a miracle. "The woman refused to die."

By late October, Susan was back in Los Angeles. Prior to leaving Emory her doctor warned her that the tumors would eventually take away her ability to speak, then her memory would fail, and then finally she would lose the ability to swallow. At that point, her only alternative would be to be fed intravenously or she would die.

With each day her condition worsened, but still she would not give up her fight. She kept as active as she could and in touch with friends. Her body weight had shriveled to a mere eighty pounds and she was now completely paralyzed. Despite her weight loss, her face never changed. She never wore make up and still she was beautiful.

At the end of February, she could no longer swallow and was advised to check into a hospital which she refused to do. Her lungs were beginning to fill with fluids; and yet she kept struggling to stay alive with every ounce of strength left in her. Susan was conscious at all times, until she suffered another seizure and went in a coma again. Even in a coma she put up a fight to stay alive.

Finally on March 14, 1975, Susan's eyes flew open and at that moment, she was gone. Her physician requested that her body be taken to Century City Hospital, where an autopsy was performed.

Susan's son Tim tried his best to honor his mother's wishes for a small service. He gave the Hollywood press an incorrect date of burial, so they would not descend on the small cemetery in Carrollton. The news leaked out locally and people lined the seven miles of highway from the Alton Funeral Home to the cemetery. On Sunday, March 16th, her local fans watched as her body was driven by.

In a chilly drizzle, sons Timothy and Gregory, helped to carry their mother's rose and orchid covered coffin to the grave site and like her husband, Susan was buried. The grave is located on the east side of the church which faced her home at 320 Sunset Boulevard.

Our Lady of Perpetual Help Catholic Church
Old Center Point Road
Carrollton, Georgia
Directions: Take Hwy 61 to Hwy 27 make a right. Look for an Ingles Supermarket on your left and an intersection, this is hwy 113, make a right and travel about 5 miles or so. You will pass many churches and cemeteries along the way none of which is her's. Look for Old Center Point Road and a sign for the church on your left. Turn. As you approach the church you will see a small cemetery, her tombstone is a large monument closest to the church.

Rita Hayworth
October 17, 1919 - May 15, 1987

Sexy and talented Rita, screen star of more than forty films including, "*Pal Joey*" and "*Gilda*," had a life that most would never believe. She married five times to men who were wrong for her. The first husband, who was a drifter and con_man, Eddie Judson, was close to her father's age. The only good thing that he did was help turn the chubby young dancer into a screen legend. His methods however, were very questionable; offering her body to those in Hollywood whom he felt could further her career.

Another marriage, this time to Aly Khan, who had a notorious reputation for womanizing produced a daughter, Yasmin. Fed up with his promiscuity, she left him to return to America with Yasmin in tow. Once at home she resumed her career to make some very memorable movies.

In 1955, as her mother before her, Rita was beginning to show the effects of early Alzheimer's disease. Most people close to her attributed her odd behavior to alcohol abuse. It was common knowledge, that she had been drinking excessively since her failed marriage to Aly Khan. There is no real evidence on how alcohol effects Alzheimer's disease. It is known however that since alcohol destroys brain cells, the disease could then manifest earlier than it normally would have, as it probably did with Rita.

By the late 1960's Rita's mind was now paralyzed with fear. She became very forgetful, so working was almost impossible. So many projects never materialized due to Rita's inability to memorize and remember lines. By the time she made "*The Wrath of God*," in 1971, she had to be fed line for line as it was filmed in sections.

RITA HAYWORTH
BELOVED MOTHER

✝

OCT. 17, 1918   MAY 14, 1987

TO YESTERDAY'S COMPANIONSHIP
AND TOMORROW'S REUNION

Holy Cross Cemetery, Culver City, California

Also she suffered from mood swings, that were intensified when she drank. She became defiant and paranoid, hearing noises and hallucinating. While having these episodes she would often call the police claiming that someone was trying to break in. When the police would arrive there would be no evidence of any attempted break-ins. When not calling the cops, she could be seen out in her yard cursing at a tree or tossing bottles at her neighbor, Glenn Ford's antenna.

On April 29, 1979, a hearing was finally scheduled to appoint a guardian to handle her affairs and to care for her. The cruel press packed the courtroom in hopes to catch a disheveled Rita in complete mental collapse. To avoid this humiliating scene, Yasmin sent her mother to a clinic in Connecticut until things could be ironed out. While in her daughter's care, Rita had totally given up alcohol and was looking better.

Although Rita still looked good on the outside it was just a mere shell to her existence. She was invited to do a benefit with Cesar Romero. As they danced, she constantly stepped on his feet; and was unable to follow his lead. The Alzheimer's had robbed her the ability to gracefully dance as she once had..

Finally in 1981, she was legally put in her daughter Yasmin's care. Never did her daughter ever consider putting her mother in an institution. Instead Yasmin chose to put her
own career on hold to lovingly care for Rita. This was no easy task because Rita later became violent and had to be put on Haldol to control her rages. Eventually she lost her ability to recognize people and was confined to diapers.

The end came on May 15, 1987, as a nurse rolled her over to change her garments. All that were close to her knew of Rita's intense fear of death and were thankful that she appeared unaware of the end.

Rita is buried next to her mother, in a section of Holy Cross Cemetery called the grotto. It's a beautiful part of the cemetery surrounded by gardens and a little grotto where you can light candles for the dearly departed. She is not far from another Hollywood legend, Bing Crosby.

Holy Cross Cemetery and Mausoleum
5835 W. Slauson Avenue
Culver City, California
Directions: Take the 405 to 90E get off at the Slauson Avenue exit the cemetery is on your left Once in the cemetery get a celebrity map and proceed to the Grotto. Park as soon as you see the cave like structure (the Grotto in the Grotto Section). Walk towards it and you will see a little patch of grass next to it with a few graves. She is there. The Grotto, #L196

Margaux Hemingway
February 16, 1954 - July 1, 1996
They say that one romantic night in Portland, Oregon, a couple shared a bottle of Choateau Margaux and conceived a daughter whom they named after said wine. This girl whose last name proceeds her, went on to become a famous model and actress of the 70's. Margaux grew up the rural surroundings of Ketchum, Idaho, where she spent her time fly fishing in the mountains near her home. This simple life unfortunately, was shrouded by a family whose legacy was that of alcoholism and suicide. A total of twelve people in her family had killed themselves.

Her life has been typically *Hemingway*; made up of a lot of mental highs and lows. Like her famous grandfather, Margaux suffered from bouts of clinical depression, one of which landed her in an Idaho psychiatric hospital in late 1994.

Despite her personal problems Margaux seemed to be successful, co_starring with little sister, Mariel in a the film, "Lipstick." Their sometimes turbulent relationship was constantly publicized, perhaps being responsible for a lot of Margaux's mental anguish.

In 1975, she won a million dollar contract as the fresh faced image behind Faberge's Babe perfume, only to lose it along with a lot of sleep and dignity as she became a member of the perpetually sloshed at Manhattan's decadent *Studio 54* set. Margaux's partying eventually turned into an out of control alcohol problem.

MARGOT LOUISE HEMINGWAY
FEB. 16, 1954
JULY 1, 1996

FREE SPIRIT FREED

LOVE

Ketchum Cemetery, Ketchum, Idaho

Unlike most of the Hemingways; she eventually beat her alcoholism and remained sober. She turned her life around and was given a job hosting *"Wild Guide,"* an outdoor adventure series scheduled to air on the Discovery Channel. This she felt would jump start her acting career. Despite all positive events in her life, some close friends felt that she appeared strangely forlorn. When asked what was wrong she would respond with, "Oh nothing, I'm not feeling so good."

Neighbors commented that on occasion they would see the statuesque beauty on the street looking disturbed and haggard. In contrast, Margaux seemed happy in her new sunny Santa Monica apartment.

In the last week of June, close friend Judy Stabile made many attempts to call Margaux. Each call went unanswered. Finally on June 1st, Judy drove to the former model's home. Outside she saw Margaux's white Ford Bronco with Idaho plates parked on the street. After Judy's repeated knocking went unanswered, she found a ladder, climbed it and looked in the window. There was her friend, lying on the bed, her hands folded over her nightgown. Judy got two construction workers to go inside. Once inside they realized that she was dead.

It is a mystery as to what went wrong in the last moments of her life. The initial details of her death were unclear. But as the toxicology report came back, it was clear that she died of an overdose of Barbiturates. It turned out, (as the thoughts of the *Hemingway curse* entered everyone's mind), she did commit suicide. Some of her closer friends however, resisted these thoughts and believed that she succumbed to a fatal attack of epilepsy, a disease that she had struggled with since childhood. Or that perhaps she accidentally took too much medication; she was notorious for over or under medicating herself.

After she was released from the coroner; she was cremated and her ashes were given to her family. They brought her back to her hometown of Ketchum, Idaho where she was first entombed and then later buried.

Ketchum Cemetery

Hwy 75

Ketchum, Idaho

Directions: From Hwy 93 go north past Twin Falls to Hwy 75 north into Ketchum. Drive past all the neat little shops as if you were going to leave the town. Keep looking to your right and slow down the cemetery will be coming up. It is easy to miss. Once inside drive to follow the 2nd road to the middle of the cemetery. Ernest has a large tombstone that's not hard to miss. Margeaux's smaller marker is a little bit past him to the left. This cemetery is so small, you won't have much trouble finding her.

Jayne Mansfield
April 19, 1933 - June 29, 1967

Vera Jayne Palmer was raised in a home of great privilege in the Pennsylvania town of Pen Argyl. Perhaps feeling that she had nothing to lose by pursuing her dreams, she traded the safe haven of home and family for the precarious Hollywood existence.

She married and became a mother while still a teenager, and felt as though her life was being predetermined. This, plus the yearn for stardom made her work even harder to achieve her goals. Jayne quickly found that performing outrageous stunts would get the attention she needed to succeed. Jayne was not above a swim in the buff if it meant catching the eye of someone who could further her career.

Whatever parts came her way were usually glitzy, bimbo roles that fitted the image she created. But like most sexpots, she yearned for the role of substance that constantly eluded her. To add insult to injury, the end of the 50's marked the end of the blond bombshell and she was out on her shapely bottom. She was demoted to signing in small night clubs and seedy lounges.

Fairview Cemetery, Pen Argyl, Pennsylvania

JAYNE MANSFIELD

APRIL 19, 1933
JUNE 29, 1967

WE LIVE TO LOVE YOU MORE EACH DAY

(Actual Grave)

JAYNE MANSFIELD

1938 — 1967

WE LIVE TO
LOVE YOU MORE
EACH DAY

CENOTAPH

Hollywood Forever Cemetery, Hollywood, California

Jayne's last performance was on June 29, 1967, at the Steven's Supper Club in Biloxi, Mississippi. Jayne agreed to be a last minute replacement for friend Mamie Van Doren, whose own show was held over at its current location in New York. After the show, Jayne traveled by car to the next engagement. As they drove, they encountered some thick fog which impaired all visibility. Before they could do anything, they had slammed into the back of a slow moving truck. Jayne, her boyfriend, Sam Brody and the driver were killed instantly, but her three children who were sleeping in the backseat were spared with minor injuries.

James Roberts, a mortuary official who was in charge of Jayne's case, denies the report that she was decapitated. The false report came when a bouffant blond wig was found near the accident scene, and mistakenly and prematurely identified as her head.

Mansfield has two grave sites. Although her family had planned to have her buried in her home town, her ex-husband perhaps thought she owed it to her fans to have a second symbolic site in a Hollywood cemetery.

Fairview Cemetery
202 S. Schanck Ave
Pen Argyl, Pennsylvania
Special Thanks to Melody who with a car load of family, went out of her way to escort me personally to Jayne's final resting place.
Directions: From Rt 33, take the Wind Gap exit, make a left at the end of the ramp towards Pen Argyl. This is S. Broadway. Follow the signs that say 512N (Pennsylvania Ave). Until you see a flashing light, bear left and continue on 512N which becomes E. Main Street. When you see the Pen Argyl Pizza Parlor, make a right, that'S. Main Street. Follow this until you see the cemetery which will be on your right. Keep going to the 2nd entrance. Once inside follow the road around as if you are going to head for the exit. Stop halfway. Look for a tombstone with "Raines" on it, that is to your right and on the road. She is behind that.

Jayne's Cenotaph
Hollywood Forever Cemetery
6000 Santa Monica Blvd.
Hollywood, California
Directions: Take the 134 west to 101 south to Santa Monica Blvd. The cemetery is between Gower Street and Van Hess Avenue. Special thanks to Bob Coffey Sr., retired Seabee, who volunteers at the Hollywood Forever Cemetery and helps visitors find the graves of the stars. He helped me to find Jayne who is not listed on the cemetery map and a little difficult to find. As you enter the cemetery, you might want to spend the $5.00 and purchase a celebrity map. If not, follow my directions. Make a left as you go through the gates on Lakeview Avenue. Continue to Section 8, it is the only section with a lake in it. You should see the Cecil B. DeMille white crypt from the road. Park. Walk past the crypt in the direction of the mausoleum, but stay close to the lake. If you see Janet Gaynor you are right in the area. Jayne is by a clump of trees.

Marilyn Monroe
June 1, 1926 - August 5, 1962
You would have to be either born yesterday or sequestered on some island for the last forty years not to know this blond beauty. She had a phenomenal career as a sex symbol starring in such films as *"The Seven Year Itch"* and *"Some Like it Hot."* Although these movies were successful at the box office, they left poor Marilyn unsatisfied as an actress. Wanting to broaden her skills as an actress she studied under Lee Strasberg in an attempt to be considered for the serious roles that eluded her. Unfortunately her hopes to bring fulfillment to her career turned out to be just another disappointment. The public and the studio could not see beyond the sexy persona she had worked so hard to create.

All her success did nothing but make her life more complicated. Three marriages, a couple of miscarriages, abortions, two suicide attempts and an addiction to drugs and alcohol, all took it's toll on the fragile Marilyn. On August 5, 1962, she was found dead from an apparent overdose of barbiturates at her Los Angeles home. The newspapers were quick to print that she was found naked, laying in bed, clutching her telephone, forever leaving the public wondering who she was attempting to call.

Pierce Brothers owner, Guy Hockett, was called to remove Marilyn's body at 7:30 the next morning Believe it or not, her body remained unclaimed for several hours before ex_ husband and close friend, Joe DiMaggio stepped in to handle all the arrangements for the services and her entombment. One of the first things he did, was to ban all her Hollywood "friends" because he felt that they were indirectly responsible for her death. Due to her alleged
affairs with both Kennedy brothers, *all* Kennedys were also barred from her funeral. A shocked Pat Kennedy Lawford, who made a special trip from the east coast, to pay her last respects was turned away.

The service was held at the Westwood Memorial Park Chapel, a then obscure place, and was attended by only thirty one mourners. This was hardly a typical Hollywood funeral one would expect for such a monumental star.

Founded in 1904 the Pierce Brothers Westwood Memorial Park was a quiet neighborhood cemetery; that is, until 1962 when Marilyn moved in. Prior to her entombment it was considered "unfashionable" to be buried there. Now it is considered to be one of the most expensive cemeteries in the U.S., with an average price of interment being $22,000. Hugh Hefner reportedly paid $85,000 to spend eternity next to the girl who launched his magazine with her famous photo. It could be speculated that Joe DiMaggio, who has the reputation to shun the limelight, chose this quiet place for her.

"Somewhere Over the Rainbow" played softly as she lay in an open bronze casket lined with champagne colored satin. She wore her green Pucci dress and a green chiffon scarf. In her hands was a small bouquet of pink teacup roses, a gift from DiMaggio, who had sat vigil the night before. After the funeral, DiMaggio set up an account with a local florist to have roses delivered to Marilyn's grave twice a week, for the next twenty years. It was a promise that he made to her on the night that they wed. That if anything were to happen to her he would honor her in some special way, as William Powell did Jean Harlow.

Allan Whitey Snyder, who did her makeup for years, kept his promise to Marilyn and applied her make up for the last time. A flask of gin was needed to get the job done. The two had made a pact in jest many years earlier, that should anything ever happen to her he would be the one do her makeup as usual. Marilyn gave him a gold money clip from Tiffany's inscribed with: "Whitey Dear, While I'm still warm, Marilyn." to remind him of his promise.

Long time hairdresser to Marilyn, Agnes Flanagan, did her hair. However, due to the damage that the autopsy had caused, Agnes had to find a wig similar to the style Marilyn wore in her last movie.

Though the initial medical examination determined her cause of death as a suicide. Many conspiracy theories have linked the Kennedys and/or the Mafia as the real cause for her premature demise. Perhaps it is because her death has been shrouded in mystery that she remains eternal as an icon for future generations to enjoy.

Rumor has it that Marilyn was entombed with a million dollar diamond necklace. One night two very stupid thieves attempted to break into her crypt hoping they could steal the necklace and maybe her too. They, however, didn't take into consideration the 500 pounds of concrete they would have to break through to reach Marilyn. To this day, her crypt is framed by cracked marble from the unsuccessful attempt.

Her grave is always adorned with gifts from friends and fans from all over the world. In fact, in front of her crypt is a bench that was erected in her honor by her fan club, so mourners can have a place to sit while paying their last respects.

MARILYN MONROE
1926 — 1962

Westwood Memorial Memorial Park, Los Angeles, California

Westwood Memorial Park
1218 Glendon Avenue
West Los Angeles, California
Directions: Take the 405 to Wilshire Blvd. exit. Travel east to Glendon Ave. Make a right.
SLOW DOWN! You see some parking garages and office buildings, look for a black sign to
your left, Pierce Brothers Mortuary, Westwood Memorial Park, turn. You will enter an "oasis of
tranquility," so the brochure says. It is pretty amazing. Once inside the make a left and park. Walk past
Mel Torme and keep going. You'll pass 3 Sanctuaries, that look like little rooms, on
your left. At the end of the last one you'll see a hallway, a little bench and Marilyn's crypt. Corridor of
Memories, Crypt #24 See the empty crypt next to her? Supposedly that is the crypt will someday be
occupied by Hugh Hefner.

JIM BACKUS

DARLING HUSBAND

FEB 25, 1913 – JULY 3, 1989

Chapter 2 - Rebels Without a Cause
Jim Backus
February 25, 1913 - July 3, 1989

Ohio born actor Jim Backus' stage career began in summer stock, where, according to his then roommate Keenan Wynn, he was as well known for his prowess with the ladies as he was for his on-stage versatility. Backus continued acting in New York, first in vaudeville and then in radio during the 30's and 40's. He was a regular on radio's *"The Alan Young Show,"* portraying Eastern Seaboard snob Hubert Updike III, a precursor to his *Thurston Howell III* character he later played on *"Gilligan's Island."*

In 1949, Backus provided the voice of the nearsighted *"Mr Magoo"* cartoon which he did until 1970. Backus claimed he created Mr. Magoo's character from his father's true life personality.

Jim branched out into movies making his first appearance in *"Easy Living."* His most famous screen role was that of James Dean's weak willed father in *"Rebel Without a Cause."*

Television was another medium where Jim found his niche. First co-starring with Joan Davis in 1950's sitcom, *"I Married Joan."* Then playing the lead role of the fast talking news service editor Mike O'Toole on *"Hot Off the Wire"* (a.k.a. *"The Jim Backus Show"*). In the 1960's, he played what would be his most memorable role on *"Gilligan's Island."*

After an accomplished career in radio, movies and television, he along with his wife, Henny, collaborated on several amusing volumes of memoirs. Their last two books *"Backus Strikes Back"* and *"Forgive Us Our Digressions"* comments humorously on a deadly serious subject: Parkinson's Disease, the ailment which would eventually take his life.

Jim was diagnosed with Parkinson's disease and had been living with it's effects for many years. That is until June 13th, when he was admitted to St. John's Hospital in Santa Monica, after contracting pneumonia. He died several weeks later at the age of seventy-six.

Westwood Cemetery
1218 Glendon Avenue
Los Angeles, California

For directions to the cemetery see Marilyn Monroe in the Glamour Girls Chapter From the entrance walk in the direction of the office. Stop when you get to the end of the grassy area. You should see a lot of little niches or grave markers, these are the cremated people. Just above that you'll see the larger markers that look like regular graves. Count approximately 8 to the right of the street. Jim is slightly obscured by a bush in that area.

James Dean
February 8, 1931 - September 30, 1955

Dean was born in Marion, Indiana, a small farming community, ten miles north of Fairmount. Although the family lived a comfortable life in Indiana, they chose to move west to California for a better life. Young James' life seemed typically normal until at the age 9, when his mother died of cancer. He was sent back to Fairmount, alone, to be raised by his paternal aunt and uncle while his father remained behind in California. Apparently his mother's bedside confession revealed that the young James was not the biological son of her husband, thus forever estranging the boy's relationship with his father.

While James attended Fairmount High School in 1945, he became interested in acting. He placed first in the Indianan State Contest of the National Forensic League with his presentation of *"The Madman"* by Dickens.

After graduation, he left Fairmount to be with his father in California and pursued a career in pictures. There he attended UCLA where he became a theater major. His first real acting job was in a Pepsi commercial for which he earned $30. Soon he received bit parts in a couple of movies, but still he longed for more roles of substance.

In September, 1951 Dean left Hollywood's tinsel town to pursue the serious roles that the New York City stage had to offer. There he was cast in several live television dramas before being cast in his first Broadway play, *"See the Jaguar."*

Park Cemetery, Fairmount, Indiana

JAMES B. DEAN
1931 — 1955

It was in this Broadway play that director Elia Kazan spotted the young Dean. Kazan arranged a screen test for him and then cast him in John Steinbeck's classic *"East of Eden."* From there he went on the make films like, *"Rebel Without a Cause"* and *"Giant."*

After completion of his first real famous film,*"East of Eden,"* Dean purchased a Porsche Spyder 550 to celebrate his success. James had always had a great interest in car racing, and participated in many small races, as long as his film schedule would permit it.

On September 30, 1955, Dean decided to drive with friend and mechanic, Rolf Wutherich, to Salinas, California to enter a race with his new Porsche. While en route to Salinas, Dean was stopped by Highway Patrolman Otie V. Hunter who issued him a speeding ticket at 3:30 pm, just outside Bakersfield. Dean was clocked at what would typically be considered a snail's pace for him, 70 mph.

This was not good for Dean, he had just finished a commercial for highway safety and did not need the gossip magazines to find out about his speeding ticket, especially after *his* preaching about the evils of speed on the highway.

The highway patrolman had only succeeded in momentarily slowing Dean's speed, soon he was once again speeding and driving recklessly along Hwy 446 (now renamed Hwy 46). Prior to Dean's horrific accident, witnesses had seen his car weave recklessly in and out of traffic at a high rate of speed sometimes narrowly missing cars along the way. On one occasion he almost drove head on into a car driven by Clifford Hord, who at the time was traveling with his two young children and his wife. Clifford had no choice but to drive off the road to avoid a collision.

Robert White an accountant from Paso Robles witnessed the accident. He saw the car speed past him at a high rate of speed, perhaps over 100 mph. Of course a car traveling at that rate of speed could no way stop in time to avoid an accident.

Unfortunately it would be Donald Gene Turnupseed who would find out the hard way that a speeding sports car cannot stop on a dime. As Turnupseed approached the intersection where Hwy 41 turns off, he proceeded to turn after seeing that there were no other cars in close approach. Then out of nowhere, the sports car was on top of him. Donald slammed on his brakes and turned his wheel to the right to avoid the crash, but it was too late.

White watched the whole accident transpire before his eyes. He saw Dean's car try to swerve to avoid the collision to no avail.

Dean's car flipped a few times before landing next to a telephone pole, just barely missing it. The other driver, Turnupseed, had minor injuries in contrast to the others, he sustained just a few cuts and bruises. Dean's companion had been thrown from the car and was lying on the ground approximately six feet from the driver's side of Dean's Porsche. Dean and his friend were still alive. It was unknown to those at the scene, the extent of Dean's injuries. He lay there barely conscious and bleeding.

A nurse, Mrs. Coombes, that was passing by the accident stopped to see if she could assist anyone. She saw right away that Dean's neck had been broken and that he had a faint pulse. Dean did not have much time left.

Friend Bill Hickman who had also been traveling to Salinas for the races, had finally caught up with Dean at the intersection. He recognized the wrecked Porsche as Dean's car and ran over, only to see his friend moments before his death. Hickman held Dean in his arms as the ambulance drove up. Then suddenly Dean stirred and then he let out his last breath. This young man was gone before his time, all because of a stupid preventable accident.

Dean was brought to the War Memorial Hospital in Paso Robles were he was officially pronounced dead by Dr. Bossert, the doctor that was on duty that night. He instructed the ambulance drivers who brought him to the hospital to take him to Kuehl Funeral Home on Spring Street.

Martin Kuehl was the undertaker that was going to take care of Dean. Hickman had arrived at the funeral parlor to do what he could for his friend. Kuehl gave Hickman Dean's wallet. There was no money; the ambulance men had apparently rolled the deceased star. This was a omen for Hickman to stay close to his friend.

Kuehl prepared to process the body. He moved his head and noticed that Dean's neck was broken, perhaps at the base of the skull. The left side of his face was damaged and particles of glass were embedded in his face. HIs his jaw was broken. It was apparent that his face had obviously absorbed most of the collision's impact. The bones in both arms were broken. The only intact part on his body were his legs. .

Officer Ernie Tripke, who was investigating the accident requested a blood sample to determine whether Dean had been drinking. Kuehl had to poke and prod because there was hardly if any blood left in his body.

On Saturday, Dean's father Winton, arrived in Paso Robles escorted by chief of security from Warner's Bros. He met Hickman at Kuehl's where he quietly asked the undertakers to be careful that none of his son's possessions were left behind to fall into the wrong hands. He selected a coffin and handed over the suit he had brought for his son to be buried in. The torn and bloodied clothing were thrown away.

Winton had first wanted his son to be buried next to his mother in Grant Memorial Park, he instead chose Park Cemetery, a place closer to the Jonesboro house where his aunt and uncle had raised young Dean.

On Tuesday morning, John Stander loaded the casket with Dean's body into the black hearse and began the long drive down Hwy 101 to the Los Angeles Airport.

At 10:17pm a Hunt Funeral Home hearse was there to meet the plane as it landed in Indianapolis, Indiana. His body was taken to the same funeral home that a year ago, friend Dennis Stock had photographed Dean posing inside one of the caskets, flashing a victory sign. A wake was held; open to the public.

On October 9, Dean was buried. The service was at 2pm in the Back Creek Friend's Church, where his Aunt Ortense was organist. It was the largest funeral in the history of Fairmount, with 3000 in attendance. However, hardly anyone from Hollywood had attended. His pallbearers were high school friends and few guys from his basketball squad.

After Dean was buried, guards were hired to patrol the grave for two weeks to keep those who might steal a memento from their fallen star away. In 1983, the original headstone was taken, but then recovered, only to be stolen again, but this time never found. It has since been replaced with the one that now sits on his grave.

Later, the present stone was also stolen, but recovered after Tippecanoe County Sheriff's Deputy, Aaron Gilman, was driving on a dark, deserted country road one night. Suddenly he hit something, which suddenly tore out the transmission of his car. Turns out the culprit was the missing marker, which deputies promptly carted down to the county jail.

It is amazing that anyone could steal the marker because it weighs approximately 400 lbs and it is secured to the base with metal bars and glue. Well it just goes to show you, that you should live fast, die young and leave a good looking tombstone. Sorry...

Park Cemetery
Fairmount, Indiana
Directions: From I-69, exit at the Hwy 26 and go left. Go to Main Street and make a right. The cemetery is a half mile north of Hwy 26, you can't miss it. It is on your left hand side. There are signs throughout town guiding you to the cemetery and once you've entered the cemetery there is another sign pointing to the gravesite

If you are ever visiting the central coast of California, you should visit the crash site in the town of Cholame. There is a restaurant that is located approximately 900 feet from where the actor was killed. In the parking lot there is a monument to Dean. It is this very modern, silvery looking sculpture that explains what happened on that fateful day.

Once you enter the restaurant, you'll notice a non stop array of James Dean photos, articles, and memorabilia for sale and on display. This place looks more like a shrine to James Dean, than it does a restaurant. I didn't want to look at the menu, because I would have gotten sick if I would have seen James Dean Burgers or something.

SAL MINEO
JAN. 10, 1939
FEB. 12, 1976

MICHAEL MINEO
MAR. 14, 1937
JUNE 28, 1984

-30- GOD'S CARE

Gate of Heaven Cemetery, Hawthorn, New York

Sal Mineo
January 10, 1939 - February 12, 1976

This quiet kid from the Bronx, went on to become one of Hollywood's most popular film prodigies. Little did he know that, not only would he aspire to be in one of Hollywood's most famous motion pictures of it's time, *"Rebel Without A Cause"* but also he would fall prey to it's alleged curse.

Despite his many memorable contributions to the movie industry, the newspapers painted him as pathetic washed up teen idol, that was now living in the 'slummy' part of West Hollywood. His plan was to do away with these rumors and recapture his fallen fame.

On February 12th, Sal was preparing for the Los Angeles opening of *"P.S., Your Cat is Dead."* He left rehearsal around 9pm, and his co-star Keir Duliea was one of the last people to see Sal alive. Keir later said, "Sal was in tremendous spirits. He had always talked that this play was a major one for him, one which would launch the second phase of his career."

Sal parked his blue Chevelle in the garage of the two story apartment complex at 8563 Holloway Drive, where he had lived for the past three years. At approximately 10pm neighbors heard someone screaming "Oh God! No! Help! Someone Help!" His cries were followed by the sound of a struggle, more screams and than silence. By the time his neighbors had reached Sal, they claimed that they saw a young white man fleeing the scene. Stories conflicted on his description; some said he had long dark hair, others said he had blond hair. The only thing that everyone agreed upon was the fact that the assailant wore dark clothing. None of the neighbors chased the man, because they were in a state of shock over the events that had just transpired.

Ray Evans, one of the first neighbors on the scene, found Sal in a fetal position with a stream of blood ten yards long flowing from his massive chest wounds. Things did not look good for Mineo who had by now taken on an ashen color. Evans attempted mouth to mouth resuscitation to keep him alive. "He kept gasping and after about 5 or 6 minutes, his last breath went into me and that was the end of it." said Evans. Sal Mineo died before the paramedics arrived, of a deep knife wound near his heart.

The coroner's office performed an autopsy on Sal. It showed that he had died of a massive hemorrhage due to a stab wound to the chest, that penetrated his heart. A heavy type knife was the weapon used to kill him. Medical examiner, Don Drynan, said there were no other injuries apparent. This report, however, conflicted greatly with eye witnesses who claimed they had seen several other wounds to his body.

The murder was investigated as a possible drug crime or a crime of passion, due to the fact that it occurred on the notoriously kinky Sunset Strip. Robbery was not the motive because his wallet, watch and ring were still on his person. One speculation was that maybe he resisted a robbery attempt and was stabbed. Numerous calls and tips were made to the authorities, however, none of them panned out.

The following Tuesday, Sal's body was flown back east to Mamaroneck, New York, for his funeral and burial. Long time friend, David Cassidy, accompanied his body home. That same day, detectives revised their description of the suspect: to a 20-30 year old male, Caucasian of medium build with dark brown or black hair, approximately 5 feet 7 to 10 inches. Still the police were without a motive or a lead.

At the wake, Sal's father had an open casket. Some of Sal's West Hollywood friends claimed that he would not have liked the idea of people parading past his dead corpse.

There were 250 people who attended his funeral at Holy Trinity Roman Catholic Church. Dozens more stood outside; 300 curious on lookers crowded the streets and pressed their noses against the windows. The services were performed by Rev. Gerard DiSenso.

A slight rain fell as the mourners marched out to the church behind the brown coffin and a priest who scattered drops of holy water, recited: "We pray for our brother Sal who died in Christ." He was then taken to his final resting place, Gate of Heaven Cemetery in Hawthorn. A few people lingered outside the church to gawk at the stars in the crowd. He was interred next to his father on a peaceful hill overlooking a lake.

Westwood Memorial Park, Los Angeles, California

Gate of Heaven Cemetery
10 W. Stevens Avenue
Hawthorn, New York

Special thanks to Gloria who went out of her way to escort me to the cemetery. See the people of New York are friendly.

Directions: Take the Taconic Pkwy north to Stevens Ave. The cemetery is on your left. As you enter the cemetery, go to the office and get a map. Even though the cemetery map provides you with lettered locations. It is still sometimes hard to find the grave. On the map find the Section 2 or "S," for the area in which he is buried. When you get there you'll notice a row of mausoleum type houses and graves markers in front of them. Look for "Buckley" and "Forstman" and then look to the right by a little cement path. He's not far from the street perhaps 2 or 3 rows.

Natalie Wood
July 20, 1938 - November 29, 1981

Natasha Gurdin was the daughter of Russian immigrants who lived in Santa Rosa, California. Her father was a laborer who could barely speak English and did the best he could to support his family. Still Natasha's mother had to be resourceful with whatever money he brought into the household.

The family's big break came when the movie *"Happy Land"* with Don Ameche and Frances Dee was being filmed in their town. The movie put out a call for extras, and one of the first to show up was Natasha and her mother. This could be a way for the family to generate more money. After the initial 'test,' the director hired five year old Natasha.

Months went by and the same director, Irving Pichel, called Mrs. Gurdin to see if her daughter could come down and test for his new film, *"Tomorrow Is Forever."* With that Natasha's mom packed up the whole family and headed for Hollywood.

Once in Hollywood Natasha unfortunately flunked her test. This was quite a crisis for the family. They had no money, and were now in a strange city. Thankfully, Mrs. Gurdin had the diligence to march over to Twentieth Century-Fox and talk her way into the office of Mr Pichel's. She charmed Mr Pichel into giving Natasha another screen test. This time she passed the test and got the job and a new name: Natalie Wood.

Unlike most child stars she continued to act into adulthood. By 1954, she made *"Rebel Without a Cause,"* a film that remains very popular to this day. When she wasn't at the studio, she attended Van Nuys High School like any other teenager. Unlike most teenagers though, she was beautiful, famous and drove a brand new pink Thunderbird convertible. Being that birds of a feather flock together, she hung around other teen stars like Dennis Hopper and Sal Mineo.

By 1956 she had met the love of her life, Robert Wagner and a year later they were married Like most Hollywood marriages it was doomed to divorce. But unlike most Hollywood marriages their paths would cross again; which would lead them to marry once more. This time the union lasted until her death.

Together they purchased a yacht called *"Splendour."* Frequently they boarded their yacht and headed for their favorite vacation spot, Catalina. On Thanksgiving weekend, Robert and Natalie invited their friend, Christopher Walken to accompany them aboard their yacht for a trip to Catalina. There were many rumors circulated as to what happened that fateful night. Lana Wood, Natalie's sister, believes that her sister was not murdered nor did she commit suicide.

Although Natalie sometimes drank a little too much, she wasn't considered an alcoholic. When under pressure she *would* overindulge, also on occasion she would take sleeping pills and Valium to calm her down.

What probably happened that night was that Natalie had a little too much to drink . The coroner's report confirmed that her alcohol level exceeded that of a drunk driver. The dinghy was banging on the side of the boat preventing her from sleeping, so she got up, put on her heavy down filled robe, and attempted to retie it. While doing this she possibly slipped and fell into the water. She must have tried to cling to the side of the dinghy, but the weight of her water drenched robe pulled her under. Coroner, Thomas Noguchi's first reports states that she became unconscious almost immediately and died. If this did occur, it spared her the agony of confronting her fear of water and worst of all death.

Later he told the family that she did indeed struggle to stay afloat in a futile attempt to save her life. Dr Noguchi kept the first story going for a year to spare the family additional grief and to protect his career. In the past, he had been severely criticized for his comments about the deaths of William Holden and a number of other celebrities. Eventually he was removed from office.

He caused a lot of controversy in the press, by divulging testimony saying that RJ and Walken had a heated argument prior to the incident. Both have denied this allegation. Another report said that Natalie and Chris had spent the night in a motel on Catalina. The truth was that yes they did spend the night there; but in separate rooms.

Her funeral was held in a small chapel and then she was buried in Westwood Cemetery. Her funeral was a typical Hollywood affair with practically every star in attendance.

Westwood Memorial Park
1218 Glendon Avenue
Los Angeles, California

For directions to the cemetery see Marilyn Monroe in the Glamour Girls Chapter As you drive into the cemetery make a quick left and park. Go to the corner of the large grassy area (the corner where you turned walk down approximately 6 or 7 rows then walk to your left approximately 12 plots. She is in this area. Her grave is D-60. This cemetery is not clearly marked nor does it seem to have any kind of order. This makes it hard to pinpoint an exact location. One thing to your advantage it that it isn't large and while you are looking for one grave, you are bound to stumble upon another.

Chapter 3: Famous Brothers
Marx Brothers

All products of "Stage Mother" Minnie Marx, the brothers were organized into a vaudeville act. In 1910, and later became the Marx Brothers. Although their group name changed, their characters remained the same: Groucho, the semi serious wise cracking straight man, Chico, the pun happy Italian, Harpo, the silent dervish, and Gummo, the helplessly lost straight man. There was one thing that all the brothers did have in common: that was the ability to play an instrument at an accomplished level.

Groucho
October 2, 1890 - August 19, 1977

Born Julius Henry, he was the third oldest Marx Brother and first to take the show biz plunge. At the age of fourteen he took a job as a boy soprano with a group called the *LeRoy Trio*. This engagement was nearly his last when Groucho who became stranded in Colorado, was forced to work his way back home. Marx was more than willing to trade the theater for a career as a doctor. Once again his mother, determined to keep her son in show business, paired him with his brother Gummo and a minimally talented girl.

His shaky beginnings graduated him and his brothers to the film industry where throughout the 20's and 30's they made many movies. This left the Marx Brothers, with exception to Chico, very wealthy.

However after a successful run, Hollywood considered the Marx Brothers to be washed up and gave them less and less projects to do. Groucho welcomed the lull in film making because it now gave him time to socialize with writers and novelists who made up his close circle of friends. He felt comfortable with these people because he had always considered himself more a writer than a comic. Throughout his lifetime, he produced many witty books and articles. In the 1960's, his letters to and from his friends were installed in the Library of Congress. All quite an accomplishment for a man who never finished grade school.

By the 1940's he was back in films. Not really for personal creativity but to bail out the eternally broke brother, Chico. After his last film, Groucho went solo and kept busy with radio and television. His most famous show was *"You Bet Your Life"* which lasted fourteen years.

By the 1960's, he worked less frequently only to have his films "rediscovered" by young hippy types. His films reflected a total lack of respect for the "establishment" and class division, all qualities that appealed to this younger generation.

The 1990's brought ill health for Groucho. He had suffered a stroke and was extremely frail. Divorced and on his own he needed a secretary/companion to assist him with his daily duties. He hired a young girl, Erin Fleming, who on the positive side encouraged Groucho to return to performing on TV. Work was the best therapy for Groucho as it gave him a new lease on life.

On the negative side, Erin began to take advantage of Groucho. As his health failed so did his mind, and Erin saw this as an opportunity to take advantage of him. This relationship caused an estrangement between Groucho and his family and many close friends. Later it caused the family to become embroiled in a heated legal battle over the disposition of his estate. During the height of all this controversy, Groucho peacefully passed away at the age of 86. His family finally prevailed in their suit against Erin.

It is rumored that Erin is now a bag lady somewhere in Hollywood.

Security is very tight at Eden Memorial for two reasons. One, the controversial Lenny Bruce is buried there and two, Groucho ashes were stolen in May, 1982. I don't know how valid this story is but, it sounds pretty good so that's why I'm including it. First of all, I contacted every Groucho site asking for more info on the theft. Everyone ignored my questions, apparently this is a very tacky question to ask a real "Grouchophile." It turns out that a very good source who told me the story, knew the guy who stole Groucho.

GROUCHO MARX

1890 ✡ 1977

Eden Memorial Park, San Fernando, California

-36-

As the story goes, the thief was a former employee at Eden Memorial Park where Groucho is interred. Angry because his boss had fired him, he concocted a plan to get him back. The best course of revenge he could think of, was to steal Groucho. He pried the cover off Groucho's niche with a screwdriver, stole him for the night, and brought him to his home in Burbank. He and another friend claimed they opened the urn and found little pieces of dentures and such.

This part I don't believe because when a body is cremated, there are still a lot of big pieces that don't burn completely. I guess it looks like a camp fire that burns itself out. The funeral director who does the cremating, takes the remains, your bones, etc., and pulverizes them into powdered ashes. You would not see any pieces. Another thing, they remove all items that would melt so they don't ruin their crematorium.

Another reason why the thief brought the ashes to Burbank was to negate a famous quote that Groucho had said, "I would never be caught dead in Burbank." After the thief was done with his sick mission, he dropped off the urn with the ashes on the doorstep of Mt. Sinai Cemetery. The urn was shipped back to Eden Memorial and a locked gate erected. The gate, however, remains unlocked during the day. Apparently the screwdriver marks around his niche have gone unrepaired.

Eden Memorial (CLOSED SATURDAYS)
11500 Sepulveda Blvd.
San Fernando, California
Directions: Take the 405 to the Rinaldi exit east. Follow the cemetery to the Sepulveda Blvd, that is where the main entrance is. Don't bother asking for a map or any directions, they won't give you any information. The directions are a little difficult to follow, but once you find it, it seems so obvious. Face the crypts. The most outstanding feature is a structure in the center with a Star of David on it. Walk to the left and you'll see the wall go in and a little door in the corner. Enter through this door, this is where he is. Groucho is on the back wall, in the center of all the niches.

Gummo
October 23, 1893 - April 21, 1977

Mother Minnie was at it again; she paired brothers Milton (Gummo) and Julius (Groucho) with a female singer to form the *Three Nightingales.* When the girl left the group in 1909 Harpo replaced her. Together they developed their comedic skills and later became the Marx Brothers that we know today.

In 1918, Gummo went into the army, so their youngest brother Zeppo replaced him by joining the troop. Gummo was relieved to leave the group because he was never enthralled with show business and was thankful the army gave him an excuse to leave. Also The Marx Brothers were becoming less of a song and dance act, which made him feel less and less a part of them.

On Thursday, April 21, Gummo died in Palm Springs. He was known to be extremely upset at Groucho's predicament and had been lonely and melancholy since the death of his wife, Helen, the year before. A spokesman for the Eisenhower Medical Center announced that he had died of natural causes. Zeppo was quoted as saying, "I guess his heart just gave out." . He had lived to the fullest, in his own quiet way, his long life of eighty five years.

Groucho was never told of his brother's death due to his fragile health. By then, Groucho was aware of very little anyway.

Forest Lawn Memorial Park - Glendale
1712 S. Glendale Avenue
Glendale, California
For directions to the cemetery see Jean Harlow in the Glamour Girls Chapter. Get a map, but don't ask for any locations. Go to the Freedom Mausoleum. Walk into the main entrance and go downstairs, find the Sanctuary of Worship. He's towards the top.

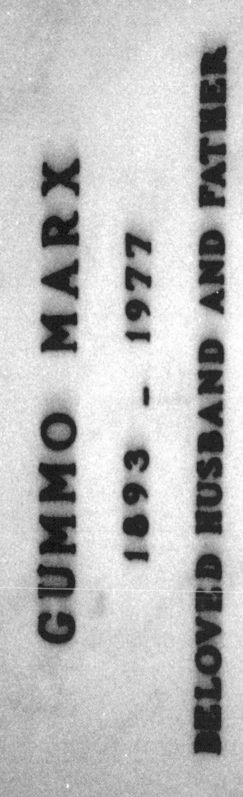

Forest Lawn Memorial Park, Glendale, California

Chico
March 22, 1887 - October 14, 1961

Born Leonard, he was the second son (the first son died in infancy) of Sam and Minnie Marx. Both who were German/Alsatian immigrants in search of the American dream..

In 1907 at the age of twenty, Chico had settled in Pittsburgh. He had gotten a job with a song publishing firm, Shapiro, Bernstein & Co of Philadelphia, and had proved so capable that they transferred him to manage the company's other branch.

It wasn't Chico's nature to stay in one place or one job for long, So he conceived a plan to return to the stage. But first he needed a partner, so he convinced his assistant Arthur Gordon, to trade their steady jobs for a career in vaudeville. Before quitting their jobs, they spent many hours perfecting their craft. Unfortunately their rehearsals got in the way of their jobs and they were promptly dismissed.

Later Chico chose to go at it alone as a free lance pianist in orchestras, saloons and "bawdy houses." After his stint as a pianist he joined his brothers in a "*schoolroom act,*" and drew upon his expertise with dialects by playing an Italian comic.

The Marx Brothers achieved great success with their films and by 1937 had earned enough money to consider retiring. But Chico's success in films was eclipsed by his tumultuous personal life that was marred by womanizing, divorce, but worst of all, compulsive gambling. At times, he ran up high tabs owing considerable sums of money to notorious gangsters. The brothers felt obligated to their wayward Chico and continued to work in an attempt to pay off his debts..

During the 50's, he paid his bills by headlining state fairs with brother Harpo. By early 1959 his health was beginning to fail as he toured with *"The Fifth Season."* This was the first time he acted without his brothers and without his Italian accent. He was charming and endearing on stage. Even though typecast as an Italian comic, the audience was able to see past this and loved him.

But after each performance he had to lie down. Sometimes he would amaze the other performers, because he would be so out of it before each show. They would give him his first line and then have to push him on stage. Once on stage he seemed fine

After the play closed Chico went to England for a one week concert tour, but recurring attacks of nausea forced him to cancel the engagement and return to Los Angeles. Upon his return, Chico was hospitalized in Cedars of Lebanon hospital. The Hollywood press said he was hospitalized for "chest congestion," in reality it was his second heart attack.

The last time Groucho and Harpo had seen their brother was after he was released from the hospital. Still gravely ill he was permitted to go home with a nurse to attend him.
Perhaps sensing that the end was near, he told his daughter, "Remember, honey don't forget what I told you. Put in my coffin, a deck of cards, a mashie niblick and a pretty blonde." The next day he was dead.

Groucho once told his son Arthur, that he always predicted that Chico's life would end in bed. But from shotgun wounds, not angina pectoris and not his own bed, but in some other husband's.

The funeral services were held two days later at the Wee Kirk O' the Heather Chapel at Forest Lawn Memorial Park in Glendale, Friday October 13th. At the funeral, Harpo turned to Groucho and asked how he was feeling. "Better than Chico," he replied. "Wanna make a bet on which one of us goes next?" asked Harpo "I'll give you three to one, and take either corner." Harpo lost the bet.

Forest Lawn Memorial Park - Glendale
1712 S. Glendale Avenue
Glendale, California
For directions to the cemetery see Jean Harlow in the Glamour Girls Chapter. Get a map, but don't ask for any locations. Go to the Freedom Mausoleum. Walk into the main entrance and go downstairs, find the Sanctuary of Worship. He's in there.

Forest Lawn Memorial Park, Glendale, California

Harpo
November 23, 1888 - September 28, 1964

Born Adolf Arthur he became famous not only for his comedic talents but for his skills as an accomplished musician who played the harp, hence the name "Harpo." He was perhaps the most endearing as he playfully chased women and communicated only by a series of whistles and gestures.

I remember him best in a cameo he played on "I Love Lucy" where he traded moves with Lucille Ball who was imitating him.

Harpo died on September 28, 1964, soon after undergoing open heart surgery. He was seventy-five. He is cremated and allegedly sprinkled on one of his favorite spots: the 9th hole of the Rancho Mirage Golf Course.

Warner Bros.
Harry
December 12, 1881 - July 27, 1959

He was born to poor immigrant parents from Poland in 1881. To escape poverty Harry's father ventured alone to the promise land to make enough money to later send for his family.
As the two year old "Hirsch," his sister and his mother walked through the custom gates into America, his father noticed that his son was shirtless. A shawl had been wrapped around his shoulders. Yet the boy was shivering in the cold winter air.

"What's this?" asked his father, "You come to your new country half naked?" Apparently the shirt was full of lice and needed to be discarded. This story became famous with Hirsch's grandchildren as he would often comment that he came to this country with not even a shirt on his back.

One of the first things Hirsch's father did was Americanize his children's names. Hirsch became "Harry" and Anna became "Annie." He believed that you should forget your past and focus on your future to be successful. Perhaps another reason for the Warner's success was their "all for one and one for all" ethic. Something that their father instilled upon them at an early age.

The Warner Brothers had their start in the shoe business and then later show business. The man behind the financing and decision making was Harry. In 1917, he sent his brother Jack to Los Angeles to make a serious bid for success in the rapidly growing movie industry. He needed to be closer to the action that appeared to be centering in the little town of Hollywood.

These brothers seemed unstoppable until 1934, when a massive fire swept through the Burbank studio, causing half a million dollars worth of damage. The studio's net loss for the year was $2.5 million

Warner Bros, were made up of all four brothers: two remained in New York, while Harry and Jack were in California. These two brothers fought constantly as their very different personalities clashed. The first big wedge in their relationship was Jack's string of affairs that culminated in his abandonment of his wife and small son.

Harry was the stable brother who was morally conscience. Who believed in the sanctity of marriage and family. He was also the conservative brother when it came to spending. Something that the extravagant Jack knew nothing about.

The brother's fighting at the studio became legendary. On one occasion Harry was seen chasing his brother with a three foot lead pipe. It was a shock for their employees to see two respected business men at each other's throats in such a childish way.

The hate Harry had for his brother sometimes distorted the reality that Jack was making great pictures. As far as Harry was concerned, Jack was nothing but a first class screw up that chased skirts.

Eventually the fighting took its toll on Harry causing him to have a heart attack. Soon after, while still in the hospital, he suffered a stroke leaving him with impaired walking ability. His doctors gave him a cane and told him to remain in the hospital. Just before his death Harry would sustain two more strokes

WARNER

On August 23, 1957, Harry and Rea celebrated their golden wedding anniversary with their family. A larger party at the Beverly Hills Hotel had been planned earlier, but had to be canceled, as Harry's condition worsened. He spent the festivities propped stiffly in an armchair near a window where he could watch the outdoor activities.

The end came on July 27, 1958, when he died of cerebral occlusion at the age of 76. Funeral services were held at the Home of Peace Cemetery close to where his only son Lewis was buried. Among the mourners were actors Edward G. Robinson and Jimmy Stewart. Absent was his brother Jack.

After the funeral his wife Rea, was appalled that Jack had not attended. She said that her husband didn't die; Jack killed him.

Home of the Peace (CLOSED SATURDAY)
4334 Whittier Blvd
Los Angeles, California
Directions: Take the 10 east to Hwy 60. Exit on the Downey Road South turn right on Whittier Blvd. Get a celebrity map and proceed to Section D. You'll see more than one Warner mausoleum with Warner on it. Look at my photo to find the correct one, look inside and see Harry's crypt.

Jack
August 2, 1892 - September 9, 1978

Jacob was the fifth son of Benjamin and Pearl's twelve kids. This "American" was born in London, Ontario in 1892. In his early teens, he changed his name to Jack and then adopted a middle name Leonard, because he thought it sounded classy. He was the first brother to travel to Los Angeles in 1917, to make a serious bid for success in a rapidly growing movie industry.

The brothers who had been raised with their father's ethic of "all for one and one for all" worked hard to make Warner's Brothers the monumental institution that it became. Jack betrayed his brothers especially Harry, and went against their father's "ethic" by selling out the company to strangers, so he could succeed as Warner Bros. president.

Jack worked hard to convince brother Harry that the sale of their studio was necessary and it would enable them both to retire. Too tired to fight him, Harry gave in. After the deal was signed, sealed and delivered, Jack was installed as president and Harry was out. All this, plus the constant fighting drove Harry over the edge and he had a heart attack that would eventually end of his life.

While Jack was vacationing on the Rivera, he received a telegram that his brother Harry had died. Instead of rushing back to the States to pay final respects to his dead brother he had his secretary send a wire saying, "Unable to attend. Please pay my respects."

As if there is such a thing as divine retribution from the grave; Harry finally got his brother back. Four days after Harry's funeral, Jack was involved in a car accident that almost killed him. While in the hospital, his sister showed up just to tell him, that God had punished him for not going to Harry's funeral. Jack had her removed and they never spoke again. Not only that, when she died he didn't show up at her funeral either.

In 1972, Jack had reached the "big eight oh!" as he put it. Throughout the remaining 70's, Jack suffered from a host of health problems. The coup d' grace occurred when he took a fall while playing tennis. From that point on he began to act disoriented. His wife felt that it would be in his best interest to be kept inside the house while she nursed him.

By Christmas, 1977, he had suffered a stroke and was confined to a wheelchair. The next stroke took his sight. September 9, 1978, was the end of the another Warner Brother. Jack died of edema, he was 86.

Bitter to the end, his will stipulated that no other family members be allowed to visit his grave and that it should be placed far from the other Warners.

Home of Peace (CLOSED SATURDAY)
4334 Whittier Blvd.
Los Angeles, California

JACK WARNER
IN MEMORY OF YEARS OF DEVOTION
1892 — 1978
ANN WARNER
1908 — 1990
TOGETHER

Home of the Peace, Los Angeles, California

See Harry Warner in the Famous Brothers Chapter for directions to the cemetery.Get a map, the people in the office are very nice and extremely helpful. From the office follow the road to the right of the of the round-a-bout. His grave is the garden grave to your right.

CURLY-JOE DeRITA
"THE LAST STOOGE"

JULY 12, 1909

JULY 3, 1993

Valhalla Memorial Park, Los Angeles, California

Chapter 4: Five Stooges?
Joe Derita
July 12, 1909 - July 3, 1993

Born in Philadelphia, as Joseph Wardell, he was introduced into show business at an early age by virtue of his parents. His father was stagehand, his mother a dancer called *"The Girl in the Moon"* because, suspended by a wire, she'd swing across the stage over the audience in a moon. DeRita traveled across the United States with them and once he caught the whiff of greasepaint, he too, became hooked on the stage.

DeRita made his stge debut at the tender age of seven, at a Red Cross benefit during World War I, and soon was teamed with his mother and sister in a stage act called *DeRita Sister and Junior.* That led to seven seasons of playing the title role in *"Peck's Bad Boy,"* once again alongside his mother and his sister, Phyllis.

DeRita went solo by the age of eighteen. Able to sing, dance and tell jokes, he became a staple of the burlesque circuit and moved up to films, making his debut in *"Dough Girls"* for Mark Hellinger at Warner Bros. But DeRita's first love was performing before live audiences, and he was a regular participant on road shows staged for U.S. servicemen, teaming up with everyone from Randolph Scott to Bing Crosby. Once back he settled into a contract with the Minsky Burlesque in 1950, working at the Rialto Theater in Chicago and the Dunes Hotel in Las Vegas for eight years.

When approached with the offer to become a Stooge, DeRita didn't exactly jump at the chance to join them. His widow, Jean DeRita, recalls that Joe was in Mexico, playing the villainous hangman alongside Gregory Peck in the Fox film, *"The Bravados"*

"When he finally got back to L.A., he had a lot of messages on his machine from them," said DeRita's wife. "The decided to put something together to see how it would work. They got some routines out, and well, they were old routines that Moe had, and Joe didn't like them. They put some together and they went somewhere and tried them out but they didn't go very well. They were all disappointed. Joe and Moe got out the old trunks of Joe's with the burlesque things and they picked some old things out from there, put a new act together."

DeRita had worked on stage with the likes of Abbott and Costello. And his trunks of memorabilia contain a slew of carefully clipped news write-ups from papers across the country. All praising DeRita for stardom on the big screen. Though he did numerous features and shorts for MGM during the 1940's , he did not become the star MGM hoped. He signed a deal at Columbia in 1946 to make a few shorts for them, some directed by Jules White, at a weekly salary of $600. But stardom never happened, and he returned to the burlesque stage, where he remained until the fateful visit from Moe Howard and Larry Fine.

They needed some routines for a new act and DeRita offered his archive of jokes and routines to Moe and Larry. His trunk contained volumes of carefully typed routines that DeRita either wrote himself or picked up during his long stage career. There are jokes, cataloged by subject, for nearly every occasion. All of them are typed and filed alphabetically. His widow said Joe typed them all himself, using one finger, and not a typo could be found. There's even a verbatim copy of the *"Who's on First"* routine made famous by Abbott and Costello.

A letter written to DeRita from his agent., Al Kingston, indicates that joining the Stooges wasn't an easy call. Kingston was against DeRita joining the group thus turning his back on his own opportunities as a solo act

But DeRita had made up his mind. He shaved his head to closely resemble the original Curly, whose shorts were the favorites on TV. According to Jean DeRita, it was a decision he never regretted.

Actually, there was little time to reflect, once the shorts became the top-rated series across the country for children. The Stooges were in demand all over. The tour began in Pittsburgh, with children and their parents packing shows all day. From there, they guest-starred on *"The Steve Allen Show,"* with *"Curly Joe"* performing the nearsighted rajah routine first done by Curly Howard in *"Three Little Pirates."* The skit ended with DeRita throwing a knife that wound up in the stomach of Allen, who closed the gag with a triple slap of the Stooge faces.

Soon the Stooges played everywhere, though Larry Fine preferred when they avoided the casinos, since by his own admission, he'd end up losing more at the tables than earned in salary.

Multiple appearances followed on *"The Ed Sullivan Show,"* highlighted by Sullivan's inability to remember their names in which he introduced them as the Ritz Brothers. After realizing his mistake he said, "Oh, it looks like the Three Stooges." At that point, he might have been about the only person in America unclear as to who they were.

Though TV brought them back form the dead, the boys decided to try once more to land a series. Moe's son_in_law, Norman Maurer, came up with an idea that he called *"Kook's Tour."* The pilot, narrated by Moe, featured the Stooges taking a vacation, visiting national parks around the country. They had made a decision to shoot the pilot without a script, relying on events the boys might get into while fishing and hiking through the woods. Hopefully this would lead to some very funny scenarios. In fact, there was very little humor and the shoot proved to be a nightmare. Moe and DeRita took falls that were not advisable for men in their late fifties and sixties. Several times the boys got lost in the boat. Once they got caught in a torrential down pour far from shore. Another time, while they were shooting footage of Snake River, (where rapids had earlier taken the lives of eleven explorers), the engine died. They had to sit for five hours, praying that the tide wouldn't turn and send them into rapids, where they'd surely drown.

While filming the end of *"Kook's Tour,"* Larry suffered a debilitating stroke. The tour was over and so were the Stooges. When Larry died five years later, Moe soon followed. Surviving Stooge Joe DeRita attempted one last time to carry on the act, but he found that the original Stooges could not be replaced.

A year prior to his death, like Larry, as his health failed him, and he too was forced to move into the Motion Picture Country Home to get the constant care he needed. After many strokes, and just nine days before his 84th birthday, Joe died from a bout with pneumonia. His small funeral was attended by less than 30 people. Some fans purchased the black granite tombstone with Joe's face etched in it. There might have been more than three Stooges, but due to his longevity, he was dubbed the last Stooge.

Valhalla Memorial Park
10621 Victory Blvd
Los Angeles, California

Directions: Take the 101 and exit east on Victory Blvd. The cemetery entrance is on the left. As you enter the cemetery, get a celebrity map from the office. From the office follow the road to the right, stop. This should be lot 19, look for section #338 and Block D.

Larry Fine
October 5, 1906- January 24, 1975

Born Lawrence Feinberg in Pittsburgh, Pennsylvania. His desire to enter show business started at a very early age. As a two year old he danced for relatives on top of a jewelry display case at his parents watch repair shop.

As a young boy, Fine took up the violin as therapy to rejuvenate an arm that was injured when his father accidently spilled a bottle of acid on it. He became so proficient at playing, that in his teens he won several amateur contests. He later contributed his talents in many of the Stooge's shorts.

Another thing that may have prepared Larry for a career as a Stooge was a few amateur boxing bouts. Soon he grew tired of the beatings and he left boxing forever, to perform in the less painful vaudeville. Little did he know that he would someday suffer a onslaught of blows in the name of success.

Larry was discovered by the Stooges in 1925, while in a Chicago club. He was doing a Russian dance in high hat and tails, while playing the violin. Larry agreed and joined the group.

For the years to come, Larry and Moe played with an assortment of third men. Stooge leader Moe was in a predicament and needed a replacement for his brother Shemp who was leaving the group. The best choice for replacement would be his very funny brother, Curly. So in 1934, Curly joined them and remained with the Stooges until his heath failed him.

LARRY FINE

1902 – 1975

Forest Lawn Memorial Park, Glendale, California

On March 6th they signed a contract with Columbia Picture for 190 film shorts. From there the Stooges quickly established the roles that would carry them through the next four decades: Moe the leader, Curly the smart aleck and Larry the guy always caught in the middle.

The end of the 50's and 60's proved bittersweet as Columbia ended its twenty four year relationship with the group.

Larry's personal life was not going so great either. In 1961, his son was killed in a motorcycle accident then six years later he lost his wife Mable. He lived alone in the Knickerbocker Hotel, before moving into a room above the garage in his daughter's house.

In 1970, while filming the Stooges final TV pilot, *"Kook's Tour,"* Larry suffered a debilitating stroke that left him paralyzed on his left side. He then moved to the Motion Picture Country Home where he spent the rest of his life. While there he entertained the showbiz veterans and had a visitor list that included the likes of James Cagney.

By the mid 70's he suffered a couple of stroke that eventually ended his life. His exact cause of death was cerebral thrombosis. He was 72, He had a small funeral at the Church of the Recessional at Forest Lawn where he is entombed next to his wife.

Forest Lawn Memorial Park - Glendale
1712 S. Glendale Ave
Glendale, California

For directions to the cemetery see Jean Harlow in the Glamour Girls Chapter. Go to the Freedom Mausoleum and enter through the main entrance. Go downstairs and look for the Sanctuary of Liberation. On the bottom row count 4 rows over he's right there.

Moe Howard
June 19, 1897 - May 4, 1975

Born Mose Horwitz in 1897 in Brooklyn, New York he was determined to get into movies. Moe, then going by his middle name Harry, went to the Brooklyn based American Vitagraph studios in May 1909, and volunteered to run errands for the stars and crew for free, while others charged for the service. This impressed Maurice Costello, who brought Moe inside and introduced him to the company. Soon, he was appearing in dramas with Costello and comedies with John Bunny and Flora Finch.

At first, he didn't tell his family about his movie work. But, when they thought he was crazy because he was acting like his characters at home, he told them about his extracurricular activities. Unfortunately most of his films from this period were lost when the Vitagraph film library burned on July 2, 1910.

In 1922, he joined Ted Healy, forming the act that would later become the *Three Stooges*. He toured Vaudeville and appeared in films with Healy for ten years before they broke up the act to pursue a separate career. Moe appeared in more than 250 films during his 66 year career, including 190 Three Stooges shorts. Over the act's 50 year history, the Three Stooges went through several personnel changes. Moe who was Stooge head, had a legal agreement with his fellow Stooges stating that he reserved the right to choose Stooge replacements.

At the end of his life, Moe finished writing his memoirs just shortly before his death. He had been suffering from lung cancer for six months but choose to keep his illness to himself. Finally when the illness progressed to where he could no longer remain at home he was taken to Hollywood Presbyterian Hospital where he died Sunday, May 4th. His funeral was two days later at the Hillside Memorial Park where he is buried.

The Stooges were a dedicated bunch; the only thing that could break them up was illness or death. Although Moe was 77 years old when he died, his Stooge films will live on forever.

Hillside Memorial Park (CLOSED SATURDAYS)
600 W. Centinela Avenue
Culver City, California

Directions: From the 405 and get off at the Sepulveda-Centinela exit. Go south on Sepulveda Blvd, then turn left and proceed to the cemetery Go to the office and get a celebrity map. If you have any problems the ground keepers are extremely helpful. After you leave the office walk towards the chapel. Walk around it towards the back and you will see the Love section. Go through here and you will see a small alcove in the right hand corner enter Moe is next to his wife on the wall to your right. He's the 2nd crypt up from the floor.

Jerome Howard
October 22, 1903 - January 18, 1952

When the fifth child of Jennie and Solomon Horwitz arrived they were a little surprised. Jeannie had prayed for a girl after four boys, but instead she got Jerome Lester who would later become perhaps the funniest of all the Stooges,"Curly."

As Curly grew up with brothers Moe and Shemp in Bensonhurst, New York he frequently took center stage and stole the show when the boys put on plays. In these neighborhood shows, Curly, aged seven, loved to prance around in front of the audience. The sound of applause only egged him on to perform again and again. His brothers would sometimes cast him as the female; a role he didn't mind.

Throughout the career of the Stooges, Curly and his brother Shemp would alternately replace each other, mostly out of necessity due to illnesses on both of their parts.

In 1934, Columbia had offered Moe, Larry and Curly a contract. It was agreed that Moe would become manager for the team. For the next seven years of their contract, the Stooges longed to make a featured film. However, Columbia wanted them to only make shorts because the studio felt that a comedic featured film would not be marketable..

Just the same these shorts brought them big money and Curly spent it as fast as he made it. Moe had his hands full trying to get him to 'save for a rainy day.' But Moe's advice fell on deaf ears as Curly continued to spend his new found fortune on wine, women, cars, dogs, and houses.

Curly performed in ninety seven Stooge comedies for Columbia. Most of the films were very violent and Curly endured many bruises and injuries. He survived the battering his bald head went through, may it be squashed in a printing press, slammed in a door jamb or smashed by a hammar, the show went on.

Once after suffering a severe head injury that left him with a huge gash in his scalp, the studio doctor had to seal his wound with collodion, and a little makeup, so the cameras could continue to roll. Curly continued on very wobbly legs as if nothing happened. The abuse didn't stop there, in public, people were always challenging his endurance for pain, because after seeing him take these blows they thought he was invincible.

On January 25, 1945, Curly checked into the Santa Barbara Cottage Hospital where he underwent some tests. The doctor's findings were scary. He was diagnosed as having high blood pressure, malignant hypertension, a retinal hemorrhage and obesity. His EKG showed definite evidence of myocardial damage. As usual the very serious Moe panicked upon hearing the news and began advising the carefree Curly to change his lifestyle. Once again it went in one ear and out the other. As the years progressed Curly's health had begun to fail due to the rigor of abuse he had taken throughout his career.

In addition to the ninety-seven Stooge shorts, Curly had made appearances in twenty-three other projects; including *"Hold that Lion"* where he played a cameo role in a Shemp short. The 50's were not good for Curly health wise. On August 29, 1950, Curly was admitted to the Motion Picture Home for the second time, this time for a stroke. He spent several months there getting the best care available until he was released on November 15th.

MOE HOWARD
1897 - 1975

Hillside Memorial Park, Culver City, California

During the next three months, Curly's improved condition began to deteriorate again. He suffered a stroke which left him paralyzed and bedridden. The following month he suffered another stroke and this time he had to be returned to the hospital for good. While at the North Hollywood Hospital he lost his ability to walk or talk. He lost so much weight he was a mere shadow of his former self. Curly asked Moe if he could have his dog, Lady, stay with him at the hospital. Moe agreed and brought Lady to his ailing brother. Lady who was accustomed to sleeping with Curly, refused to enter the hospital room and instead chose to sleep in the doorway.

Eventually Curly, due to his mental degeneration, became difficult to handle. The doctors suggested that Moe have him transferred to a mental institution. Moe would in no way put his brother in a mental institution, instead he moved him to the Baldy View Sanitarium in San Gabriel, California where he spent his final days. On January 18, 1952, Curly was gone at the age of 48. Years of physical abuse, greasy food and excessive drink had finally taken it's toll.

His funeral services were held on January 20th at 2pm at the Mallnow & Simons Funeral Home. He was then taken to his final resting place, the Home of Peace Cemetery in Los Angeles. California.

Home of Peace Memorial Park (CLOSED SATURDAY)
4334 Whittier Blvd.
Los Angeles, California
For directions to the cemetery see the Warner Bros. in the Famous Brothers Chapter. Get a map and from the office follow the rod on the right until you see the Western Jewish Institute. He is in the 5th row, grave 1.

Shemp Howard
March 17, 1895 - November 22, 1955
Like his brothers, Shemp was born in Brooklyn, New York. Also like his younger brother Moe, was much better at creating mischief than getting good grades. A chronic complainer and prankster who later became famous for his hypochondria and fear of, well everything.

Shemp caught the acting bug from his brother. He teamed with Moe to put on plays and comedy routines. When they did they often dragged along their little brother, Babe (Curly), who would inevitable wind up the butt of their jokes.

Shemp and Moe were very close and confided in one another about everything. That is why Shemp was shocked when Moe announced that he was running away to Mississippi. He was more concerned about Moe's plans than his parents were. "It began during the summer," said Moe's daughter, Joan. "Having parents who were brought up in Europe, they were a different animal. His mother was bright but couldn't speak English well, and father was into his religion. I think that with five kids to look after, and my dad next to youngest, that at that point they probably didn't pay much attention. Not that she didn't love her sons. The only one nervous about him leaving for Mississippi was Shemp and maybe he was jealous because he didn't have the courage to go himself. Shemp was a worry wart."

When Moe returned he joined Ted Healy forming an act that would someday become the Three Stooges. Shemp joined the troupe and remained with them until he got a better offer. It hurt Healy when Shemp left, because out of all the Stooges, Shemp was his favorite.

Ever the worrier, Shemp had to be reassured by his brother before leaving, fearful his exit would break up the act. He was reluctant to go, saying, "Well, what are you going to do for a third man?" Moe later recalled,. "And I said, "Don't worry, Shemp. We'll take Curly, we'll break him in, and we'll take him along." That decision was to be one of the defining moments in Stooge history.

Shemp pursued his own interests until Curly suffered a stroke and left the Stooges suddenly short handed. At a moment's notice Shemp was back in to fill Curly's shoes. That is until he could no longer perform....

Home of Peace Memorial Park, Los Angeles, California

There was no bigger fight fan other than Shemp, he loved boxing. One night as he was returning home with a couple of buddies after watching a fight card at the Hollywood Legion Stadium, his friends suddenly smelled something burning in the back seat. It was Shemp and his cigar slumped over, dead from a heart attack at the age of 59. The official cause was acute coronary occlusion according to his obituaries. In an attempt to save his life his friends rushed him to St. Joseph's Medical Center in Burbank where he was pronounced dead.

He too kept secrets about his illnesses, his own brother Moe had no idea that he was taking nitroglycerin pills for a heart condition.

Home of Peace Memorial Park (CLOSED SATURDAY)
4334 Whittier Blvd.
Los Angeles, California
For directions to the cemetery see the Warner Bros. in the Famous Brothers Chapter. Get a celebrity map and head over to the mausoleum. Go into the main entrance and walk up to the "Corridor of Memory" make a left. Make a right at the stairs past eh "Corridor of Harmony" past the "Corridor of Benevolence," make a left. Got to the "Corridor of Eternal Life" and on your right side, crypt #W215 approximately 3 sections down is him.

SHEMP HOWARD
BELOVED HUSBAND AND FATHER
1895 — 1955

Home of Peace Memorial Park, Los Angeles, California

San Fernando Mission, Mission Hills, California

Chapter 5: The Little Rascals
Scott Beckett
October 4, 1929 - May 11, 1968

In typical Hollywood fashion, Scotty got his big break when he caught the eye of a casting director who immediately had the young boy tested. His successful screen test led to his debut in a 1933 drama, *"Gallant Lady."*

Hal Roach thought the cute little youngster had a wistful Jackie Coogan_ish quality and signed him to a long term contract. His next step was to pair the boy with another scamp, Spanky. The two were successfully teamed in many Little Rascals shorts throughout the 1930's.

Scotty's trademark attire became that of an oversized turtleneck sweater along with a baseball cap always worn sideways. During his tenure at the Hal Roach Studios, Scotty appeared in a total of fifteen shorts. He performed in his first short at the age of four entitled, "Hi Neighbor!" and three years later he filmed his last short, "Our Gang Follies of 1936. While in high school he took time off from film assignments to try his luck on the stage. He was fortunate to be one of the rare child actors who made the transition into adolescence without it distroying his chances of a continued career in show business. He was cast in many lead roles such as that of young Al Jolson, in the *"Al Jolson Story."* Also he worked on a regular basis for MGM, starring in many films with other now adolescent child stars. Despite his good fortune, his life became turbulent in the late 1940's and early 1950's.

In 1948, he was arrested on suspicion of drunk driving. The following year he eloped with Beverly Baker, a tennis star. It was predictable that the marriage would fail within a few months. A second marriage produced one son, Scott, Jr. This marriage seemed to temporarily keep Scott on the straight and narrow path, until 1954, when he was arrested for passing a bad check and for carrying a concealed weapon.

Despite his brushes with the law his career still prospered. He was offered the role of *"Winky"* the comic sidekick in the popular TV show *"Rocky Jones, Space Ranger."* This would be his last gig.

The last ten years of his life were filled with divorce, violence, drugs and arrests. After show business waned he was forced to sell real estate, and then cars. Some speculate that he sold drugs to supplement his income.

Towards the late sixties, he was admitted into a rest home after an attempt to slash his wrists. He had made a personal promise to clean up his act. But it wasn't long before he resumed taking drugs and drinking.

On May 8, 1968, he checked into a Hollywood nursing home for injuries suffered in a serious beating. He died two days later at the age of 38. Although there were pills and a suicide note present, no conclusion had ever been made by the coroner as to the exact cause of death.

San Fernando Mission
11160 Stranwood Avenue
Mission Hills, California

Directions: Take the 405 to the San Fernando Mission Blvd. exit. Follow it to the cemetery. Get a map at the cemetery and go to Section B and find #1089 on the sidewalk. Find "Dowd" which should be 2 markers down from the 1089, start walking up while counting 21 markers.

Hollywood Forever Cemetery, Hollywood, California

Darla Hood
November 4, 1931 - June 3, 1979

Born in Oklahoma, Darla's opportunity for success seemed slim. She was however, encouraged by both her mother and a teacher to perform. To enhance her talent, Darla's mother invested in dancing and signing lessons for the young child with later paid off. Her teacher, aware of Darla's talent and appeal, took special interest in her and brought her to New York City. While there she was invited to sing with the band leader at the Edison Hotel in Times Square. The crowd loved her and coincidentally, Hal Roach 's casting director Joe Rivkin happened to be dining in the audience. Upon seeing the talented young girl he arranged for an immediate screen test for Darla. Roach liked the test and whisked her away to Hollywood where he signed her to a seven year contract with a starting pay of $75 a week.

Her first Roach short was *"Our Gang Follies of 1936."* The film was already in production; and Roach had her hastily written in. From that moment on, she became "Our Gang's" leading lady.

At age six her career as Our Gang's Sweetheart was beginning to wane. After that came a difficult period of adjustment for her. She never attained the on camera attention, that she once did as a child. Fortunately her career took a behind the scenes turn for the better, where she was the voice of one of the Campbell Soup Kids, the Tiny tears doll and sang the Chicken of the Sea jingle.

In 1979, Darla was hospitalized for Hepatitis. While there she seemed fine and on the road to recovery. She was talking to friends and walking around. Two days later while still in the hospital, she was suddenly dead, as her family put it, 'of suspicious circumstances." She was only 47.

Hollywood Forever Cemetery
6000 Santa Monica Blvd.
Hollywood, California

For directions to the cemetery, see Janet Gaynor in the Glamour Girls Chapter. Go to the Abbey of the Psalms. Find G-4 which is located to the left just before the main entrance steps. G-4 is also the Sanctuary of Light. Look for 2081 on the right side way up at the top.

June Sprigg - Miss Crabtree
November 6, 1903 - March 10, 1984

Her stage name was June Marlowe, but she was really Gisella Goetten of St. Cloud, Minnesota. As a student, she studied for a career in art. In the early 1920's, her father's health was not good and the family thought it best to move west for the better weather so his condition could improve. Once in California, Director Mal St Clair saw her in a school play and invited her to the F.B.O. Studios for a test. Producer Sol Lesser renamed her and soon she was making pictures under contract to Warner Bros.

She came out to the studio and met with Hal Roach, whom she had known through a mutual friend. Roach suggested a blond wig to match Jackie Cooper's light colored hair. The wig dramatically transformed her appearance and instantly she became "Miss Crabtree."

The schoolhouse Miss Crabtree taught in was originally built to teach kids on a huge ranch back when Southern California really was the wild West. Hal Roach purchased the schoolhouse when it was going to be sold or demolished to make room for a larger building, and moved it to the studio location ranch. In the 1960's when the Little Rascals became popular again, June was approached by a publisher who asked her to write some children's stories. She completed one called "Beesy" and one called "Furry." Soon Parkinson's disease made it impossible for her to continue to write these adventures.

In later years, June moved back to Los Angeles with her husband, Rodney Sprigg. She traveled back home to Minnesota as often as her delicate health would allow. She died in 1984 at St. Joseph's Hospital in Burbank, from complications attributed to Parkinson's disease. She was eighty years old.

San Fernando Mission Cemetery (CLOSED SUNDAY)
11160 Stranwood Avenue
Mission Hills, California

BELOVED SISTER

JUNE SPRIGG

1903 — 1984

BELOVED BROTHER

San Fernando Mission Cemetery, Mission Hills, California

Directions: See Scott Beckett in the Little Rascals Chapter. Once inside the cemetery go to the office and get a celebrity map. Proceed to Section B and find 656 on the curb. Find "Smith" a marker that is close to the curb, not far from 842 (not marked) from "Smith" walk up 7 rows and there she is.

Carl "Alfalfa" Switzer
August 8, 1927 - January 20, 1959

Famous for his role as the freckled faced kid in the Little Rascals movies. His tenure in Hollywood would leave him broke, troubled, and a has been at a young age. As with most child stars that grow up and become unmarketable in the movies, he became haunted by his own demons that constantly got him in trouble, which culminated in his murder.

Carl was constantly in trouble with the law and the studio was forced to bail him out of his messes to prevent bad publicity for the newly syndicated "Little Rascals" films. It is even rumored that the studio had grown tired of coming to his assistance, and had his murder set up to silence the troubled star once and for all.

On one occasion he was arrested for selling Christmas trees that he cut down from the Sequioa National Forest. He was fined $225 and put on a year probation. Another time he was involved in a drive by shooting, where he narrowly missed getting shot. This incident was the result of a drug deal gone bad. In 1958, he attempted suicide.

The final thing that did him in was a fight with an acquaintance over a lousy $50. It was 1959, and Alfalfa was 31 years old. Apparently his friend, Stiltz's, hunting dog was missing. The friend put out a reward of $50 for the dog's return. Apparently Alfalfa found the dog, but was never paid for his efforts. On the night of January 21st, Alfalfa and his other friend Piott paid a visit to their friend Stiltz. Alfalfa started banging on the door to be let in, threatening to kick the door in. Stiltz opened the door to Alfalfa and Piott and Alfalfa demanded the fifty bucks he felt that was due him. The two men got into a violent argument over the money and a fight ensued. During the fight Alfalfa grabbed a glass clock and smashed it over Stiltz's head. Stiltz then grabbed for a gun that was in the bedroom dresser. Alfalfa was not afraid and lunged for the gun. During the struggle the gun went off once, hitting no one but the ceiling. Alfalfa then pulled a knife and threatened to kill Stiltz. That's when Stiltz shot again this time hitting Alfalfa and killing him. The knife was found beside the body on the living room floor of the ranch style home. The police determined that Stiltz's action were done in self defense so no charges were filed against him.

Alfalfa is buried in Hollywood Memorial Park Cemetery in the Highland Section. Most of the graves were once in ill repair before the new owners took over, but Alfalfa's was well groomed. Also I noticed a hunting dog on the tombstone. I am suspecting that it was because at one time Alfalfa and his friend and murderer, Stiltz, were partners in a bear hunting scheme in which Alfalfa worked as a guide, one of the many varied jobs he worked during his later years. I would hate to think that it was someone's sick joke, because that's what he lost his life over, a hunting dog.

His grave is located by his father and another relative, perhaps his uncle. On his father's tombstone, there is a photo of a washer machine and a slogan, "the Switzer Method." Could he have been the precursor to the Maytag man?
Hollywood Forever Cemetery
6000 Santa Monica Blvd.
Hollywood, California
Highland Section
For directions to the cemetery see Janet Gaynor in the Glamour Girls Chapter From the office go up Pinelawn Ave to Maple Ave. and make a left. Go up halfway and park. On your left is the Highland Section/Section 6. Alfalfa is close to the road by three tall trees

BELOVED FATHER
SON AND BROTHER
CARL "ALFALFA" SWITZER
AUG. 7, 1927   JAN. 21, 1959

Hollywood Forever Cemetery, Hollywood, California

William Thomas- "Buckwheat"
March 12 1931 - October 10, 1990

Born in Los Angeles in 1931 he appeared in his first short *"For Pete Sake,"* at the age of three. While at Hal Roach studios he appeared in ninety-three "Our Gang" comedies, over a period of ten years.

In February 1934, Hal Roach personally staged the first of many talent contests at the Lincoln Theater on Central Avenue, a predominately black community of Los Angeles. Thousands of kids headed for the theater for these Saturday tryouts in hopes to reach Hollywood stardom. Each month Roach himself, selected four kids for screen tests back at the studio. This left hundreds of disappointed stage mothers, who would not take no for an answer. These parents wanted a second chance and camped outside the studio, looking for Hal Roach.

Throughout 1934, many of these kid applicants were auditioned, lots were tested, and only two were given six month contracts, neither worked out. Then on October 10th, the tryouts ended when Mattie Thomas answered the Wednesday "open call" at the studio gate, and gained entry into Hal Roach's office, where he was finally hired. After a long run in the series, Billie Thomas did some work away from Our Gang. From 1943 to1945 he completed three pictures.

By the fall of 1945 he had dropped out of movies and entered public school. It was the first unpleasant experience in his life. Kids teased him, but he adjusted well, and later joined the Army after high school. There he served in the Korean War. After the Army he wasn't interested in pursuing a continued career in show business. Instead he embarked on a steady job as a film laboratory technician with Technicolor in Hollywood..

The last time he appeared on TV was on the *"Tomorrow Show"* with Tom Snyder in 1974. There he was reunited with Darla, Spanky, and Stymie. Buckwheat really didn't associate or keep in touch with the other "Our Gang" alumni, with exception to Stymie. Their relationship only lasted for the last six years of their lives.

He was divorced and living alone near the University of Southern California, when he died of a heart attack at age forty nine. It was forty six years to the day, that his mother first brought him through the gates of Hal Roach Studios.

Inglewood Park Cemetery
720 East Florence Avenue
City of Inglewood, California

Directions: Take the 405 to Manchester Ave exit, continue to La Brea make a right continue to Florence Avenue make a right. The office is towards the back, follow the dotted lines to get to it. Once at the office ask for a celebrity map and head for the Acacia Slope section. Go to the far right hand corner of this section. It is approximately 2 rows of markers down from the end and two rows in from the street. He's in Grave D, Lot 773.

Petey the dog

Perhaps my most favorite character. I wanted to get his tombstone, but unfortunately I could not. I traveled to the **L.A. Pet Cemetery in Calabassas**, where he is buried. The office would not give me the exact location of his grave, the best they could do was point me in the general direction. Even the cemetery workers wouldn't cooperate. Usually they will go ahead and tell you but these guys were steadfast in keeping their stupid little secret.

While I searched each tombstone I found at least four different "Peteys." Non of which I felt was the genuine artifact. So alas we are without Petey.

Oh yeah, cause of death: poisoned by a disgruntled person.

Inglewood Park Cemetery, City of Inglewood, California

WILLIAM B. THOMAS
PFC US ARMY
WORLD WAR II
MAR 12 1931 ● OCT 10 1980

George "Spanky" MacFarland

He lived the latter part of his life as an entrepreneur in Dallas, Texas. With exception to an occasional "Our Gang"reunion or a fund raiser, George MacFarland led a quiet existence far from the Hollywood spotlight. He died of a heart attack in 1993. He was cremated and his ashes given to his family.

Forest Lawn Memorial Park, Glendale, California

Chapter 6: The Rat Pack

The name "Rat Pack," did not originate with its owners, so they claimed. They, Sinatra, Lawford, Davis, Martin and Bishop, said that they did not like the term and that it was a result of Time Magazine.

What probably started the whole thing, was that Sinatra and his crew were among those who belonged to Humphrey Bogart's, "Holmby Hills Rat Pack," in the early 50's. When Humphrey Bogart died in 1957, Sinatra took over. Most of the original members quit and the new group was made up of Frank, Sammy, Joey and Dean. Peter Lawford was added later.

They epitomized "cool," by driving expensive cars, carrying a martini in one hand and a cigarette in the other. They were constantly surrounded by beautiful woman, stayed only in the penthouses of the best hotels , and had their own "cool" language.

Sammy Davis Jr.
December 8, 1925 - May 16, 1990

Born in New York City, Sammy Davis Jr. entered show business at the age of two. His first exposure to show business was in an act with his father where they toured the vaudeville circuit. To bypass the strict child labor laws, Davis was billed as "Silent Sam the Dancing Midget." Later at the age of seven, he debuted in his first film, "Rufus Jones for President."

As a patriotic gesture, Davis then still an adolescent. attempted to sign up for the army when Pearl Harbor was bombed. He was too young at the time, but one year later signed on for what was to be an a very long stretch in the army. Sammy had to endure basic training eight times; apparently the army was quite a challenge to someone of his slight stature. His speciality was song and dance and as you know the army does not have too many slots for variety artists. In addition to the basic training problems, Sammy endured a salvo of racist attacks, belittlements, assaults, slights and slurs. Ultimately, this treatment fed his desire to become a star.

After getting out of the army, Sammy, Uncle Will and his father continued to struggle. It was at this time that Sammy first met Frank Sinatra, who was at the peak of his drawing power as a teen heartthrob. Sinatra was huge, but Sammy was still trying to get to the next level to become more than just another flash dance act.

When Sammy met Frank, his career took on a more positive direction, especially when he became a member of the Rat Pack. Although Sammy still was faced with a lot of racial barriers. Sinatra opened many doors of opportunity for him.

On November, 1954, while driving from Las Vegas to Los Angeles, Sammy was involved in a near fatal collision which resulted in the loss of his left eye. The accident generated enormous publicity for the rising young star. Finally he saw the light at the end of that long tunnel to show business. From that moment on he worked hard to keep his name in the papers as he entertained audiences. Many times his attention getting antics would overshadow his artistic achievements, but nothing could diminish the incredible strength of Sammy's talent.

During the 70's and 80's things in show business were changing. The traditional lounge acts that were popular in the 50's and 60's were now becoming a thing of the past. It was no surprise that Davis would now find it hard to fit in during the late 70's and early 80's. The only thing left for Sammy was to settle on entertaining in the showrooms of Las Vegas, Reno, Atlantic City or Lake Tahoe. Variety shows that appeared on television were now near extinction, so this was no longer an option for him either. Unfortunately too late for Sammy, was a re-emergence of performers in the 90's, who like Davis had faded away.

Sammy Davis' lifelong habit of inhaling enormous volumes of cigarette smoke resulted first in cancer of the throat. After many unsuccessful treatments, it spread to the rest of his body. On May 16, 1990, Sammy Davis Jr. died in Beverly Hills.

When Sammy Died , the lights on the Vegas strip went dark for an unheard of ten minutes in tribute to their beloved "Mr. Bojangles" The only other times the lights had been dimmed were for.President John F. Kennedy and later, briefly for Dean Martin

PETER SYDNEY LAWFORD

BELOVED HUSBAND, FATHER & FRIEND

SEPT. 7, 1923 - DEC. 24, 1984

(Has since been removed)

According to his daughter Tracey Davis, the first hours after Sammy's death went badly. Ignoring Sammy's last request that his headstone should simply read: "The Entertainer," his wife, Altovise, changed it to read: "The Entertainer. He Did It All: Your Loving Wife Altovise, Father of Tracey, Mark, Jeff and Mann." Manny was a young man who was never adopted by Davis. Also against Davis' wishes, he had an open casket, revealing his thin body that had been ravaged by cancer. And worse yet, a photographer had appeared out of nowhere and had taken pictures of Sammy in the casket.

Tracey, almost hysterical, had called their dear friend Shirley MacLaine and told her about the incident. Shirley told their mutual friend, David Steinberg, who confronted the photographer with a lie that Sinatra would have him killed if the photos weren't turned over to the family. The shaken photographer immediately complied. Tracey later discovered that it was Altovise who hired him to take the pictures.

Sammy's death was the lead story in newspapers, on the radio, and television. When the motorcade left Sammy's house, it looked like a presidential procession, thousands of people lined the streets, taking off hats, crying, and shouting "Sammy we love you." Legions of celebrities showed up for the services. People were led through the park in groups to accommodate the many thousands of fans that showed up.

He once said, "You name it and I've done it. I'd like to say I did it my way. But that line, I'm afraid, belongs to someone else." Well his grave is quite spectacular, it is located in Forest Lawn in Glendale. He is locked in the Garden of Honor, with fellow singer Sam Cooke. As you can see he has a beautiful white marble statue with "DAVIS," inscribed in it. Sammy is not the only Davis under that statue, he is buried with his father, grandmother, and Uncle Will.

Forest Lawn Cemetery - Glendale
1712 S. Glendale Ave
Glendale, California
Garden of Honor

For directions see Jean Harlow in the Glamour Girls Chapter. Get a map, but don't ask for any locations. Drive to the Freedom Mausoleum and park. Walk up the center of the court of Freedom. To the left of that is the Garden of Honor. Sometimes it is locked and sometimes it's not. Inside is Sammy Davis is located to the right side of the garden along with his father They are located below a family statue that simply says "Davis."

Peter Lawford
September 7, 1992 - December 24, 1984
Date exhumed May 18, 1988

Hailed from a privileged British upbringing, his family had suddenly found themselves broke. But thankfully due to their social status they were permitted to stay with several wealthy friends in their guest houses. When this was no longer an option they made the move to West Palm Beach, Florida and lived in a small cottage as they attempted to stretch their meager income. Peter got a job as a valet, parking cars to help make ends meet. One of his frequent customers was none other than his future father-in-law, Joseph Kennedy, who allegedly criticize him severely for befriending a black valet. The incident almost cost him his job, when the senior Kennedy complained to the management.

Later he moved with his family to California, where he became an MGM studio star almost overnight. Finally with a new career and bigger paycheck he was able to afford better living conditions for his family. What would be considered a *not so honorable* profession in the social circles he once was a part of, was now his and his family's salvation.

This new lifestyle not only provided a decent living, but also provided him with the excesses of the Hollywood. As a young eligible bachelor he was frequently seen out on the town with several current day starlets. He would party at the best clubs, drink the finest champagne and eat the best food. Nothing was too good for this star.

One of his romances was with starlet Ava Gardner, whom at the time was ex-girlfriend of pal Frank Sinatra. This relationship caused a huge rift between the two that never quite healed. Frank's bad temper and extreme jealousy almost caused Lawford's days to be numbered. The only thing that perhaps saved him was his connection with the Kennedys.

Later after many flings with major Hollywood glamour girls, Peter settled down and married Patricia Kennedy; sister of John and Robert Kennedy. Life with the Kennedys was not going to be easy. His father-in-law was frequently quoted as saying that he would never want any of his daughters to marry an Englishman or an actor. Perhaps Peter should have taken that as an omen.

The Kennedys did little for his career and shattered his self-esteem, as he became the brothers' link to the Hollywood lifestyle. His Santa Monica beach house served as a playground filled with a bevy of naked beauties swimming and laying around the pool. It is rumored that many neighbors have commented about seeing the President and the Attorney General also naked in the pool.

All the pressures of trying to balance the Kennedy lifestyle with the Hollywood lifestyle took it's toll. Soon he developed a severe dependence on drugs and alcohol. In effect, he was slowly killing himself despite anyone's attempt to help save him. Despite his many trips to rehabs, he still found a way to the booze and drugs.

That became evident to his last wife, Patty Seaton after she happen to stumble across some American Express receipts for a helicopter rental. It is alleged that while Peter was supposedly "drying out" at the Betty Ford Clinic, he was having drugs flown out to him in the desert. He confessed that he would go on long walks into the vast desert to meet the scheduled flight. He would do his 'stash' then return to the clinic as if nothing happened. No one ever suspected a thing.

Towards the end of his life as the drugs and alcohol firmly took hold of him, he became unemployable and his career waned. No one wanted to deal with him, because he would be late or not show up at all. If he did show up he would be incoherent and unable to say his lines. His abuses not only caused him to lose any opportunity to get work, but it ended his life as well. Days before his death, his wife found him laying on the kitchen floor, unconscious and bleeding. Peter was admitted to Cedars-Sinai Medical Center (hospital for the stars) in serious condition. His body was dying; as his kidneys and liver were failing. He had lost the ability for his blood to clot, so surgery was out of the question. Peter was put on life support system and doctors tried to detoxify him the best they could. His skin was yellow and the chance for survival was extremely slim.

On December 19th he slipped into a coma and remained that way for the next four days. At 8:50 am, on December 24th, Peter moved for the first time in days. His upper body rose, muscles contracting involuntarily and suddenly blood spurted from his mouth, his nose and ears. He fell back onto the mattress and was dead. The Christmas day newspapers read, "Peter Lawford dead at 61."

Peter was cremated on Christmas Day, and the following evening a small group of family and friends attended a closely guarded funeral at Westwood Village Mortuary. In a cold driving rain, Patty, his children, Caroline Kennedy, Bobby Kennedy Jr. and several more of Peter's longtime friends heard him eulogized by both a Catholic and an Episcopalian priest.

After the thirty minute service, which included the playing of John Lennon's "Love," Peter's ashes were entombed in a double crypt just several yards from friends Marilyn Monroe. and Dean Martin.

When I visited Westwood Memorial Park, I was led over to an empty crypt. According to the author James Spada who wrote his biography, he states that Lawford had died heavily in debt.

In 1988, Peter's funeral expenses had never been paid. The mortuary warned Peter's wife that if she did not come up with the balance, which was only about $7000, they would be forced to remove his ashes. His children said they would pay the balance, if Peter's widow would relinquish control of the crypt. She refused to give up her rights and told them that she was going to have the ashes removed and scattered at sea. Everyone agreed and his kids paid the disinterment fee of $430.

On May 25,1988, the cemetery workers pried open the crypt and handed Patty the urn containing Peter's ashes. She traded the National Enquirer, photo privileges for a ride in a Limousine to Marina del Rey and a boat ride to scatter Peter's ashes in the Pacific. The crypt is now the new residence of Jack Lemmon. This crypt seemed unusually large to house only an urn with ashes. Maybe he had purchased it when things were not so financially bleak for him. I was told that those crypts can cost anywhere from $80,000 to $100,000.

Westwood Memorial Park
1218 Glendon Avenue
Los Angeles, California
For directions to the cemetery see Marilyn Monroe in the Glamour Girls Chapter. As you first enter the cemetery bear left and park. Just past the Armand mausoleum you'll see several horizontal crypts, one of which is inhabited by Truman Capote. All of them have names on them with exception to one, this was Peter's crypt.
Exhumed on May 25, 1988 ashes scattered at sea.

Dean Martin
June 7, 1917 - December 25, 1995
Born Dino Paul Crocetti, the son of Italian immigrants, he spoke only Italian until the age of five. English was his second language and made him insecure about speaking in public. He once said, "When Jerry Lewis and I were big, we used to go to parties, and everybody thought I was big-headed and stuck up, and I wasn't. It was because I didn't know how to speak good English, so I used to keep my mouth shut."

He gained fame through his union with Lewis in the 40's and 50's. Later after the team's break up he became a member of the "Rat Pack." He is remembered for his smooth baritone voice, a constant drink in his hand accompanied by a cigarette.

For many years he successfully mixed cabaret and film work without any prospects for a recorded hit. In 1964, things changed as he reached number one with "Everybody Loves Somebody." The song became the theme to his long running, "The Dean Martin Show."

After forty years in the public eye, Dean became semi-retired and took refuge in his Beverly Hills home. Occasionally he would make an appearance with Frank in Vegas or Jerry on his telethon.

In 1987, Martin's son, Dean Paul, was killed in a fiery plane crash. With this he lost the will to live and became reclusive. Two weeks before his death, while having lunch alone at the Friar's Club in Los Angeles, Milton Berle came by his table to say hello. Dean kept the conversation short and said, "Goodbye, old friend."

Martin's mental collapse, plus his life long habits of heavy drinking and smoking killed him on Christmas morning, 1995. His cause of death was respiratory failure due to emphysema. Private services were held at the Westwood Village Memorial Chapel. He is interred in the sanctuary of remembrance. The epitaph on his crypt says it all: "Everybody Loves Somebody Sometime."
Westwood Memorial Park
1218 Glendon Ave
Los Angeles, California
Sanctuary of Love
For directions to the cemetery see Marilyn Monroe in the Glamour Girls Chapter. As you enter the cemetery make a left and follow the drive around to the Sanctuary of Remembrance. It is the third sanctuary before the end. He's on the left wall, third column over and third from the bottom. His parents are in the Sanctuary of Love behind him under the name "Crocetti."

Frank Sinatra
December 12, 1915 - May 14, 1998
Born in 1915, in Hoboken, New Jersey, Francis Albert Sinatra was thought to be stillborn. But thanks to the quick thinking of his grandmother, a former midwife, who doused him with cold water, he was okay. Maybe his slow start in life was why he grew to be a rather scrawny child. But what he lacked in physical stature, he made up with a charismatic, strong willed personality that most said he inherited from his mother.

Westwood Memorial Park, Los Angeles, California

DEAN MARTIN
JUNE 7, 1917 - DECEMBER 25, 1995
EVERYBODY LOVES SOMEBODY SOMETIME

Sinatra's start into show business was the successful win of first prize in the 1935 radio talent program, Major Bowes Amateur Hour. Within a few years he was a regular, singing with that show and playing the occasional club and radio gig. In addition to that he held down a $15 a week job as a singing MC and headwaiter at an Englewood, N.J. eatery called the Rustic Cabin. There he was discovered by trumpeter and bandleader Harry James, who was looking for a featured singer for his band.

While Sinatra sang with Harry James, it was rumored that his manager planted frenzied females in the front row to get the crowd going. It seems that he really didn't need this because all of his appearances were sold out and his records ruled the charts.

In the late 40's, Sinatra became interested in pursuing an acting career. His charismatic personality was exploited in a string of "cool", generally music-oriented films.

Then the early 50's he became his gloomy period. First, a scandalous affair with screen sex goddess, Ava Gardner, led to the break up of his marriage. When news got out that he left his wife and three small children to marry Gardner, the press had a field day that almost destroyed his career. Then the following year, his vocal cords suddenly hemorrhaged. With all this bad luck, his music career foundered in neglect, his film career stalled out and his personal life ended up in shambles. The 37 year old Sinatra was clearly considered a write off when he was dropped by Universal, CBS TV, Columbia Records, and worst of all his agent.

In 1953, things began to turn around for Sinatra. He landed a role in "From Here to Eternity," and embarked on a new recording contract with Capitol Records. Sinatra's phoenix_like creative renaissance was due to Ava Gardner's help in securing him that movie role.

Almost twenty years later, Sinatra announced his retirement from both recording and acting in 1971. However, he did do a television special and album, "Ol Blue Eyes Is Back" 1973. Then in 1980, he played in an urban crime drama, "The First Deadly Sin." His last project was an album entitled, "Duets" (1993) that was followed by "Duets II" that he did in 1994.

Although Sinatra continued to perform in the early part of the 90's, his health began to trouble him. Years of smoking and heavy drinking had taken their toll on his body. On one occasion he lost consciousness as he was performing and had to be rushed to the hospital where he spent time recuperating. Realizing that he could not perform as he once did, he retired to his home. He occupied his time by painting, which allowed him to take the final years of his life a little easier.

His heart problems became progressively worse in 1997 and he was in and out of hospitals on a regular basis. Finally the end came on Thursday night, May 14th, when Frank died of a heart attack at Cedars-Sinai Medical Center in Los Angeles. As reported from the Sinatra web site, he went out fighting. His children said. "Please know that Frank was courageous and fought very hard, and that he never gave up, not even at the very end. He came in fighting for his life, and he went out fighting for his life." His last words were, "I'm losing."

Sinatra's Funeral took place at the Good Shepherd Catholic Church. His casket was covered with his favorite flower, gardenias, which also hung in wreaths above each of the three doors of the church. And as usual for "ol blue eyes" it was a standing room only crowd minus the screaming girls in the front row. More than 500 mourners, including his widow and children packed the church, which was covered with white flowers.

Frank's wife, Barbara, and some of the family accompanied the casket to Palm Springs on a private jet, where he was buried beside his parents, Natalie "Dolly" Sinatra and Anthony Martin Sinatra.

Like Sonny Bono, Frank is buried in Palm Springs, California. When I found his grave, I also found the graves of practically his whole family and friends. They almost took up the whole row, squeezing out Zsa-Zsa Gabor's mother and sister into the next row. First is Frank's dad, his mother, his uncle Vincent, then Frank, then a spot (perhaps for his current wife, Barbara), then his friend Jilly, and then his mother and father-in-law. Amazing in life he was always surrounding by many wives, children, and assorted family members, and in death he mimics this. I wonder if there is space left for wife #1, and Mia as well. As for Ava she's better off in North Carolina, there she has a crowd of family members of her own.

THE BEST IS YET TO COME

FRANCIS ALBERT SINATRA
1915 † 1998
BELOVED HUSBAND & FATHER

Desert Memorial Park   Cathedral City, California

Shortly after Frank's death, it appears that he reached out from the great beyond to protect something dear to him, a life size portrait of himself that hangs on the wall of the first club he worked in. When the 500 Club, owned by friend Skinny Damato was burned to the ground the only thing that survived unscathed was Sinatra's picture.

Desert Memorial Park
69920 E Ramon Road
Cathedral City, California
Directions: I-10 to Ramon Road exit and go south, the cemetery is on your right. Go to the office and get a map. Park any where and walk up 8 rows to B8 Sinatra is about the third or forth in. His grave is #151

Woodland Cemetery, Dayton, Ohio

Chapter 8: Forever Etched in Stone
Erma Bombeck
February 21, 1927- April 22, 1996

Erma Louis Fiste was born to a typically middle class home in Dayton, Ohio. She inherited her lighthearted wit from her family who faced life in a cheerful way. Despite what most would think, Bombeck's first love was tap dancing, not writing. She was only a year older than 1934's brightest child star, Shirley Temple. Had she been in Hollywood instead of Dayton who knows what could have happened. In truth, it was more of a dream for Erma's mother to see her daughter hit the bright lights of Hollywood, than it was for the painfully shy Erma.

As a young woman she took a job at the Dayton Journal Herald as a full-time newswoman. Soon she became unsatisfied with the objective tone expected. She wanted projects that she could put more of herself into. It was inevitable that in that era she would end up doing a women's page column with her own elements of humor thrown in. This was a time before feminist issues had changed most women's point of view about housework and family. The columns she wrote were as Erma put it, "a sort of sick 'Hints from Heloise'.... I told people to go clean their johns, lock them up and send the kids to the gas station on the corner." the column became known as *"Operation Dust Rag,"* a humorous view of housework.

Newly married she grew bored with her column and longed for a child. For the next two years, she experienced a host of fertility problems. After many failed attempts the Bombecks decided to adopt. Soon after January, 1954, they adopted a seven month old girl, Betsy. Despite what doctors had told her, she became pregnant with a son, Andy. Then three years later another son, Matthew was born.

After her kids were grown and in school, she returned to work. She started a column called *"At Wit's End."* which paid a big $45 a week. Within five years, however, the column appeared regularly in 500 newspapers. In 1988, she moved the column to Universal Press Syndicate so her column could get more exposure.

In the early 1960's, Doubleday and Company expressed interest in publishing a compilation of Erma's best columns. For Erma the prospect of writing a book was an exciting experience that would be the icing on the cake of her career. Her book, entitled *"At Wits End,"* finally came out in 1967. Although it wasn't an instant best seller it did put Erma's name on the literary map.

By 1978, Erma was hot. She had written several books, columns, and a 'made for TV' movie: *"The Grass is Always Greener Over the Septic Tank."* She was now being offered another deal: to develop a sit-com for TV, called *"Maggie."* It was based on her family, set in her hometown, Dayton, Ohio. *"Maggie"* debuted in September 1981, and unfortunately only lasted eight weeks. There was no real reason for it's cancellation; it just didn't get the ratings needed to survive.

On April 23, 1982, Erma learned that she had developed breast cancer and was forced to undergo a modified radical mastectomy of her left breast. She was lucky the cancer hadn't spread, making it possible for her to conquer this horrid disease. Unfortunately she would not be so lucky with her kidney disease.

Erma had inherited polycystic kidneys from her father. This disease which is lifelong and progresses slowly, causes cysts to grow on the outside of the kidneys. Eventually the kidneys become entirely covered and they can no longer function. The only cure is a transplant. On July 1, 1993, she became extremely ill from the disease that she was diagnosed with in her twenties. It had finally shut down her kidneys entirely. The first thing doctors did was to hospitalized her to make sure the cysts were not cancerous. Upon her release, she was instructed on how to administer the dialysis she needed four times a day to sustain her life. The only good news was that she was on a list to receive a kidney transplant. The bad news was that she would perhaps have to wait for a year before one would be available that matched hers.

Westwood Memorial Park, Los Angeles, California

Sticking to her optimistic attitude, she signed a contract for two more books with Harper Collins. In the meantime, the kidney bank didn't have good news, Erma was now told she might expect a new kidney in the spring of 1994. Unfortunately the time came and went and still there was no kidney. Erma's health grew worse and she was now in great pain constantly from kidney failure. She had to be hospitalized once again, this time to remove one of her kidneys, the one with the most cysts. After surgery and five weeks rest, she was back to writing. She was sent home with a beeper, so if a kidney was found she could be rushed to the hospital for a transplant.

On April 1996, the beeper went off and a kidney had been found. She was flown to the University of California at San Francisco Medical Center where the transplant operation was to be performed. The transplant performed by Dr. William J. Amend, on Wednesday, April 3rd was a success. At the same time her eleventh book *"All I Know About Animal Behavior, I Learned in Loehmann's Dressing Room."* was released.

Everything looked good until things took a sudden turn for the worse. Erma's transplant had developed complications arising from the operation. Several days after the transplant she suffered from post operative pneumonia. Not only that she had developed gallbladder disease and jaundice. Her condition worsened to serious. Within three weeks it became apparent that the transplant was not the success that they originally thought.

On the night of April 21st all her family visited a cheerful Erma. The family said their good byes and slipped out quietly later that night. On the early morning of April 22nd, Erma died of heart failure. She was 69.

The funeral was held at St Thomas the Apostle Catholic Church. Upon her request, the services were open to the public. Twelve hundred people came to bid their farewells to their favorite author. Her body was then transported to Woodland Cemetery in her hometown of Dayton, Ohio. In honor of their literary daughter, Dayton named a street after her.

Her tombstone is an unusual one, a giant rock from her Arizona home. It arrived in the cemetery on April 23, 1996 and yet to date, it still has no marker.

Woodland Cemetery
118 Woodland Avenue
Dayton, Ohio
Directions: I-75 to 35 E and get off at the main Street exit take Main Street exit. Then take main Street to Steward Ave, make a left to Erma Bombeck St, make a left to Woodland Ave, make another right..As you drive into the cemetery park and get a map. For her grave you really don't need a map because if you look to your left from the office/entrance you'll see a huge rock. That's her grave.

Truman Capote
September 30, 1924 - August 25, 1984
His first published work was at age 25, when he documented his lonely, troubled childhood in Alabama, in a series of short stories featured in a novelette called *"Other Voices, Other Rooms."* He is most famous, however, for his novel, *"In Cold Blood"* an impersonal account of an actual murder.

Capote led a colorful life plagued by a well publicized addiction to alcohol and drugs. He along with other avant garde types were permanent fixtures at the legendary Studio 54 in New York City.

Eventually he became ostracized by most of his Studio 54 celebrity chums for publishing a revealing story about their secrets and their lives. This and the rigors of alcohol and drugs took its toll on his diminutive body. With his health failing he decided to visit his friend Joanna Carson on the west coast and leave his sordid east coast life behind.

While staying with close friend Joanna Carson, he fell ill and became bedridden. The years of alcohol and drug abuse had forever ruined his liver. On the morning of August 25th, Joanna entered his room only to find Truman near death. "He was cold and didn't look good." she said. She offered to get him a cup of tea and he gripped her arm and begged her to stay, he then slipped away. He was only 59.

Ketchum Cemetery, Ketchum, Idaho

Per his request he was cremated and half of his remains went to Joanna and the other half went to former lover, Jack Dunphy who lives in Sagaponack, N.Y. The reason for this was that he wanted to be eternally bi-coastal.

Enshrined for four years in the Bel Air home of his friend Joanna, he was stolen during a Halloween costume party. At 11:40 pm, she notice that he was missing along with some of his mementos and $200,000 worth of jewelry. Then six nights later a mysterious car screeched in and out of Carson's driveway, leaving Truman's remains in a coiled up garden hose on her back steps. Happy that she recovered her friend's remains; she no longer felt he was safe within her home. So Joanna purchased a crypt for him at Westwood Memorial Park, where he could be near his friends Marilyn Monroe and Natalie Wood. At noon on November 11th, two mausoleum officials removed the pink marble face plate from a coffin size crypt so that Joanne could place the urn and a few mementos inside. Also she included a letter to Truman that read, in part, "True love,... Wait for me. I'll be joining you in time and we'll sail kites against the clear blue sky... As you once said 'Living on this planet will kill you.'... Just don't take your eyes off me for a second."

Westwood Memorial Park
1218 Glendon Avenue
Los Angeles, California
For directions to the cemetery see Marilyn Monroe in the Glamour Girls Chapter. As you enter the cemetery make a left and park. Walk over to the wall of crypts on your left he's there.

Ernest Hemingway
July 21, 1900 - July 2, 1961
Nobel and Pulitzer Prize winner, he influenced generations of writers. His novels included *"The Sun Also Rises"* and *"For Whom the Bell Tolls,"* where he used brutal themes to weave his tales.

A man with a death wish, Hemingway enjoyed things that put his life in constant danger. He felt that life was for the living and that you should jump in with both feet and worry about the consequences later. His loves were big game hunting under the worse conditions, deep sea fishing, bull fighting and any other macho activity. Professionally he also tempted fate as a war correspondent who reported from the front lines. Like a cat with nine lives he managed to walk away from two plane crashes. His yen for a daring lifestyle was probably inherited from his father, an ambitious man who was one of many Hemingways who eventually committed suicide.

Due to his over indulgences, his health was extremely poor. He suffered from a host of ailments including high blood pressure, high cholesterol, and a failing liver. All of which may have played an important role in contributing to his overwhelming depression.

During his lifetime, Hemingway had visited countless hospitals and doctors to help him deal with his depression. On November 30th, he made the trip to the Mayo Clinic in Rochester, Minnesota along with his fourth wife, Mary. While there he received a course of electric shock treatments twice a week during the months of December and January. The treatments seem to go well with exception to their common side effects which are headaches and temporary memory loss. This became a bit of a catch 22 for Hemingway. If he didn't get the treatment he would be depressed and if he got the treatment he would suffer memory loss and then he couldn't write which would depress him further. There seemed to be no solution to his problems. Except the drastic one he eventually took.

Another thing that added to his depression was the fact that the treatment interfered with his social life. While still in the clinic, he received an invitation to then President-elect John F. Kennedy's inauguration ceremonies. A once in a life time event, that he had to watch on television along with everyone else.

He was finally discharged in late January and flew back to his home in Ketchum, where he attempted to write a little each morning. Ernest did everything he could to follow his doctor's instructions, which included a hike in the afternoon. Yet, things weren't right. He was quiet and withdrawn, not his usual self.

DOROTHY KILGALLEN KOLLMAR
BELOVED WIFE AND MOTHER
1913 — 1965

IN GOD'S CARE

Gate of Heaven Cemetery, Hawthorn, New York

23-121-6

Soon after many depressive episodes, he began to harbor suicidal thoughts. Mary came downstairs only to discover her husband standing there in his red robe, holding his shotgun. Quickly thinking she stalled for time after calling the doctor who were on their way. She spoke quietly to him for a little over an hour until the doctor arrived. Successfully she persuaded him to give her the gun. After this episode, she took him to Sun Valley Hospital for observation. It was determined that he needed to return to the Mayo Clinic right away. The minute they arrived at home to pack for the trip, he picked up the gun again and held the muzzle to his throat. Once again his wife had to disarm him, before he could inflict harm on himself or her.

During their flight back to the Mayo Clinic, he attempted to kill himself again as the plane stopped for refueling in Rapid City. Hemingway tried to walk into the blades of the whirling propellers of a taxiing plane.

Upon arrival to the clinic he underwent another series of shock treatments. After that they felt they could do no more and they discharged him. A shocked Mary became very upset because she knew that it was only a matter of time before he would attempt to kill himself again. She arranged for a transfer to a psychiatric institute in Hartford. The Mayo Clinic advised her against this, so with little other options, she decided to take her husband home. She rented a Buick and headed home with her husband.

Perhaps the trip did Hemingway some good because when they arrived home his condition seemed to be improved. One Saturday evening on July 1st, he shared a happy evening with his wife singing an Italian song, *"Tutti mi Chiamano Bionda."* Mistakenly Mary thought that perhaps this time he was finally cured. The next day was beautiful and sunny. Everything looked better than things had been in a long time. Unfortunately Mary could not see what lurked in her husband's troubled mind.

Ernest woke up early, put on his red robe and went downstairs while his wife still slept. He took the keys for the basement from the window ledge behind the kitchen sink, and quietly made his way down the basement stairs. He unlocked the storage room where Mary had put the guns and chose a double-barreled Boss shotgun. Then after grabbing a handful of shells, he locked the door and came upstairs to the front foyer and small entryway. He loaded the two shells, put the butt of the gun on the floor, and pressed the twin barrels against his forehead just above his eyebrows and pulled both triggers.

Upon the news of his death, some friends described him as despondent while others thought him to be in good spirits. To protect her husband's memory, Mary issued a statement saying that Ernest had *accidently* shot himself while cleaning the firearm and that services would be held at the Lady of the Snows Church.

His house has since been purchased by the Nature Conservancy. It can be seen from Saddle Road off State Highway 75, three quarters of a mile north of Ketchum The best view is from the west side of the highway . Take the Saddle Road extension toward Warm Springs Road, then turn right on Northwood Way and look uphill to the left. His former house has four big windows with green trim and a green balcony.

Ketchum Cemetery
Hwy. 75
Ketchum, Idaho
Directions: I-75 through town it will briefly turn into Main Street, bear right and keep going on I-75 the cemetery is on your right. Drive into the cemetery follow the 2nd road. Ernest is on your right side midway through the cemetery by a four pine trees to the right.

Dorothy Kilgallen
July 3, 1913 - November 8, 1965
Another person who fell prey to the JFK conspiracy of silence, was the noted reporter, columnist, and television celebrity, Dorothy Kilgallan. As millions watched the popular game show, *"What's My Line?,"* few knew that she had any involvement with the JFK story. Dorothy had broken the convention of silence in the press and written openly in her column about discrepancies in the official story. Then suddenly she was dead.

MARGARET MITCHELL
MARSH
BORN ATLANTA, GA.
NOV. 8, 1900
DIED ATLANTA, GA.
AUG. 16, 1949

MARSH

JOHN ROBERT
MARSH
BORN MAYSVILLE, KY
OCT. 6, 1895
DIED ATLANTA, GA.
MAY 5, 1952

Oakland Cemetery, Atlanta, Georgia

She had revealed secret transcripts of Ruby's testimony in her column after conducting a half hour long interview with him. There she learned that the Dallas underworld met, three weeks before the assassination, at Ruby's strip joint, *"Carousel Club."* The *"Big D's"* mobsters frequented his club discussing a plot to assassinate the president. Also present were Ruby, Officer J.D. Tippit, Benard Wiesmann and later she would learn a fourth party.

Lee Israel, author of *"Kilgallen,"* reports that Ruby, himself a TV fan, had developed a trusting bond with Kilgallen. She had gained his confidence and had several conversations with him in the courtroom.

When Dorothy returned to New York, she told friends that she had discovered that Ruby and the slain Officer J.D. Tippit had been friends. They had been seen together in Ruby's *"Carousel Club"* at a meeting two weeks before the assassination in the company of Bernard Weissman, who had placed the *"JFK- Wanted for Treason"* newspaper ad in Dallas newspapers on November 22, 1963. Studying the Warren Commission Report, Killgallen deduced that the meeting had also been reported to Chief Justice Warren and that the identity of the fourth man, which she had been unable to ascertain, had been reported to Warren as *"a rich Texas oil man,"* a description used in the official transcript.

Kilgallen had told Israel about a very mysterious and sinister player in the JFK assassination plot called David Ferried, another known associate of Jack Ruby. He was involved in gun running, the Marcello mob and other anti_Castro operations from Florida to Texas.

"Nightlife's," producer, Nick Vanoff, pleaded with her not to talk about the subject on the air. She had arrived at the studio with a folder full of pertinent and explosive notes and documents. Throughout the interview she kept the folder closed. Thankfully, Vanoff, asked her agent, Bab Bach, to send her a dozen long stemmed roses.

On the early morning of Sunday, November 8th, Dorothy was found dead, sitting fully dressed, upright in bed. The New York City Police investigated and the coroner found that she had died from the ingestion of a lethal combination of alcohol and barbiturates. All her notes and the article on which she had been working, that would have blown the JFK assassination wide open also disappeared.

After Dorothy's death the code of silence went unbroken. The New York Times and The Daily News both noted the coroners findings of death by suicide. No one questioned anything, not even the fact that she was not a substance abuser, nor did they question why would a woman who was at the height of her career want to kill herself?

Gate of Heaven Cemetery
10 W Stevens Avenue
Hawthorne, New York
For directions to the cemetery see Sal Mineo in the "Rebels Without A Cause" Chapter. Once inside the cemetery get a map from the office and head for Section 23. Look for "DeSIMON" across the street and go to that spot. From the Section 23 sign walk 19 headstones to "BELLAMY" and then turn right and walk 1 up and there she is.

Margaret Mitchell
November 8, 1900 - August 16, 1949
Margaret was most famous for her book, *"Gone With the Wind."* This 1,037 page novel brought her $1 million in royalties, movie payments and the Pulitzer Prize. She felt that her fame had robbed her the time she could contribute to writing.

The end came one evening when Margaret and her husband decided to catch a movie. Instead they stopped for some cocktails at the Atlanta Women's Club on Peachtree Street. As they were attempting to cross at 13th and Peachtree, a speeding taxi driven by Hugh Gravitt rounded the blind curve. Startled by the car, she panicked and darted out in it's path. The driver had been going anywhere between 35 to 50 m.p.h. in a 25 m.p.h. zone and (the skid marks were 67 feet long) could not stop in time. Hugh Gravitt was later convicted of involuntary manslaughter and sentenced to 10 months and 20 days in prison.

JACQUELINE BOUVIER KENNEDY
ONASSIS
1929 — 1994

Arlington Cemetery, Arlington, Virginia

Margaret died on from brain damage and other internal injuries. She was only 49. Her funeral was held on August 17th, where only 300 invited guests were allowed to attend. After the service, fans converged, and tore apart the floral arrangements for souvenirs. She was buried in the historic Oakland Cemetery in Atlanta.

Recently the Margaret Mitchell Estate has initiated a law suit against a black woman who felt the need to re-tell *"Gone With the Wind"* from a slaves perspective. Her claim was that she felt that Mitchell's novel was a slap in the face of all black people because she only represented them as slaves. Right or wrong, weren't there slaves in *that* era?

Oakland Cemetery
248 Oakland Ave SE
Atlanta, Georgia
Directions: Take I-20 to Boulevard, the first exit east of I-75/85. Turn left on Boulevard and then left on Memorial Drive and right on Oakland Avenue. Once in the cemetery go to the office and purchase their map, $1.00. It pretty historic and gives you all the information you need to see the entire cemetery. From the office go left and walk straight to a path that's off the road she is 3 plots away to your left.

Jacqueline Kennedy Onassis
July 28, 1929 - May 19, 1994
During the summer of 1929 Janet Lee Bouvier was driven fifteen miles to the nearest hospital in Southampton. An hour later Jacqueline Lee was born. Jacqueline grew up in a privileged home with a cold self absorbed mother and a hard drinking playboy for a father. Despite all this, money was able to steer the young Jacqueline in the right directions.

She married a senator who succeeded to the White House. Survived her husband's assassination and then became a widow with two young children. Later she entered into a controversial marriage with a Greek tycoon.

After becoming a widow for the second time and once her children were grown, Jacqueline became restless and needed something to do with her life. A friend suggested publishing and Jackie embarked on a career as an editor with two major publishing houses, first Viking Press and then Doubleday.

During the summer of 1993, Jackie contracted what she thought was a flu. Still sick three months later, long time companion, Maurice Tempelsman, suggested that she slow down and reduce her hectic schedule. That perhaps rest would put an end to her illness.

But one Saturday afternoon in November, Jacqueline took a fall from her horse. Unconscious for a few moments, she was taken to a Virginia hospital, where a physician found a swollen lymph node in her groin. Assessing it as a sign of infection, he treated her with antibiotics. When she returned to New York, she felt weaker than ever and was compelled to cancel a few editorial meetings.

Jackie and Maurice began a Caribbean Cruise during Christmas week, but suddenly she became ill with severe pains in her back and abdomen. Now there was a second swollen lymph node in her neck. They returned at once to New York and Jackie checked in New York Hospital-Cornell Medical Center for a battery of tests. When the tests came back the news was grim, she had non-Hodgkin's lymphoma, a particularly virulent form of cancer that can spread rapidly throughout the body. The swollen lymph nodes in her groin and neck were the classic first signs of this disease.

She embarked on chemotherapy and radiation treatment in hopes to abate the cancer. The four courses of chemotherapy took a toll as terrible as the disease itself. On April 14, Jackie collapsed at home and was rushed to the hospital for surgical repair of bleeding ulcers caused by adjuvant steroid injections. At the time of its discovery the cancer had already spread deep into her lungs

Maurice faithfully stayed with her throughout her ordeal, helping her to the doctors and catering to her every need. By the end of April, the cancer had spread to her spinal cord and brain. She was experiencing severe pains in her arms and legs. On occasion, she would have periods of frightening confusion. More treatments entailed a tube being inserted directly into her skull to reduce pressure and to deliver appropriate drugs. Soon her speech and gait were affected.

Green River Cemetery, East Hampton, New York

On Sunday, May 15, Jackie accompanied by Maurice, daughter Caroline and grandchild Jack ventured out to Central Park for the last time. Jackie enjoyed the warm sun and recalled memories of her youth as she sat on the bench. That night she was restless and in terrible pain. By Monday morning she developed chills and a violent headache. She was taken to New York Hospital where she was given antibiotics for pneumonia. She seemed to do better, but then went into a sudden decline. Another scan showed that the disease had now invaded her liver and her kidneys were failing.

Suddenly lucid and without fear Jackie asked that all treatment be withdrawn and that she be taken home. Once home she slipped in and out of consciousness and her breathing became erratic. On Thursday, May 19, the family asked for a priest to perform the final rites. Just after 10pm, there was one long deep sigh and Jackie was gone.

But according to Sarah Bradford's book *"America's Queen,"* a throughly researched and documented biography, that Jackie took her own life to prevent her family's prolong agony as they watched her waste away from cancer.

According to Bradford, on May 19, 1994, a thin Jackie, wearing a purple silk turban to hide her hair loss from chemotherapy, called her beloved children John and Caroline, and other relatives, to her Fifth Avenue apartment in Manhattan. They were all ushered into her darkened bedroom, where the curtains were pulled tight to keep out the sun and the noise of the traffic below. "Once my eyes adjusted to the near darkness, I could see her bedroom was filled with dozens of bottles of pills and medical equipment of all kinds. There was even a respirator to aid her breathing." says a Kennedy family source.

Jackie had a personal goodbye for each and every visitor to her chamber. "Almost everyone important to Jackie came and listened to her final words, she thanked some, chided others quite harshly and told all her loved ones to take care of each other." said the source.

"She told her son John it was her wish that he marry and have children and since she wouldn't be around to approve of his choice for a wife, he should rely on his sister Caroline's judgment."

"She told Maurice, that he brought joy to her life and had been a wonderful surrogate father to her children. Also she told him the get on with his life and fall in love again, if he met the right woman."

"Jackie even joked that the one thing she'd change is if she had to do it all over again would be to spend even more of her second husband, Aristotle Onassis' fortune on designer clothing."

Jackie then took the pills, washed them down with Evian water and drifted slowly away. Her funeral was held at the St. Ignatius Loyola Roman Catholic Church in New York City. After that she was buried next to her first husband, John F. Kennedy in Arlington Cemetery.

Arlington Cemetery
Arlington, Virginia
Directions: I-66 to the Theodore Roosevelt Memorial Bridge this will turn into the Jefferson Davis Hwy get off at the Memorial Drive exit and follow the signs to the cemetery. Get a map from the office, as you leave make a left on Schley Drive, then a right on Roosevelt Drive then another right on Weeks Drive which will lead you right to her grave.

Jackson Pollock
January 28, 1912 - August 11, 1959
His entrance into the world was perhaps just a traumatic as his exit. On January 28, 1912 Jackson was the last of five kids was born. After his birth the doctor forbade his mother to have any more children. Apparently Jackson had become entangled in the umbilical cord and was strangling in the birth canal. When he finally was born he was black. Upon examination there were no signs of any permanent abnormalities in the infant. It is hard to say, however, whether the lack of oxygen contributed to later emotional and physical problems.

In 1930, Jackson and his brothers, Charles and Frank, ventured to New York to study art. It was Charles that encouraged Jackson to make the move from Wyoming. In New York he prospered, because after art school, he quickly turned into one of the most gifted American painters.

Like most gifted artists he was extremely self destructive. Jackson drank hard and drove fast, frequently taunting death. His temper was volatile, especially while under the influence. It was common to see him staggering through Penn Station or spilling a tableful of Thanksgiving dishes all over his wife in a drunken rage. As a typically tortured artist he was arrogant and abusive.

His move to Long Island established an artists' colony in East Hampton. He broke through the walls of traditional art with Abstract Expressionism. Later there was an emergence of other artists to follow: Willem de Kooning, Larry Rivers, Franz Kline, and Joan Mitchell.

On Saturday, August 11, 1956 at 10:30am Jackson went to the only bar in the area that would serve him. Previously he had thrown a brick through the window of another local bar, Sam's Bar, and was permanently banned.. Jackson had a reputation for trouble when he drank, so few bartenders wanted to serve him.

He asked the bartender for his usual 'eye-opener,' a gin. Two girls were on their way from the city to visit him, so he waited at the bar for their train to arrive. By the time they finally reached East Hampton, he was half in the bag. They all headed for his house and he went to bed and tried to persuade one of the girls, Ruth to join him. But Ruth decided to go out with the other girl, Edith instead.

For dinner he washed down a steak with gin and they all discussed whether or not to go to a concert that evening. Shortly after 10:00 pm, Jackson and the two girls Ruth and Edith were in his car driving very fast. The girls sat in the front seat next to a very drunk Jackson. Edith began screaming for him to slow down. While both girls were pleading for their lives, Jackson laughed madly and drove faster. On a curve, he lost control of the car and it headed for some trees.

The first person on the scene after the accident's occurrence, was a mechanic who saw an upside down convertible on the shoulder of the west lane. A woman was approximately ten paces in front of the car crawling on her elbows. The other girl was under the car. Jackson was no where to be seen. A cop who was looking through the woods for Jackson found him by a tree. He was just laying there with his eyes wide open. He had been thrown a good fifty feet hitting the tree dead on with his head. When the cop turned him over, there was a little blood running down from his forehead. There appeared to be no other damage other than a swollen neck from impact and some facial scratches. The woman under the car was pronounced dead at the scene. She didn't have a scratch on her.

This accident was no surprise to those who knew him and lived in the area. He was notorious for drinking and driving very fast. It was just a matter of time before he claimed his life and/or someone else's.

The funeral director, Frederick Williams, assisted Dr. Francis Cooper in the Jackson Pollock case. Frederick Williams had concurred that Jackson's immediate cause of death was due to a compound fracture to the skull, laceration of the brain, laceration of both lungs, and hemothorax shock. Another words, a piece of his skull had pierced his brain. Being that his face and neck were all cut up, the best that the Mr. Williams could do was to prepare, preserve, and then place him in the casket. Jackson was dressed in blue jeans and looked pretty good after they were done with him.

He was taken to the Green River Cemetery on Accabonac Road.

Green River Cemetery
Acabonack Road
East Hampton
From Montauk Hwy (27) go east to Acabonack Road which will be on your left side. Go north or left on Acabonack Road until a little bridge. Continue up the road about three to five miles, until you see the cemetery on your left. Go in either entrance and travel all the way to the rear of the cemetery. You'll see a huge rock, that is Jackson's tombstone.

Andy Warhol
August 6, 1928 - February 23, 1987
Andy was small town boy, turned legendary icon, who rubbed elbows with movie stars, rock stars, designers, artists, CEO's, and heads of state. Also he celebrated his avant garde status with parties, galas, interviews, art openings and spent his evenings at chic clubs and restaurants.

In 1965, he started making films that featured nudity, profanity and boredom; topics that were quite risque for that time. He was best known, however, for enshrining everyday images from soup cans to photos of celebrities like Marilyn Monroe, as high art in the form of repetitive silk screen reproductions. Andy's preoccupation with popularity led to his theory that in the future, everybody would be famous for at least 15 minutes.

Andy Warhola arrived in New York from Bethel Park, Pennsylvania (a small town outside Pittsburgh) in 1949. His lack of finances forced him from time to time, to share apartments with friends until he was able to get his art career going. Eventually Andy's mother suddenly appeared in New York and they moved in together. She remained with him for many years until she suffered a stroke; she then returned to Bethel Park to live with her other sons.

In 1972, she died in a nursing home; years later, whenever someone would ask Andy, "How's your mother?" he would reply, "Oh fine." He was very odd like that.

As finances improved and Andy's art became famous, he moved into a loft on 33 Union Square West, in which he called the "Factory." The "Factory" was a place where his art could grow. There he would make movies using "characters" he would find in the back corners of Max's Kansas City. Max's was a hang out for people who wanted to be in his films. Including the psycho that shot him in 1968.

Valeria Solanis, 29, who was the founder of S.C.U.M. (Society for Cutting Up Men). She had put an ad for her organization in a local newspaper. Andy read it and thought it was a joke so he hired her to act in one of his surreal films. The film he wanted her in was entitled, *"I, a Man."* Valeria wanted something in return for efforts. She wanted Andy to make movie from the script she had written. When Andy declined, she shot him, firing two bullets into his chest and abdomen as he spoke on the phone.

In 1969, after surviving his brush with death, Andy decided to start a magazine. The magazine's objective was to get stars to talk candidly about anything, and he would print their words unedited. This low budget magazine was called inter/VIEW. The magazine achieved two things for Andy: an opportunity to expand his creativity and it kept him from fading into sixties history by meeting creative new people.

Andy's greatest fear was that of going broke. That and getting cancer. Any headache or freckle was always a possible brain or skin cancer. Ironically, it's apparent now in retrospect that when he was really worried about a health problem, he scarcely mentioned it. Like the lump in his neck in June, 1977 which doctors finally diagnosed as benign and the gallbladder problem that led to his death.

On Saturday, February 14, 1987, he went to Dr. Karen Burke for a collagen treatment. During his visit he complained of pains in his gallbladder. The next day he stayed in bed all day and the pain finally went away. Monday, Dr. Burke called Andy to see how he was doing; again he was experiencing sharp pains. His doctor suggested he see his regular doctor, Dr. Denton Cox. That Tuesday, he had to make a "celebrity appearance" at a Japanese fashion show. While he was there he was in severe pain all night. Finally at 6:30 am he took a painkiller and a sleeping pill which enabled him to sleep through the night and past Wednesday. Thursday, at 9am Andy answered the phone; it was his secretary. He was breathing heavily and informed her that Dr. Cox had recommended that he go to "the place" to have "it" done. Andy was petrified of hospitals and any surgical procedures. He was so phobic that he couldn't bring himself to say the words. But he needed to face reality, If he didn't have the operation he would surely die.

On Friday, February 20th he was admitted to New York Hospital as an ambulatory emergency patient. The surgery to remove his gallbladder was to be performed the next day. After it was removed he appeared to be recovering well from the procedure. He watched television and made phone calls to friends.

By Sunday morning he was dead. Apparently his private nurse, did not detect the malfunctioning IV, over hydrated him, causing him to drown in his own fluids. When she had looked in on him around 3:00 am he seemed okay, very pale but that was a natural look for Andy. If it had be anyone else, she said would have been alarmed by his color.

He had two services a quiet one for family and a huge one for his friends which seemed like a day time Studio 54.

St. John the Baptist Catholic Cemetery
Connor Road
Bethel Park, Pennsylvania
From I-70 to Rt. 19 (Washington Road) make a right on Connor Rd and you will soon see the cemetery on your right side. Enter and drive up the hill, his tombstone is up on the hill to your right clearly visible from the road.

MORTON

LUCILLE
1911 – 1989
BALL

Forest Lawn Cemetery, Hollywood Hills, California

Chapter 9: Season Finales
The 1950's Posthumous Pilots
I Love Lucy
Desi Arnaz
March 2, 1917 - December 2, 1986

Lucy's ex-husband was the third cast member to go. He died of lung cancer after a highly publicized life of cigarette and alcohol abuse. Although Lucy and Desi's divorce was far from amicable, they remained friendly towards the end of his life. After he died at his home, he was cremated and his ashes given to his family to be scattered.

Lucille Ball - "Lucy"
August 6, 1911- April 26, 1989

Born Lucille Desiree Ball in Jamestown, New York. The strong willed redhead became fatherless at age four and despite the lack of guidance from her father, she developed a strong work ethic as a child. One job she had was that of a "seeing eye kid" for a blind soap peddler.

It was common in the era for children to take piano lessons. You could entertain friends and family, teach or turn it into a career if you were talented enough. Lucille was no different from anyone else she too took lessons as a child. She however, never pursued it as a career, instead she was interested in acting. As a teen, she did amateur plays for the Elks Club and her high school. At one point she starred, staged, and publicized a production of *"Charley's Aunt."*

In 1926, Ball enrolled in the John Murray Anderson dramatic school in Manhattan, where Bette Davis was also a pupil, but due to her extreme shyness she was discouraged by her teachers to continue. Nevertheless, Ball plugged away until she got a role as a chorus girl. A few modeling jobs gave her a few bucks but little encouragement from her peers.

Ball had been in a serious car accident that left her with recurring stomach ailments which interfered with her theatrical career. Still, she was no quitter and in 1933 managed to become one of the singing and dancing "Goldwyn Girls"for movie producer Samuel Goldwyn.

Another set back occurred when her MGM contract expired, the film industry thought she was washed up and refused to give her parts. Now she had to work even harder to propell herself into stardom.

In the studio's commissary Lucille met the man of her dreams, Cuban Bandleader Desi Arnez. Although seven years his senior, their romance was extremely passionate. In 1940, they married and despite an obvious strong affection for one another, they had separated and considered divorce numerous times during the war years. Hoping to keep her household together, Ball sought out professional work in which she could work with Desi. She was finally offered her own starring TV series in 1950, but refused to do it unless Arnaz would co-star with her. The television executives were not favorable about having Lucy portray the wife of a Cuban and put up a lot of resistance before succumbing to Lucy's demands.

Televison was a godsend for the Arnazs. Desi discovered he had a natural executive ability, and soon he was calling all the shots for what would become *"I Love Lucy."* From 1951 through 1957, *"I Love Lucy"* was the most popular sitcom on television. Ball was finally, after years of career stops and starts, firmly established as a mega-star in her role of a zany, disaster prone Lucy Ricardo.

When her much publicized baby was born in January 1952, the story received bigger press coverage than President Eisenhower's inauguration. With their new Hollywood prestige, Ball and Arnaz were able to set up the powerful Desilu Studio Production complex, ultimately purchasing the facilities of RKO, where both performers had once been contract players. Professional pressures and personal problems had taken it's toll on their marriage and in 1960 Ball and Arnaz were divorced.

Lucille's last television appearance was just weeks before her death. She appeared with Bob Hope, who was in many respect her male counter part in show business. Together they presented a production number featuring rising young talent on the 1989 telecast of the Academy Awards.

Lucille who was a perfectionist, had a reputation for sometimes using salty language or a distant persona to get her point across. One of my girlfriends who was a stewardess that worked in first class for a major airline, had an encounter with Miss Ball.

On this one occasion according to my friend, Lucille was on the plane with her personal secretary. When my friend attempted to ask Miss Ball if she wanted anything, her secretary interrupted my friend and said, "I'm sorry, but you must speak to me, Miss Ball does not talk to the help."

Also being difficult at times were not the only things that ate away at her health. She smoked like a chimney as well.

On April 19th, just eight days before her death, she complained of chest pains and was taken immediately to Cedars-Sinai Medical Center. Cardiologist Yuri Busi diagnosed, a dissecting aortic aneurysm, which in laymen's term, is a hole in the wall of the largest artery, the aorta, that feeds blood to the body. Lucy was sent to surgery within an hour. The surgeons performed an operation, that would take seven hours and forty minutes, in an attempt to save her life. A team of specialists worked to replace her aortic valve and a portion of the aorta itself. The heart must be stopped, making this procedure very risky.

At first she began to recover rapidly, which is no easy feat for anyone who has undergone such an extensive operation. Also a woman of her age, has a higher risk of postoperative complications.

When her daughter visited she lifted her oxygen mask and said, "Wouldn't you know this was the day I was suppose to get my hair color done." The next morning she got up and sat in a chair, and the day after that she was walking around her room with a little assistance. Things looked good for Lucille, as the worst seemed to be behind her.

The last time Dr. Busi saw Lucille, she was in high spirits, looking forward to getting on with her life. But the unforeseeable happened, on April 26th, just before dawn she woke with severe back pains and died within minutes. Her aorta had ruptured again, this time at a point fairly distant from the repaired location. A team of doctors and nurses worked feverishly to revive her, but there wasn't anything anyone could do. She was gone at the age of 77.

There was a question on whether or not the doctors should have replaced the entire aorta. Could that have saved her life? Doctors say that, theoretically it is possible to replace the entire aorta, but due to it's complexity, the operation is seldom performed.

Lucy is now interred in Forest Lawn Cemetery, Hollywood Hills in the Court of Remembrance. I walked into two other little rooms before entering the Columbarium of Radiant Light where she is interred. Out of all the little rooms I entered, I immediately felt that she was there. It was fragranced from all the flowers that were left behind for Thanksgiving. And there was a tree in the middle which was also very nice. She shares that room with Walter Lantz creator of Woody Woodpecker. Her remains, (I would have to guess that she is cremated because she's in a niche), are located to the right as you walk in. There is a bronze plaque that reads, "MORTON," the name of her last husband. Then beneath it is Lucille Ball. Next to her is "Dede," her mother.

Since her death her last husband, Gary Morton, has died. He is interred elsewhere; perhaps because after Lucy died he remarried. She does however, share the Court of Remembrance, with many other stars such as Bette Davis, and Liberace.

Forest Lawn Cemetery - Hollywood Hills
6300 Forest Lawn Drive
Los Angeles, California
For directions to the cemetery see Bette Davis in the Glamour Girls Chapter. Ask for a map at the gate, but don't ask for any celebrity directions or they will throw you out. Follow the main road, Memorial Drive to Evergreen Drive make a left. Then at Ascension Road make a right. Follow this to Vista Lane, left. You will be in front of the Court of Remembrance. Walk past Bette Davis into the Court. Once inside you'll notice you are in a square court, walk to the back left corner to the Columbarium of Radiant Light. Look on the right hand wall towards the corner, look for "Morton" that's where she is.

Photograph by Anne Parisi

San Fernando Mission Cemetery, Mission Hills, California

IN LOVING MEMORY
WILLIAM C. FRAWLEY
FEB. 26, 1887 ✝ MAR. 3, 1966

William Frawley - "Fred Mertz"
February 26, 1887 - March 3, 1966

Bill who was a native of Burlington, Iowa started out in Vaudeville introducing such standards as *"Melancholy Baby"* and *"Carolina in the Morning."* before making the move to Hollywood in 1928. Most of the films he appeared in were comedies. He was in both versions of *"The Lemon Drop Kid,"* respectively in 1934 and 1951.

But William became best known for his character as "Fred Mertz," the Ricardos' landlord at the fictitious address of: 623 East 68th Street, in Manhattan. That address is so fake, that if you were to try to find the address you'd end up in the East River.

Fred's tenure with *"I Love Lucy,"* lasted from 1951 to 1960 when the show ended. Although a prolific actor that appeared in over 150 movies, he had developed a reputation for somewhat of a heavy drinker. Lucille was extremely skeptical about hiring him for the part of Fred, fearing that his drinking might interfer with the show. Husband, Desi, who was also a heavy drinker convinced Lucy to reconsider, offering full responsibility for Bill's actions.

His last acting role was on one other TV show, *"My Three Sons,"* where he played the role of *"Uncle Bub"* for five years. He stayed with the show until his health began to fail forcing him to retire.

One evening after seeing a movie, William and his nurse, were strolling along Hollywood Boulevard when suddenly he was fatally stricken by a heart attack. Despite being rushed to nearby Hollywood Receiving Hospital, he was pronounced dead; a week after his 79th birthday. Rumor has it that the Knickerbocker Hotel is haunted by Frawley's ghost because he died right outside.

Frawley was the first cast member of "I Love Lucy" to die. Desi Arnaz showed his sympathy for his old friend by paying for a full page ad in the "Hollywood Reporter,"which appeared on the day of his funeral. It featured a picture of Frawley along with the dates of his birth and death, and the words, "Buenas Noches, Amigo!" (Which means, "Good Night, Friend!")

San Fernando Mission Cemetery (Office Closed Sunday)
11160 Stranwood Avenue
Mission Hills, California

For directions to the cemetery see Scott Beckett in The Little Rascals Chapter. Get a celebrity map at the gate. From the office go left stop where it says 54 on the curb of the C section. Walk five up and there he is. The map's directions are a little weird, so don't pay that much attention to them.

Vivian Vance
July 26, 1909 - August 17, 1979

Vivian who played Lucy's friend and landlady "Ethel Mertz" was the second cast member to go. She died of bone and breast cancer and was cremated. Her remains were given to her family

The Honeymooners
Jackie Gleason - "Raiphie Boy"
February 26, 1916 - June 24, 1987

Herbert John Gleason broke into show business at age 15, by winning an amateur night contest. From there he went on to perform in vaudeville, carnivals, nightclubs, and road houses.

In 1940, he was signed to a film contract by Warner Brothers, and debuted on screen in *"Navy Blues"* in 1941. His career was interrupted by World War II, but at the war's end, Gleason returned to Hollywood, this time playing character roles in a number of films. His film work, however, lent little strength to his career. He briefly turned to Broadway before making the transition to television where he later achieved major success as a star. His successes were *"The Life of Riley,"* *"The Honeymooners"* and *"The Jackie Gleason Show."*

Our Lady fo Mercy Catholic Church, Miami, Florida

It was on "*The Honeymooners*" that he created such enduring characters as "Ralph Kramden" a loud mouthed bus driver and "Ed Norton" his scatter brained sewer working buddy, played by Art Carney. The show is set in the same Brooklyn neighborhood he grew up in. Not only that, the address of the building featured in the show is the actual address he lived at as a child.

After "*The Honeymooners,*" he relocated to Miami Beach where he broadcasted "*The Jackie Gleason Show.*" As a result of the comedic talents he displayed on TV, he became known as "*The Great One.*"

The Great One, was probably dubbed this for a lot of other reasons as well. One reason comes to my mind, is his invincibility to his excessive lifestyle. Everything he did was in excess. He self-destructed with alcohol, food and cigarettes. He could eat in one sitting, five heavily sauced bowls of pasta and wash it down with a proportional amount of wine. Some said he was trying to commit "foodicide." He smoked like a chimney and usually on, "*The Jackie Gleason Show,*" it was more than just coffee that made him bellow, "*Ohhh, how sweet it is!*"

In addition to that, he compulsively spent his huge income on gross displays of extravagance; his home had a playroom and a huge professional bar that could keep up with any tavern you might visit.

Athough he had achieved great success, it was as though he had a death wish. He continued his unhealthy lifestyle up until his seventies. Finally his body could not tolerate this behavior any longer, and he was now dying.

After complaining of agonizing abdominal pains, his doctor checked him into Imperial Point Hospital in Fort Lauderdale. After three hours of surgery, the doctors removed a large tumor that was blocking his colon. Unfortunately, the cancer had spread to twenty-seven of the twenty-eight lymph nodes in his groin. In addition to that his liver was also affected by the cancer. This was for sure a swift death sentence for Gleason. His doctors informed him that he would only live perhaps another six months to a year. Unfortunately, he did not last that long, he died within one month.

With mortality facing him, he threw caution to the wind and arranged to have his oxygen tent turned off so he could resume chain smoking. A couple of weeks later he had more surgery to repair his intestines that were leaking. The only thing the nurses could do was to strengthen him up, so he could be able to make the trip home to die. On June 24th, he was dead.

Personally speaking, I always liked Jackie Gleason. When I heard that he had died, I felt bad because this was a guy that we all grew up with. If it wasn't the "*Honeymooners,*" it was his show in Miami Beach with the June Taylor Dancers that we all sat around to watch. .

I forget exactly how my friend and I found out where he was having his wake. Perhaps it was in the papers, it was however, opened to the public. We went down to the Lithgow Funeral Home located in North Miami, not really knowing what we were going to see. We were in our early twenties and were kind of afraid to see this normally huge man, withered away from cancer.

We had heard terrible stories from another girlfriend of ours, who was a nurse at the hospital he was in. She said he was hardly recognizable, he was white as a sheet and looked like a ninety year old man. When we arrived we encountered a closed coffin, thank God, with a giant photo of him on top. Written on it was "the greatest card player." In the background they played the Jackie Gleason theme song, "*Melancholy Serenade.*"

Only one star showed up for the wake and the funeral, his former co-star Audrey Meadows. That didn't matter because, there were thousands of people that visited him. The people that really loved him, because he entertained them. You would have thought that the Pope had died. I guess to Miami he is the Pope. They named practically everything after him: a theater, streets, etc.

Several years later I visited his grave. He is one of those people who lived large and maintained that reputation after death. It was his wish to spare no expense for his funeral or burial. And believe me, his grave site is no little headstone. He had a huge marble edifice built overlooking a small lake. In death he also maintained a sense of humor with a suitable epitaph, "And away we go" written on the steps of his crypt. The crypt is large enough to hold two, I guess the other spot is for his widow, when she is ready. It is really something to see, this monument to him, set in the far end of the cemetery. Despite this, it is the first thing you see as you enter the cemetery.

IN LOVING MEMORY

AUDREY MEADOWS SIX

BELOVED WIFE, AUNT & FRIEND

1926 ✝ 1996

Holy Cross Cemetery, Culver City, California

Our Lady of Mercy Catholic Cemetery
11411 NW 25th St
Miami, Florida
Directions: I-95 south to the 826 get off at the NW 41st Street exit. Make a left on SW 87th Street (973) then right on NW 25th Street. Enter the cemetery and bear to your left. You'll see his white crypt by the lake, you can't miss it.

Audrey Meadows - "Alice!"
February 8, 1924 - February 3, 1996

Meadows was perhaps best known for her role as "*Alice*" on the hit television show *"The Honeymooners."* She almost didn't get the role because Gleason thought she was "too pretty" to play a Brooklyn housewife. Audrey wanted the role and thought of a way to convince Gleason that she could transform into the character he was looking for. She paid a photographer to take pictures of her with no makeup, unkempt hair and a sloppy house dress doing a variety of domestic chores. These photos won Gleason over and she remained with the show until it left New York, returning once in 1966 for the last black and white Honeymooners, *"The Adoption,"* which was broadcast from Miami.

Years later she played on another television show "*Too Close For Comfort*" in which she played Ted Knight's mother-in-law.

For many years like Gleason, she too was a heavy smoker, and unfortunately it culminated in her contracting lung cancer. She kept her illness a secret, even from her sister Jayne Meadows, until she was hospitalized. On January 24th she entered the Cedars-Sinai Medical Center where she died a couple of weeks later. Also like Gleason, she was 71.

Her grave is a sharp contrast from that of her TV husband's grave. It is a simple marker in a section that has few stars.

Holy Cross Cemetery
5835 W. Slauson Avenue
Culver City, California
Directions: Take the 405 to 90E get off at the Slauson Avenue exit the cemetery is on your left. Get a celebrity map and drive around to the north side of section F/ Holy Rosary. Park between Holy Rosary and the beginning of Section R/Resurrection. Count 26 from the road. Look for marker "Tohn" which will be by the road to guide you as to what row you need to count up from. The location is T29, grave 58.

Bewitched
Marion Lorne - "Aunt Clara"
August 12, 1883 - May 9, 1968

Marion made her stage debut in 1905, but gained her first television popularity in 1952, after she was cast as "Mrs Gurney," the fluttering bewildered English teacher on NBC's "*Mr. Peepers,*" which lasted until 1955.

Later she was cast in the role that we all remember her most, "Aunt Clara" in ABC's *"Bewitched."* She played Samantha's slightly confused aunt, whose magic was discombobulated due to her extreme nervousness. Being the only one to right her wronged spells, she would further confuse things as she forgot the much needed incantations.

During her tenure with *"Bewitched"* she died of a sudden heart attack at her home. She had no immediate survivors and her services were held at 1:00pm on May 10th at the Frank E. Campbell Funeral Home. in New York City.

Ferncliff Cemetery
Secor Road
Hartsdale, New York
For directions see Joan Crawford in the Glamour Girls Chapter. Get a map, and go upstairs in the main mausoleum. When you reach the top of the stairs go right then left go up the little steps. She's on the left wall on the bottom.

LORNE

MARION LORNE
1885 – 1968

Ferncliff Cemetery, Hartsdale, New York

Paul Lynde - "Uncle Arthur"
June 13, 1927 - January 9, 1982

Paul Lynde's successful career in television spanned the sixties and seventies, as he appeared in many sitcoms such as "*The Munsters.*" But the role that he is most famous for was that of "Uncle Arthur" on the hit sitcom *"Bewitched."*

There he played a wise cracking, practical joking warlock that menaced his nephew-in-law, Darrin. Noted for his extremely dry jokes, you were always prepared for a humorous bombshell.

Some TV-philes may not know that his first role on *"Bewitched"* was that of a nervous driving instructor hired to give Samantha driving lessons. Producer/Director Bill Asher liked him so much that he wrote him into the show.

After *"Bewitched"* ended Paul starred in his own show called, *"The Paul Lynde Show."* It was the typical format for that era: a family man living in the suburbs dealing with day to day problems. Most who had seen Paul's "flamboyant" character found this a little hard to swallow. Although popular, it only lasted a year. Coincidently, most of the writers and the production crew for his show were from *"Bewitched."*

In 1966, Paul entered American living rooms once more with the famous "*Hollywood Squares.*" He was bestowed the honor of center square. Fellow "*Hollywood Squares*" colleague and friend, Phyllis Diller, would constantly refer to him as the "Queen of Comedy."

Paul had many hidden demons that many did not know about, which unfortunately manifested in excessive drinking. This drinking led to the end of his thirteen year tenure with "*Hollywood Squares.*" Sometimes he would become so drunk that he couldn't answer the three questions needed to participate in the game.

It is rumored that once while driving intoxicated, he led the police through a high speed chase through the Valley one night. Finally he crashed into a mailbox and came to a stop. The police came to the car, guns drawn, and Paul lowered his window and told them, "I'll have a cheeseburger, hold the onions and a large Sprite."

In 1982, Lynde was found dead in his West Hollywood home. In bed and naked with a bottle of "Poppers" (Amyl Nitrate inhalant) nearby. The cause of death was a heart attack. To date, his house, for whatever reason, has been destroyed.

Paul was brought back to his home town in Amity, Ohio for burial.

Amity Cemetery
Gilchrist Road
Amity, Ohio

Directions: I-70 to exit 132 (Newark 13N). Drive through Newark, past Mt. Vernon, to Rt. 3 to Amity. Keep going until you see Gilchrist Road on your right, make a right, the cemetery is on your left. Park on the street and walk to the entrance, while standing to the right of the entrance, count four to the right and two back. There's Paul.

Agnes Moorehead - "Samantha's Mother, Endora"
December 6, 1900 - April 30, 1974

Agnes Moorehead was one of the few actresses of the century who had the courage to refine her image to her craft. Throughout her forty four year career, Moorehead acted primarily in character roles: the neurotic mother, the spinster aunt, or the dowager queen. To each role, whether on stage, radio, film or on television, Moorehead brought the same high degree of professionalism to each performance. Her forceful nature, near perfect diction, and gothic beauty impressed critics and audiences alike, which ultimately secured her a place in film history.

She was born in Clinton, Massachusetts, the older of two daughters of Presbyterian minister John Robertson and Marie Moorehead, a one time professional singer. The family moved to Hamilton, Ohio in 1904, and moved again eight years later to St. Louis. Agnes attended public school and first performed on stage in summer theater.

LYNDE

PAUL
1927—1982

JOHNNY
1929—1965

Amity Cemetery, Amity, Ohio

Though even as a child she knew she wanted to be an actress, Moorehead took her father's advice and first obtained a formal education before embarking on an acting career. From 1920 to 1923, she attended Muskingum College, a religious college founded by her uncle near her family's farm in New Concord, Ohio. She received an A.B degree and taught school in Soldier's Grove, Wisconsin and performed on the radio in St. Louis where she was billed as *"The female tenor"* before enrolling at the American Academy of Dramatic Arts in New York City in 1927. Two years later she graduated with honors.

Moorehead began her acting career in 1929 with minor roles for Theatre Guild productions, but the depression forced her into broadcasting. This economic necessity proved fortunate as her work during radio's golden age brought her widespread acclaim. A consistently hard worker, Moorehead was in thousands of radio shows, often as many as six a day. She appeared regularly in shows as *"Cavalcade of America," "The Shadow,"* and *"March of Time."* In the latter series, she occasional portrayed then first lady Eleanor Roosevelt, and was the only actress allowed to do so. Moorehead was one of the women screaming in the background in the Mercury Theater of the Air's 1938 production of *"War of the Worlds."* her performance did no go unnoticed; Orson Wells and John Houseman invited Agnes to join the Mercury Players and she was quick to accept. Following stage production of *"Dear Abigail"* and *"Julius Caesar,"* the group moved to Hollywood in 1940.

Most of Agnes's income throughout her career came from films. During the 1940's her average earnings were over $6000 a week. Although she often appeared in lesser films, she did receive three more Oscar nominations, all for supporting roles.

Agnes continued to move with ease form one entertainment medium to another. Making the transition to television, she gained wide recognition for her role as "Endora" in the series *"Bewitched,"* which ran from 1963 to 1971. She made her character memorable as she played a mother-in-law that most husbands would only dread. Constantly wreaking havoc on his name (Durbin, Dobbin, Darwood, and finally Dumbell), poor Darrin would lose his temper only to be punished by one of her life altering spells. Although she was nominated four times for an Emmy for the role of Endora, her only television award, for "Best Actress in a single performance," was given to her for an appearance in an episode of *"Wild, Wild West."*

She concluded her career by teaching in her own acting school and lecturing on acting techniques at various colleges. Her final stage appearance was in the 1973 revival of *"Gigi."*

In 1974, she died of cancer at the Rochester Methodist Hospital in Minnesota.

Dayton Memorial Park
8135 N. Dixie Drive
Dayton, Ohio

Directions: I-75 to Maxton Road, left to Dixie Drive. Go to the Memorial Abbey mausoleum, there are signs that will lead you to it. You can get a map if you'd like, they are very nice in the office. Once in the mausoleum (it's not locked, as long as the cemetery is open), flip on the lights the breaker box is next to the main entrance. Walk up the stairs ans make a left. You will be in Aisle C, count nine rows over and three up on the left wall. You should see a nice biography on her crypt that a fan left behind. Before you leave, don't forget to turn out the lights.

Dick York- "Darrin"
September 4, 1928 - February 20, 1992

Dick had finally attained stardom with a hit show, after years of hard work and obscurity. Unfortunately chronic health problems would ultimately end this long awaited success, leaving York penniless.

Prior to *"Bewitched,"* York played bit parts in a variety of films. In one film, *"They Came to Cordura,"* he suffered a severe back injury that would plague him for the rest of his life. His injury which brought him extreme pain, caused York to develop an addiction to pain killers.

AGNES ROBERTSON
MOOREHEAD
1974

Dayton Memorial Park, Dayton, Ohio

In September, 1964, *"Bewitched"* debuted on ABC, with actress Elizabeth Montgomery who played "Samantha Stevens" and Dick York as her hapless husband "Darrin." The series shot to the number two position in the Neilsen ratings by season's end. Bewitched was so popular that ABC began re-running it during weekday mornings for two years starting in 1968.

York played the role for five years, until he suffered a seizure on the set, sending him to the hospital. The crew was setting up for a special effects scene with Maurice Evans (who played Samantha's father). York was suspended fifteen feet in the air waiting for his cue. Earlier that day, he had gone to the doctor to treat the pain he experienced on a daily basis. He was put on a cycle of pain pills, that would help him sleep at night. When the pain became unbearable, his doctor would administer shots of novocaine and cortisone in his back so he could function.

This excerpt from Dick York's autobiography, *"Seesaw Girl,"* tells it all: "They were setting an inky, that's a little tiny spot that's supposed to be filling in my eyes. Someone kept passing his hand back and forth in front of the light to see where the light was falling, all very difficult, but somehow all that flickering made me feel weird and I'm sitting on this platform up in the air and Maurice is sitting there too and I'm trying to go over my lines; they don't mean a damn thing. But I know that they're a stickler for these lines being exactly the way they're suppose to be. If this line is bibbetty wham bang whoppo, that's what you better say. Anyway I'm running these lines back and forth and they're making less sense to me and this light is flickering off and on and I turn to Gibby, a friend of mine on the set, and I say 'I have to get down,' and I put my hand on his shoulder and he said, 'Sure Dick.'"

At that point York suffered a seizure, lost consciousness, and was rushed to the hospital. While recuperating in the hospital, producer/director, Bill Asher paid him a visit. At that time he asked if he wanted to quit the show and York said yes.

The actor remained on his back for the next year and through bad investments and his inability to work, York fell on hard times. The drugs had rotted his teeth and when physically possible, York along with his wife had to clean houses to survive.

The role of Darrin was taken over by Dick Sargent, who resembled York. In 1969, Bewitched dropped in ratings, and by 1971 the show ended its run.

In 1980, Dick York's life improved somewhat, he got his teeth repaired and occasionally appeared on shows like *"Fantasy Island"* and *"Simon and Simon."* His comeback was short lived as his poor health returned. As a result of years of smoking he had developed emphysema and was dependant on oxygen on a full-time basis. From his bed he devoted his life to helping the homeless. He died in 1992.

Plainfield Township Cemetery
Rockford, Michigan

Directions: Special thanks to Jackie who went out of her way to escort me to the cemetery. From Hwy 44 go to Wolverine make a right, head for Plainfield Township make a right on Rogue River. The cemetery is on the corner of Rogue and Packer. From the Packer Street entrance, he's in the first row, forth tombstone in. While there I met a very nice lady (I didn't get her name) who frequently walks through the cemetery as part of her exercise routine. She was unaware of York's grave location, but told me that his wife still lives in the area.

Elizabeth Montgomery (April 15, 1933 - May 18, 1995), who played Samantha Stevens died as a result of colon cancer that had festered in her body for years undetected. On May 18, 1995. She had no funeral, she was cremated and given to her family.

Dick Sargent, (April 19, 1933 - July 8, 1994) who played the second Darrin, died of prostate cancer on July 8, 1994. He was cremated and his ashes were given to his boyfriend, Albert Williams.

David White played Larry Tate, Darrin's boss died on **November 27, 1990** of a heart attack. He is in a community niche at Grand View Cemetery in Glendale, unmarked.

Alice Pearce (October 16, 1917 - March 3, 1966) played Mrs. Kravitz, the Steven's nosey neighbor, died of ovarian cancer. She was replaced by a new Mrs Kravitz, Sandra Could.

Sandra Gould (July 23, 1916 - July 20, 1999) the second Gladys Kravitz. She died of a stroke after heart surgery. She was cremated and scattered at sea.

RICHARD
YORK

SEPT. 4   FEB. 20
1928   1992

George Tobias (July 14, 1901 - February 27, 1980) played Mr Kravitz who died of a heart attack, went on a wild ride that would have given him another heart attack. On February 26, 1980, While on the way to the Mt Sinai Memorial Park from the Cedars Sinai Hospital, the hearse had gotten involved in a minor traffic accident on the corner of Sierra Bonita and Sunset Blvd, in Hollywood. While the drivers were exchanging information, two men jumped into the hearse and took off, unaware that they had another passenger. Once George was discovered, the thieves panicked, screeched to a halt and abandoned the hearse in the middle of traffic. George and the hearse were later found and returned to Mt Sinai safe and sound. He is buried in Mt Carmel Cemetery in Queens, New York.

Maurice Evans (June 3, 1901 - March 12, 1989) who played "Maurice" Samantha's father, died of natural causes in an upscale retirement community in Maidstone, England. He was cremated and given to his boyfriend.

Bonanza
Dan Blocker -"Hoss"
December 10, 1928 - May 13, 1972

"Hoss" was born big and at age twelve, was a whopping 6 foot and 200 pounds. So it was no surprise that he would excel as a football lineman. His childhood nickname was *"The Big Un,"* which he earned in his hometown of O'Donnell, Texas. Every Saturday night, the locals would match him with some of the toughest thugs in the town. And without fail the strapping 13 year old would pummel each man, including some that were 25 years old.

The change in his life came when he was attending Sul Ross State College in Abilene, Texas. Mrs. Freda Powell, the drama teacher, needed someone strong enough to play a part in *"Arsenic and Old Lace."* It required someone who could carry all the bodies out of the basement at the end of the play. Dan was a natural choice and from then on he was smitten by acting.

In 1956, while working toward a Ph.D at the University of California at Los Angeles, he won a solid role in *"Gunsmoke,"* then the most popular television series. A series of other Western parts followed and in 1958 the 6 foot 4 inch, 280 pound actor was selected to fill the size 14 boots of Hoss Cartwright on the new *"Bonanza"* series. The Sunday night series became so popular that President Johnson once rescheduled a television speech rather than compete with the Cartwrights on the Ponderosa.

Shooting the show's 15th season was scheduled to commence, when Blocker had to undergo gall bladder surgery. All seemed well as he was recuperating and preparing for the show's season. Before the month was over he awoke at home complaining of shortness of breath. He was rushed to Daniel Freeman Hospital were he later died of a pulmonary embolus, a blood clot in the lung.

Woodman's DeKalb Cemetery
129 N.W. Runnells (Front Street)
Dekalb, Texas
Directions: From I-30 get off on Hwy 82 exit go west. Continue pass Malta the next town is DeKalb. Go slow this is a very small town and if you are not careful you will miss the cemetery. It is located on the left hand side between two house like buildings. Once in the cemetery go to the right and all the way back. You'll see the Blocker Family Tombstone, Dan is right there.

Lorne Greene- "Pa"
February 12, 1915 - September 11, 1987

While in the process of working on *"Bonanza: The Next Generation,"* a two hour movie based on the original show; Greene's health began to fail. The first hospitalization was for surgery on a perforated ulcer. The next would be for something far worse: cancer.

B DAN D BROCKER

DEC 10, 1928

MAY 13 1972

Woodman's DeKalb Cemetery, DeKalb, Texas

During his stay at St Johns' Hospital in Santa Monica, Lorne was visited frequently by friend and co-star Michael Landon. The day before Lorne died was no exception, Michael was there to make his final moments happy.

A nurse on duty said that Michael grasped Lorne's hand with both of his, smiled and said, "How ya doin', Pa?" Although in a weakened state from the cancer and extreme pain, he responded, "Okay."

The two exchanged few words because Lorne had difficulty talking. Michael stayed with him for fifteen minutes that day, just holding his hand. Then just before leaving, he knelt down beside the bed and Lorne raised his hand. With the little strength he had left in him, Lorne began their traditional arm wrestling. Michael's eyes were filled with tears and laughter. Michael said that he never forgot his last moments with his friend. "He was Ben Cartwright to the very end."

Surrounded by his wife and children, Lorne finally died of pneumonia, a common complication from cancer.

Hillside Memorial Cemetery
600 W. Centinela Avenue
Culver City, California

For directions to the cemetery see Moe Howard in the Five Stooges Chapter. Get a celebrity map and head over to the Court of Books. At the bottom of each row of crypts are the names for each area. Look for Isaiah by the doorway. Walk straight out to the grassy area it should be the 2nd to you left. He has a ground marker not a crypt numbered 5-800-8B.

Michael Landon -"Little Joe"
October 31, 1936 - July 1, 1991

Eugene Maurice Orowitz was born in Forest Hills, New York, a vast difference from the wild west of the Ponderosa. His mother was a showgirl and his father a Broadway publicist. Despite his family background, Eugene displayed little or no initial talent for show business. As a youngster he was short and rail thin for his age as he went through an awkward stage. But like a fine wine he blossomed into quite a handsome man.

In 1952, his family left NewYork to move to Collingswood, New Jersey where they lived a typical middle class existence. It was not long before the family moved again, this time across the country to California.

After graduating high school, Eugene got a job working in a ribbon factory unloading freight cars. A co-worker asked him if he could help him with a project. Little did Eugene know that this would be the beginning of his show business career. The friend was a budding actor who needed someone to play opposite him for an audition. Eugene's good deed was rewarded as he stole the scene.

The next step was to quit his job at the ribbon factory and get a job at a gas station across the street from Warner Brother's Studio. He figured that since a lot of studio executives got their cars serviced there, that he'd get discovered in true Hollywood fashion. He was right, an executive taken with the young man's looks, told him he should enroll in the studio's acting school. One of his classmates happened to be another aspiring actor, Jim Bumgarner, who would later be known as James Garner.

In the early fifties Eugene changed his name to Michael Landon. He was waiting for his break when finally he was given a role in "*I Was a Teenage Werewolf*." The 1957 film became an overnight sensation and still remains a cult classic today. It earned Michael instant recognition and marked his first giant step towards an acting career that ultimately would make him a multimillionaire and a major TV star.

After filming "*The Legend of Tom Dooley*," Michael caught the eye of producer David Dortort, who was looking for a handsome young man to play the role of Ben Cartwright's son, in an hour long television show "*Bonanza*." His role was that of "Little Joe, " and for the first time he was in a stable position. The role paid a cool $500 a week.

LORNE H GREENE

THE WORLD'S BEST LOVED FATHER

BEN CARTWRIGHT,

THE GREAT VOICE OF CANADA —
FINALLY STILLED, BUT SILENCED NEVER
THE DEAR VOICE OF OUR LOVING
HUSBAND, FATHER AND GRANDFATHER
WILL SING IN OUR HEARTS
FOREVER

1915 - 1987

"Bonanza" debuted on September 12, 1959; it was the first western ever to be shot in color for TV. It had a long run of ten plus years which landed Michael in another role on another show.

He had matured from a son on "Bonanza" to father of Laura Ingalls Wilder in 'The Little House on the Prairie." Michael made his debut in the role of Charles Ingalls on September, 1974. He was paid eight million dollars a year during its eight year run, which made him a multimillionaire.. Eventually he wrote, produced and directed as well as acted on the show.

After "The Little House on the Prairie" ended, Michael was ready for another role, this time it was that of an angel on "Highway to Heaven." Once again he not only acted on the show but he produced it as well.

Although Michael always looked healthy; his health habits contradicted his lifestyle. In every house he lived in, he always had an extravagant gym built. There he would workout on a daily basis, yet smoke four packs of cigarettes a day. Also he was a heavy drinker who loved junk food. While working, his diet consisted of nothing but cigarettes and coffee to get him through the day.

On March, 1991 Michael decided to take his family on a ski trip. He was worried because he had been experiencing severe stomach pains for several weeks. The pains became progressively worse and he believed that he had incurred an ulcer. Prior to the trip, Michael had an upper GI done to determine the cause of the pain. The test revealed that nothing was wrong except that there was an unusual amount of stomach acid that had accumulated in his stomach. He was advised to take some antacid pills and that the cramps were probably stress related.

While in Park City the pain worsened. The stabbing pain was intolerable so Michael flew back to Los Angeles to Cedars-Sinai Medical Center to have a CAT scan done. On April 3, 1991, he learned that he had a tumor in his abdomen. It was not known whether it was malignant or benign; only a biopsy could determine that.

Friday, April 5th brought more bad news; he had inoperable adenocarcinoma (cancer of the pancreas). With exception to the encephalitis he contracted in 1974, Michael had never been sick. Instead of folding under the pressure of bad news; he was determined to conquer his disease. Unfortunately on April 24th, another CAT scan brought more bad news. The cancer had spread and the tumor had doubled in size.

To avoid bad press Michael decided to go public with his disease. He telephoned his good friend Johnny Carson and appeared on his show. They spoke optimistically about his illness and said that he was doing everything he could to conquer it. He also made jokes about his plight. He said that millions of people all over the world were sending him suggestions on how to beat the disease. One person suggested that he swim with dolphins, that the sonar they emit would destroy the cancer.

"What can I tell you ? Here I'm going to all these hospitals and I only gotta go to Marineland!" he said. According to the Nielsen ratings, that "Tonight Show" was the most watched "Tonight Show" ever.

Monday, May 13th marked his first attempt at experimental treatment. The procedure consisted of injecting a cancer killing substance into fat bubbles and then injecting the bubbles directly into the tumor. It left him weak with mild discomfort. Unfortunately the experiment didn't work because a week later he was in terrible pain. While upstairs in his bathroom the pain was so excruciating that he collapsed on the floor. His wife sped him from their home in Malibu to Cedars-Sinai Hospital, thirty miles away in rush hour traffic. Upon his arrival he was put into a wheelchair and checked into a private room. The excessive pain was due to a massive internal hemorrhage, where blood clots were found throughout his body. The clots had traveled dangerously close to his heart. The pain was so unbearable and could only be managed by morphine.

Hillside Memorial Park, Culver City, California

The end came very quickly as he grew weaker and weaker. His fatigue caused him to sleep most of the day. On Friday, June 28th, Michael requested that his family gather around him. They all kept constant vigil at his bedside as the weekend passed. Then when things couldn't look any worse, he became magically alert on July 1st. He looked around the room at everyone and calmly said: "I love you all very much, but would you all go downstairs and give me some time with Cindy?" Less than two minutes later his wife Cindy came downstairs with the news that Michael had died. It took less than three months for the cancer to take his life.

Five days after Michael's death, on the morning of Friday, July 5th, a white stretch limousine followed by a black limo, pulled slowly out of the Landon drive. His family headed to Hillside Memorial Park. Resting on Cindy's lap was a wooden box that held his ashes. Five hundred people gathered to pay their final respects to Michael. He was eulogized by former President Ronald Reagan. With a rabbi conducting the service, Michael's ashes were entombed in a white marble crypt. He left behind an estate valued at $100 million. Forty percent went to wife Cindy, another forty percent was to be divided equally among his children and the remainder was to go to charity including cancer research.

When I visited his grave I noticed that he was not on the celebrity list. Apparently his family did not want fans to know where he was entombed. List or no list; he was extremely easy to find. He's across from Max Factor and not far from his pal and former co-star Lorne Greene, in a huge white marbled crypt with LANDON written above it.

Hillside Memorial Park and Mortuary (CLOSED SATURDAY)
600 W. Centinela Avenue
West Los Angeles, California
For directions to the cemetery see Moe Howard in the Five Stooges? Chapter. Get a celebrity map from the office, but you won't see him on it. His family didn't want the location disclosed. His crypt is so big you's have to be blind not to see it. Look for Eddie Cantor, he's in the mausoleum. in the Graciousness Section #207, by the door. Walk out that door and Michael Landon will be right in front of you.

PAT BUTTRAM
A MAN DESERVES PARADISE
WHO CAN MAKE
HIS COMPANIONS LAUGH

Maxwell Chapel, Haleyville, Alabama

Green Acres
Pat Buttram- "Mr Haney"
June 19, 1917 - January 8, 1994

Born Maxwell E. Buttram in Alabama, he was the son of a rodeo circuit minister and studied theology at Birmingham Southern College. Thankfully for his fans, his religious vocation took a backseat to his acting career.

For many years he played side kick to cowboy legend Gene Autry on the television series. Using his own name on the "*The Gene Autry Show*," (1950-56) he helped Autry and his horse Champion keep peace in the Wild West. In addition to the television show, both cowboys appeared in over 40 feature movies as well as stage shows.

He is perhaps better known to younger viewers as "Mr Haney" on "*Green Acres*". From 1965-71 he played an irritating country con-man, who sells a tumbledown farm to Oliver Wendell Douglas, played by Eddie Albert and his wife Lisa, played by Eva Gabor.

In 1994, Pat entered the UCLA Medical Center and died a week later of kidney failure. He was 78.

Maxwell Chapel
Highway 5
Haleyville, Alabama

Directions: From I-65 go to Hwy 278 in the direction of Haleyville. From there Hwy 278 go to Hwy. 195 to Hwy 129 and finally Hwy 5. If you have any problems ask around everyone is pretty friendly. Once in the cemetery, he is located close to the office you can't miss him.

Eva Gabor - "Lisa Douglas"
February 11, 1921 - July 4, 1995

Eva was the first Gabor sister to immigrate to America from Hungary, she starred in a few B movies and four Broadway plays. There she was introduced to mainstream America with her role of Lisa Douglas on "*Green Acres*."

She played a socialite who marries a wealthy New York Lawyer. Her husband, Oliver Wendell Douglas, who descended from a family of lawyers would also follow the family tradition of going into the legal profession. Despite his success as an attorney he dreams of someday being a farmer. One day he gets fed up with the "rat-race" and relocates to a farm to live his dream, dragging his upper crust wife along with him. Lisa in an attempt to fit in could be seen milking a cow or cooking "hots cakes" in a lovely gown fit for a Park Avenue Penthouse.

Eva had homes in both Bel Air, California and Baja, Mexico, where she loved to vacation frequently. On June, 1995 she went to her Mexican home with some friends for a week. Apparently she had eaten some "bad" fruit and contracted viral pneumonia. She was so sick that she became weak and disoriented. As she stumbled through her house, she collapsed on a staircase and broke her hip. Unable to get a plane back to the states, and not wanting to deal with a Mexican Hospital, she called her best friend Merv Griffin who provided a private jet to bring her back to California.

On June 21st she was admitted to the fifth floor of Cedars-Sinai Medical Center where her condition worsened. She had fluid in her lungs, a fever and upon further examination, a blood clot was discovered. Doctors put Eva on antibiotics for the pneumonia, pain medication for the hip pain and heparin for the clotting. Her breathing became so difficult that she now needed a respirator.

Eventually, Eva slipped into a coma as her condition slowly deteriorated. Her family and friends prepared for the worse. Eva died at 10:05 am on Tuesday, July 4th, she was 76 years old. Her funeral was held at Good Shepard Catholic Church on July 11th, at 7pm. Where in attendance were Eva's sisters, Zsa -Zsa and Magda, Eddie Albert, Merv Griffin, Johnny Mathis Mitzi Gaynor and Rosie O'Donnell. Jolie, Eva's mother, was never told of her daughter's death, died two years later. She was cremated and buried in Westwood Memorial Park., next to Mel Torme and John Cassavetes

OUR DARLING EVA
EVA GABOR
WE LOVE YOU

YOU ARE IN OUR HEARTS FOREVER

JULY 4, 1995

Westwood Memorial Park, Los Angeles, California

JOHN F. SULLIVAN
FRED ALLEN
1894   1956

Gate of Heaven Cemetery, Hawthorn, New York

Westwood Memorial Park
1218 W. Glendon Avenue
Los Angeles, California
For directions to the cemetery see Marilyn Monroe in the Glamour Girls Chapter. As you enter the cemetery park any where. Find the "Armand" mausoleum. Eva is right in front of it, next to John Cassavettes and Mel Torme (his marker is very easy to spot.)

Also On The Tube in the 1950's and 1960's
Fred Allen - The Fred Allen Show"
May 31, 1894 - March 17, 1956
Born John Florence Sullivan in Cambridge, Massachusetts, he was the son of a bookbinder and storyteller. Young John became interested in comedy after finding a book on it's history in his father's shop. Upon further reading, he became adept in juggling and by the age of 18 he was ready for vaudeville. A successful engagement at the Palace in 1919, led to many Broadway shows, including *The Passing Show*" of 1922, where he met his future wife and radio co-star, Portland Hoffa.

After that he made the transition to radio with "*The Lint Bath Club Revue*", which premiered October 23rd, 1932, on CBS and later moved to NBC in 1933. But Allen's "perfectionism" led him to move from sponsor to sponsor.

He is best known for comically feuding with Jack Benny on the air for years. Also he became a trailblazer for future television hosts who would embark on this entirely new form of radio comedy which consisted of lampooning current events, making fun of his sponsors, and presenting skits that featured a cast of memorable recurring characters.

Unfortunately, the advent of television and Allen's constant battles with sponsors and network censors eventually drove him off the air. His humor was ahead of its time, too sophisticated for the 1940's, but it did pave the way for the success of satirist Stan Freberg in the 1950's and "Saturday Night Live" in the 70's.

On the evening of March 17th, while on a stroll near his New York apartment, Fred died of a sudden heart attack. He was 61.
Gate of Heaven Cemetery
10 W. Stevens Avenue
Hawthorne, N.Y.
For directions to the cemetery see Sal Mineo in the Rebels Without a Cause Chapter. Get a celebrity map from the office and cruise over to the "M" that is on the map of Section 17. Park on the corner of Section 44, 47 and 22. Fred is in the 1st Row, 14th down.

Bob Crane- "Hogan", "Hogan's Heroes"
July 13, 1928 - June 29, 1978
After the days of Hogan's Heroes ended, Bob spent most his time performing in supper clubs around the country. Of those who knew him personally described him as a fairly kinky character who lived the life of a swinger.

On June 29, 1978, the 49 year old actor had been found clad only in boxer shorts in his posh Scottsdale, Arizona apartment. His skull had been crushed by two blows with a blunt instrument and an electrical cord had been neatly tied around his neck.

In the days prior to his death, Crane had been seen arguing with John Carpenter (then 64), a fan and an acquaintance who had sold him some video equipment. Several smears of blood, the same type as Crane's, were found on the inside of Carpenter's rental car. But, since DNA testing had not yet been perfected, authorities had little proof to charge Carpenter of any crime.

ROBERT E. CRANE

1928 — 1978

Oakwood Memorial Park, Chatsworth, California

However, officials did later obtain the evidence needed to link Carpenter to the crime which prompted police to arrest him in Carson, California. According to a court affidavit, investigators reviewing the case had looked at pictures of the interior of Carpenter's car and noticed a speck of what appeared to be human tissue. It was presumably left by the murder weapon, which is believed to be a camera tripod that was missing from the murder scene. Inexplicably, no sample had been taken at the time of the killing. The tissue evidence was simply overlooked. Now forensic experts had declared, that when examined closely, the image in the pictures matched a small piece of tissue recovered from the bloody pillow on which Crane had been sleeping when he was attacked.

One former county attorney, Charles Hyder, who earlier declined to prosecute the case, has criticized the Scottsdale police for botching the original case. And Carpenter's attorney, Gary Fleischman, insisted that the police were hounding his client on the basis of the same flimsy circumstantial evidence as before. "How can you sit on this for 14 years and expect this man to defend himself?" he said. Carpenter who denied the charge, was then awaiting extradition to Arizona.

As for the possible motive, authorities have maintained their silence. One thing missing from Crane's apartment was a photo album containing pornographic pictures. It also turned out that the twice married Crane had an extensive collection of videotapes showing himself having sex with various women.

Eager as he is to see the culprit caught, even Werner Klemperer, who co-starred with Crane on *"Hogan's Heroes"* (1965 to 1971), thinks the case is still a long way from being solved. "I don't believe that what the police have is substantial," he said.

Oakwood Memorial Park
22601 Lassen Street
Chatsworth, California
Directions: 101 to Ventura Blvd., left on Topanga Canyon Blvd/Hwy. 27. Left on Plummer Street, right on Shoup Avenue, and Left on Lassen. Get a map. From the office follow Oakwood Drive until you get to Oak Drive, park. In the Oak Knoll section directly across from the mausoleum #2 you will see Bob. When I visited his grave, about two years ago, he was still there. I am now told that he has been moved to **Westwood Cemetery**. His family moved him there for reasons that are only know to them. He remains unmarked.

George Reeves - "Superman"
January 5, 1914 - June 16, 1959
From 1951 to 1957, Reeves played *"Superman,"* in 104 TV episodes which was broadcasted worldwide to homes in 30 countries, reaching an audience of 34 million viewers.

The part of *"Superman"* was a regular part, that brought a regular paycheck, but type casted Reeves forever as the man of steel. As he would audition for other roles in hopes of expanding his acting abilities, he would be constantly turned down. Some say this was his motive for suicide.

As a child of the sixties, watching *"Superman,"* with friends, I heard all kinds of rumors as to how he "did it." One was that he put on his Superman costume and attempted to fly off the Empire State Building. The other was that he shot himself.

Officially Reeve's death was ruled as a "indicated suicide," which means they weren't sure how he died. Others, including George's mother, many crime experts, and private detective Milo Speriglio called it a murder. There are two stories that describe his possible murder:

Those who believe he was murdered believe that his then fiancé, Lenore Lemmon shot him in a fit of rage after one of their many bitter alcohol induced fights.

According to Jim Nolt, who claims to be a George Reeves expert, also thinks it was a murder and not a suicide. There were no fingerprints on the gun, no powder burns on his hands and the gun was found between his feet. One bullet was recovered from the ceiling, two others were found in the bedroom floor and bullets were also recovered downstairs in the livingroom. Seems to be a lot of bullets flying around for a self-inflicted shot, perhaps they were just bouncing off the "man of steel."

My Beloved Son
"SUPERMAN"

GEORGE BESSOLO REEVES
JAN.6.1914–JUNE.16.1959

Mountain View Cemetery, Altadena, California

Photograph by Anne Parisi

The night before he died he had been drinking with his fiancé and some friends. Reeves had a reputation for drinking and late night parties. The autopsy revealed that his blood alcohol level was .27, well above the point of intoxication.

Lemmon had nothing to gain financially by killing Reeves, but it was well known that they had a volatile relationship, sometimes fueled by alcohol. If she did shoot Reeves in a fit of rage, it would be in her best interest to say that he committed suicide.

Suspiciously enough, the police were not called until at least 30 to 45 minutes after his death. Presumably so everyone would have time to get their stories straight and to rearrange things to make it look more like a suicide scene rather than a murder scene. The next day, Lenore left California and never returned. All the guests that were present at the party, supported Lenore story, simply because they were her friends or because they didn't really know what happened and had no choice other than to take her word for it.

The other story is very different; still it involves a gun combined with lots of alcohol.

Reeve's was involve in a very visible and torrid love affair with a married woman, Toni Mannix. The affair had been going on for many years when Reeves suddenly announced that he intended to marry another woman. Outraged, Toni began calling him late at night with death threats. Finally fed up, George called the Beverly Hills Police Department and the Los Angeles County District Attorney and filed a couple of reports on her for harassment. After their investigation, the authorities found that Toni and George were both receiving death threats. The suspect was Toni's husband, a dangerous thug who could have very easily have taken Reeve's out.

On the last night of his life, George had dinner with his fiancé, Lenore Lemmon and a houseguest, writer, Robert Condon. After dinner, the three went to the living room to watch some television. A short time later, they went to bed having consumed a lot of alcohol. Around midnight, two of Reeves' friends showed up, Carol Von Ronkel and William Bliss. The late arrival made Reeves angry, and after a few words and a drink, Reeves headed up to his bedroom in a bad mood. Lenore said, "Well, he's sulking; he'll probably go up to his room and shoot himself." She was referring to a stupid prank that George used to do. He would put a blank in his gun and pretend to shoot himself in the head. When he did it he would hold the gun a safe distance from his head to avoid powder burns.

That night however, there was a real bullet in the gun.

Reeve's mother, in an attempt to find out the truth, held up her son's cremation for three years. She hoped that his murder would be eventually solved and the perpetrators prosecuted. But unfortunately, Reeve's mother died of natural causes a short time later, before they could prove foul play was involved.

George Reeves is flanked by family members in his glass niche. His urn, simply inscribed by his mother says: My beloved son, "SUPERMAN," George Bessolo Reeves.

Mountain View Cemetery
2400 N. Fair Oaks Avenue
Altadena, California

Directions: From the 134 get off at the Fair Oaks Avenue exit go north. The cemetery is on your right. Once in the cemetery get a map or just follow the signs to the Pasadena Mausoleum. Once in the mausoleum make the first left and go past the 2nd section of urns. You might see an urn with George B. Reeves on it, that's not him. In fact, I don't know who he is and it seems pretty coincidental that two people would have such similar names and stored near one another. Perhaps he's a relative. The "real" George Reeves, has "Superman" written on his urn.

PHIL SILVERS
COMEDIAN
1911 ✡ 1985

Mount Sinai Memorial Park, Los Angeles, California

Phil Silvers - "Sgt. Bilko"
May 11 1911 - November 1, 1985

Phillip Silversmith was born in Brooklyn, the eighth child of Russian immigrants. He began his career at 12 in vaudeville as a precocious star on Broadway. It wasn't until he was 30, that he made the big move to Hollywood, where was put under contract to Louis B. Meyer. Once there, it was some time before he would be cast in any films. Most director's enthusiasm seemed to wane after they saw Silvers' screen test, in which he played the Rev. Collins from *"Pride and Prejudice."* "I have never forgotten the lines, they are burned on the lining of my brain. 'Please forgive this out boist of passion' I was asked to British it up in a very subtle manner. I had fire flashing from my eyeballs." Silvers said. A New York Jew, Silvers was an unusual choice as an English rural vicar.

Eventually, he began to get parts in musicals such as *"Coney Island"* and *"Diamond Horseshoe"*. Silvers' most famous single number in a Hollywood musical is the opening song from the 1950 Gene Kelly movie *"Cover Girl."*

Silvers was best known for his role as *"Sgt. Bilko,"* on *"The Phil Silvers Show,"* For it's brief life between 1955 to 1959, it was like no other comedy show in it's time. Silvers would leave his audiences in laughter with the brazen implausibility of his lines. When visiting a medium: "There are no lights on, she must be in." or flattering a cook with a way to steal his secret recipe: "All my life I have eaten in the finest restaurants of the world. I thought I was eating. I realize now I was merely grazing, like an animal."

He had off-screen interests, the racetrack, the ball park and the pinochle table. The gambling had begun at school and by the time he was 15. Silvers was regularly hailed by the voice that tormented Sgt. Bilko, "I hear money," Bilko tells his men. "Our money. Crying out into the night: Daddy. Take us home."

In the late 1940's Silvers' was making $5,500 a week a sum that "slipped into the bookies' hands as if it was magnetized." It cost Phil his marriage to former Miss America, Jo Carroll Dennison. "When we got divorced, he'd lost it all. We never lived expensively, or traveled, because he gambled everything away." she said. He may have had a terrible gambling habit, but one thing could be said in his behalf: he didn't drink and he wasn't a womanizer.

According to Phil's daughter death came easy for her father. After answering some fan mail, he laid down to take an afternoon nap, and never woke up.

Mount Sinai Memorial Park (Closed Saturday)
5950 Forest Lawn Drive
Los Angeles, California

Directions: Take the Golden State Fwy (5) north. Keep right and take the Ventura Fwy (134). Get off at the Forest Lawn Drive exit go left The main gate are about a mile from the exit you will see signs. Get a map they are very helpful. Go up Mount Sinai Drive to The Garden of Tradition." He is in 1A, 1004 section. It is a very small clearly marked area. You shouldn't have any problems If you do, flag down a worker with a white construction hat and they will help you. It is a grave stone in the grassy area not a crypt, but it is towards the area of the crypts.

1970's TV and Beyond
Nicholas Colasanto - "Coach," "Cheers"
January 19, 1924 - February 12, 1985

Born in Providence, Rhode Island, he gave up his job as an oil company accountant to become an actor at the age of 31. He appeared in such Broadway plays as *"Across the Board Tomorrow Morning"* (which brought him a Tony nomination) and *"A Hatful of Rain."* He performed in numerous television shows as well as films including Alfred Hitchcock's *"Family Plot,"* John Huston's *"Fat City"* and *"Raging Bull,"* in which he played a Mafia gangster.

JOSEPH COLASANTO
1917 — 1964

NICHOLAS COLASANTO
1924 — 1985

St. Anne's Cemetery, Cranston, Rhode Island

He is best known, however, as the amiable and slow witted "Coach" of the NBC series "*Cheers*," where he played Ernie Pantusso, a former baseball coach tending bar in Boston.

The 61 year old actor had been hospitalized for a long standing heart ailment and had missed several episodes of the popular TV show. While convalescing, Colasanto attended a taping of the show a week before his death. He assured the series' stars, Ted Danson, Shelley Long and others that he was feeling better and expected to rejoin the cast for the final show of the season which was to be scheduled in three weeks. Unfortunately he would never appear on "Cheers" again. While sitting in bed watching television at his home, he suffered a heart attack and died.

St. Anne's Cemetery
73 Church Street
Cranston, Rhode Island

Directions: Hwy. 2N to Scituate Avenue (Hwy.12) to Park Avenue, make a right on Cranston Street, left on Church Street. From the gate go to Section C and make a right pass D and Keep going until you come to a giant cross in a circle bear right around circle and head for a caretakers shed at the end of the road with "1903" on it. Now bear left and go to Section T you'll pass T, 3, 5, 11 section, make a left at Section 17, follow along passing 18,17,26 Section on your left side. You should now see Section 31. Park. Look for "DELSESTO" on the corner of Section 31, walk up 6 until you see "TROPPOLI" then walk 4 down to grave #211, and that's him. Phew!

Bert Convy - Game shows: "Tattletales" and "Password"
June 23, 1933 - June 15, 1991

Back in the 70's and 80's, Bert was a well known face on the game show circuit His venue, however, was not limited to game shows as he was also a guest host for Johnny Carson's Tonight Show on many occasions.

On April, 1990, while Bert was visiting his mother, he suddenly collapsed. He was admitted to Cedars-Sinai Medical Center where he underwent a battery of tests. The diagnosis was grim; the doctors discovered a malignant brain tumor. The disease quickly ran its course, only giving him 15 months to live.

Bert continued to grow ill quickly. In an attempt to keep the cancer at bay and to prolong his life, doctors operated on him twice. After spending several months in the hospital and realizing that there was no hope for survival, Bert went home to die.

On Monday, June 15th, with his wife at his side, his heart stopped at 5:20 pm and the game show king was gone. His funeral took place three days later at Forest Lawn of Hollywood Hills. In attendance was the star studded cast of mourners: Burt Reynolds, with then wife Loni Anderson, Sally Struthers, Dom DeLuise, Tom Poston, Bert's wife, kids and ailing mother.

Forest Lawn Memorial Park - Hollywood Hills
6300 Forest Lawn Drive
Los Angeles, California

For directions to the cemetery see Bette Davis in the Glamour Girls Chapter. Directions: Get a map from the information booth, just don't ask for any celebrity directions or information. Head up Memorial Drive turn left on Memory Lane and park. You are now in front of the Court of Liberty. Go to the last set of steps walk up the path and make a left go up those steps and make the 1st right. After the wall's end, walk to a 2nd little garden from left wall Look for "SUNG SOOOH FAMILY" Bert is two gardens to the right.

BELOVED

BERT CONVY

1933 - 1991

HIS STAR WILL SHINE FOREVER

Forest Lawn Memorial Park, Hollywood Hills, California

Selma Diamond - Bailiff, "Night Court"
August 5, 1920 - May 14, 1985

Selma's first movie was in *"It's a Mad, Mad, Mad, Mad, World,"* in 1963. Her initiation into show business came through writing gags for various comedians. This led to permanent writing assignments for *"The Milton Berle Show," Caesar's Hour," "The Perry Como Show,"* and even *"Ozzie and Harriet."* "She had a unique style of comedy in both writing and acting," said Carl Reiner who once worked with her during their tenure on *"Caesar's Hour,"* during the 1954 - 57 television seasons.

Miss Diamond is remembered most for her role on "Night Court," where she played a chain smoking sarcastic bailiff. Not a slave to long routines, she would walk in, drop a few snide remarks and leave.

In late April, 1985 she was diagnosed with lung cancer, and embarked on a program of treatments on May 1st. Just 13 days later she died at the Cedars-Sinai Medical Center. She was 64.

Hillside Memorial Park
600 Centinela Avenue
Culver City, California

For directions see Moe Howard in the Five Stooges? Chapter. Get a map and head to the Courts of the Book. Look for Jacob that is written on the baseboard by each doorway. Then look for I-1008, count 4 up and 5 to the right and there's Selma

Freddie Prinze - "Chico," "Chico and the Man"
June 22, 1954 - January 28, 1977

In 1972, at the age of 17, he got his first small break on Broadway, as a $2 an hour usher at a movie theater. He was fired for practicing his comedy act on company time.

Early in life Freddie showed signs of mental instability, his first suicide attempt was prompted by a breakup with a girl. He had taken an overdose of sleeping pills from which he was saved before it was too late. Although he had personal demons, his career seemed promising. His 1973 Tonight Show debut was so stellar that Johnny Carson, in a rare move, invited the unknown over to the couch to chat. A year later he was a co-star on the sit-com *"Chico and the Man."*

By time Freddie was 22 years old he was very successful. His rapid fame, made his life a total contradiction. On one hand, he was perceived as the wise cracking comic at the inaugural gala for President Carter, while later doing 70 m.p.h. in his Corvette in a school zone.

His success was not only good for him, but it open doors for other Hispanics who where trying to get into show business. Despite this contribution, he was criticized severely by his people for doing roles that they felt were too sterotypically Hispanic. One line they targeted became the catch phrase for his *"Chico and the Man"* role, was "It's not my yob!"

Fame eventually became a curse for him, and his judgment became impaired by his drug usage. He became a heavy cocaine user by 16, using five grams a day. Money and success only fueled his usage. He purchased hundreds of Qualudes a day. It is alleged that his cocaine use was so severe that it burned a hole in his nose, causing him to resort to taking the drug anally.

Another strange fascination was his obsession with the Zapruder film of President Kennedy's assassination. His favorite part was when the bullet blew off part of JFK's head.

Freddie purchased a gun and frequently played Russian roulette in front of his horrified friends. Once he clicked a gun at his head, then pointed it outside, pulled the trigger again and was knocked backwards from the blast. Another past time of Freddie's, was faking out his friend by firing a shot outside and then collapsing to the floor.

Hillside Memorial Park, Culver City, California

By January 1977, Freddie had become despondent for several weeks over work and marital problems. He was in the process of a divorce, involving their 10 month old son Freddie Prinze Jr.. Freddie mentioned several times that "I should end it all" to several friends and family members. During the few days prior to his suicide, he had in his possession a 38 caliber revolver. He kept toying with it, loading and unloading it.

The night before he died, he had received a restraining order from his wife. This didn't set well with him and sent him into a downward spiral. Early the next morning, he started making a series of goodbye phone calls. One was to Marvin "Dusty" Snyder, Freddie's business manager. Dusty became concerned, and went to Freddie's hotel room. When Dusty arrived he tried to calm Freddie down and told him that he had so much to live for. Freddie continued to make the emotional phone calls with Dusty in the room. He phoned his mother and said, "Mom, I love you very much, but I can't go on. I need to find peace." At 3:30 am, Freddie called his estranged wife, and supposedly said, "I love you, Kathy. I love the baby, but I need to find peace. I can't go on."

As he hung up the phone he put the gun to his head, and Dusty made a dive for it, but Freddie pulled away. Dusty tried again to talk him out of shooting himself, "think of you mother, and your son." But Freddie ignored him, put the gun to his head and fired. He slumped sideways with blood spilling from his head. He was still alive and Dusty called the ambulance and he was rushed to UCLA Medical Center where he underwent surgery for the gunshot wound to his head. His family kept a vigil at the hospital, and began to cry when one of the doctors announced that he was in God's hands. A priest gave him last rites.

After realizing that he was "brain dead" doctors recommended that he be taken off life support systems. He died at 1:00 pm, just 33 hours after shooting himself. He was only 22 years old.

Police later discovered a suicide note in Freddie's apartment. It said, "I must end it. There's no hope left. I'll be at peace. No one had anything to do with this. My decision totally, Freddie Prinze P.S. I'm sorry Forgive me. Dusty's here He's innocent He cared."

Forest Lawn Memorial Park
6300 Forest Lawn Drive
Los Angeles, California

For directions to the cemetery see Bette Davis in the Glamour Girls Chapter. Go through the main gates and get a map of the cemetery, but don't ask for any directions to celebrity graves. Head up Memorial Drive then main road, make a left on Evergreen Drive to Ascension Road make a right to Vista and park. Walk into the Courts of Remembrance, walk all the way back past "LIBERACE" into the Sanctuary of Light. You'll find Freddie on the left wall as you stand in the doorway, towards the back of the sanctuary.

TV Dads
Robert Reed - "The Brady Bunch"
October 19, 1932 - May 12, 1992

Interest in the series, "*The Brady Bunch*" was heightened tragically, when Reed who played architect and father, Mike Brady, died at the age of 59.

On Thanksgiving, 1991, a tumor was discovered. Surgery was followed by chemotherapy in an attempt to prolong what would be a brief battle. His death, first attributed simply to colon cancer, then later revealed to have been hastened by AIDS. His TV wife, Florence Henderson was one of many friends who knew that he was HIV positive, and yet chose to protect his privacy by not telling anyone. "I really, honestly don't think everyone on the show knew. I never discussed it with anyone except Barry Williams." she said.

Williams who played eldest son, Greg and Susan Olsen who played Cindy, both agreed that for Reed, privacy was paramount. "It doesn't surprise me that he kept that information to himself, " says Williams. "My relationship with Bob was as a friend, father and actor."

FREDDIE PRINZE
WE LOVE YOU — PSALMS 23
1954 — 1977

Forest Lawn Memorial Park, Hollywood Hills, California

As to how or when Reed could have contracted AIDS, his TV family refuses to speculate. Reed who was a homosexual, has a daughter from a prior marriage that ended in divorce in 1959.

"The Brady Bunch" series seems still more appealingly unreal than when it first turned up on ABC, Henderson characterized the show as "a traditional little show, that came along at the end of the 60's, which was a terribly turbulent time." The key to the series' enduring appeal she said, "was the fact that 'The Brady Bunch' generated an authentic, home sweet home warmth. It was one of those rare moments when the chemistry was right for everyone and we grew to love each other. As corny as it sounds, it's kinda is like a family."

As the end grew near, he checked into the Huntington Memorial Hospital on May 1st. He refused all visitors with exception to his daughter and a close friend, actress Anne Haney. "He came from the old school, where people had a sense of decorum," says Haney. "He went the way he wanted to, without publicity." Reed once made this comment which summed up his feelings about the show, "To the degree that it serves as a babysitter, I'm glad we did it. But I do not want it on my tombstone."

Memorial Park Cemetery
9900 Gross Point Road
Skokie, Illinois
Directions: I-90 to I-94 to Skokie, exit at Gross Point Road and follow it all the way up to the cemetery which will be on your left. Get a map. As you leave the office go left and pass 7 sections on your left side. On the 1st turn after the 7th Section make a left then make a right and park. Walk 11 rows and 19 up and there he is.

Danny Thomas - "Make Room For Daddy"
January 6, 1912 - February 6, 1991

In his first TV appearance, NBC's "All Star Revue," an early 50's variety show, nightclub head liner and film actor Danny Thomas bombed. He vowed never to return, blasting the medium as "only for idiots." Fortunately for us idiots, he changed his mind and his act and later appeared on many memorable shows.

In 1953, he became one of the youthful medium's most durable stars as the father on *Make Room For Daddy.* Or later seen, sporting a cigar only slightly longer than his epic nose, mixing verbal sass with moralistic schmaltz, as he shaped small screen humor along with the likes of buddies Milton Berle and Sid Caesar for over four decades.

On February 6th, he had just appeared on NBC's *"Empty Nest"* that is produced by his son, Tony. He was looking forward to doing a TV movie with daughter Marlo, when he was suddenly stricken with a fatal heart attack at his Beverly Hills home. He was 77.

He will be remembered most for his generous contribution to St Jude's Children's Hospital in Memphis where he is entombed along with his wife.

St Jude's Children's Hospital
501 St. Jude's Place
Memphis, Tennessee
Directions: From I-240 to Union Avenue go west make a left on Danny Thomas Blvd., which turns into Lauderdale St. You should be seeing the hospital. Park as soon as you see the gold domed roof. He is buried with his wife in the crypts located in the Danny Thomas memorial gardens. There isn't any indication that they are there, but security did point out their unmarked crypts behind a gate inside the garden..

ROBERT REED
1932 — 1992
Goodnight Sweet Prince

Memorial Park Cemetery, Skokie, Illinois

Robert Young - "Father Knows Best"
February 2, 1907 - July 21, 1998

Unlike his characters, Young's reality was much darker off camera as he battled alcoholism and depression throughout his life. In addition to that he attempted suicide in 1991.

He admitted in several interviews that he felt guilty playing such upright citizens when in his private life, he sought solace in a bottle to stave off depression. In a 1993 interview, he said, "When I became an actor I constantly felt I wasn't worthy, that I had no right to be a star. I held a black terror behind a cheerful face. Naturally, I tried to find a way out. Alcoholism was the inevitable result."

In the same interview, Young said it took him thirty years to realize he was drinking himself to death. He described his fight to beat alcoholism as an immensely slow, difficult process. After slipping back again and again, he felt he at last made a kind of giant step and was across the threshold to sanity and health.

Unfortunately he slipped again in 1991 when, in a fit of drunken depression, he attached a hose from his car's exhaust pipe to the inside of the vehicle. The attempt received much publicity.

Finally he did die, according to his publicist, of respiratory failure at his home in the Los Angels suburb of Westlake. He was 91

Forest Lawn Memorial Park
1712 S. Glendale Avenue
Glendale, California

For directions to the cemetery see Jean Harlow in the Glamour Girls Chapter. Get a map of the cemetery, but do not ask for any celebrity locations. Drive to the intersection where Vesperland, Sunrise Slope and Graceland all meet, park the car. You will see Graceland marked on the curve at that intersection. Look for the Thomas William Warner Statue right in front of you. From that statue count 10 rows down the hill by the curve will be the grave of "EDWIN HEARD" from there count 55 plots up the hill to the right (count the empty spots too)you will pass two trees on the way up the hill At the second tree is the grave of "CALVIN CLOUD" you will know your on the right track then. Keep gong until you finish counting the 55 spaces and there you will find Mr. Young and the rest of his family. Special thanks to Anne who helped me find him, phew!

DANNY THOMAS
Founder

St. Jude's Children's Hospital, Memphis, Tennessee

ROBERT GEORGE YOUNG

1907 — 1998

DEVOTED HUSBAND, FATHER, GRANDFATHER

Forest Lawn Memorial Park, Glendale, California

ANASTASIO

UMBERTO

1902 1957

Greenwood Cemetery, Brooklyn, New York

Chapter 9: The Wacked and the Rested
Albert "Umberto" Anastasia
September 26, 1902 - October 25, 1957

Less than five years after he surreptitiously lowered himself from an Italian tramp steamer onto a Brooklyn pier, Umberto Anastasia (in his early 20's), was already sitting on Death Row for killing a longshoreman. But by the time he won a fresh trial, every witness to the crime had literally disappeared. A pattern that would happen time and time again during his subsequent reign as the Mob's fiercest member.

Anastasia, who co-headed Murder Inc., was an equal opportunity employer whose only prejudice was against incompetence. When the law used "Kid Twist Reles" testimony to dismantle the underworld's killer elite, Anastasia pulled strings to enlist in the Army: He spent World War II serving at a Pennsylvania transportation depot. Demobilized, he returned to New York to rejoin the Luciano organization, which by now was answering to Frank Costello. Anastasia was even given his own branch of the family, a promotion owing less to his management skills than the genuine fear he inspired in Costello archrival Vito Genovese.

On the morning of October 25th, Anastasia drove from his home across the river in Fort Lee, New Jersey into Manhattan. He entered the barber shop of the Park Sheraton Hotel a little after 10:00 am, and settled back in chair four minutes later, two strangers walked through the door, waved away the barber, the manicurist and the shoe-shine boy who were administering to Anastasia. The two men began their own work with .38 caliber pistols. The mobster was shot in the hand, wrist, hip and back, but the coup de grace was a slug in the back of the head. Police found one of the murder weapons in a nearby subway station, but neither of the murderers.

Greenwood Cemetery
500 25th Street
Brooklyn, New York

Directions: Take the Bronx-Queens Expressway. Get off at the 39th Street exit drive to 4th Avenue and make a left. Once in the cemetery get a map. These people are extremely helpful. Also there is a kiosk with a computer, that when it works will help you with locations. From the main entrance go up Landscape Ave., make a right on Lake Ave. , to Sylvan Ave., make a right and park. You'll see a sign Lot 38325 walk up the steps while counting 9 double rows then count 30 graves in to your right. His is grave #182.

Humphrey Bogart
December 25, 1899 - January 14, 1957

Most Hollywood stars come from impoverished beginnings and desperately claw their way to the top. This was not the case for Bogart, who began his life on Park Avenue. He was the first born son of a Manhattan doctor and a suffragette mother, who was also a well-known illustrator who studied with Whistler (of "Whistler's Mother" fame), in Paris.

Bogart attended private schools, but he was expelled for failing five subjects and committing variety of infractions. A week after leaving school, young Bogart joined the Navy for the end of the war. While he was transporting another seaman to Portsmouth Navel Prison in New Hampshire, the prisoner smashed Bogart across the mouth with his handcuffs and tried to flee. Bogart shot and wounded him, but was left with a permanent scar on the right side of his upper lip. Allegedly the wound caused his slight lisp as well.

After his discharge Bogart decided to become an actor. Early reviews described him as giving a "rather trenchant exhibition of bad acting" or simply being "inadequate" as an actor. He bounced back and forth between Hollywood and Broadway. It took him thirteen years before he would achieve his first success as escaped killer "Duke Mantee" in "*The Petrified Forest*" in 1935.

Forest Lawn Memorial Park, Glendale, California

His success in the movie version the next year further typecast him as a criminal. It wasn't until he was offered the part of "Sam Spade" in "*The Maltese Falcon*" in 1941, followed by that of "Rick" in "*Casablanca*" in 1942, before he could get back on the right side of the law.

In his movies Bogart bravely died in many different ways, unfortunately this was no prerequisite for what was about to happen to him in real life. Years of excessive liquor and cigarettes took it's toll on Bogart's health.

Bogart had lived a long time with a dry cough that he frequently referred to as a "sensitive throat." This avoidance of reality could no longer convince others as he was finding it difficult to eat and was losing weight at an alarming rate. Just a small drink of orange juice would burn his throat so severely, that he would be pain for hours.

In 1956, just around New Year's Day, Bogart's "sensitive throat" had turned into an annoying heavy cough. While at the Romanoff restaurant, lunching with some friends, his inability to eat had worsened. One of his lunch companions, Greer Garson, was concerned and suggested that he see her physician, Dr Maynard Brandsma at the Beverly Hills Clinic.

Bogie took Greer's advice and visited her physician right away. After several tests, the worst was confirmed; Dr Brandsma told both Bogart and his wife, Lauren Bacall, that there was a malignancy in his esophagus and it would have to be removed immediately. The actor, who was in the middle of making a movie, wanted to put off the procedure, until the film was completed. His doctor responded with, "You can make the movie, and you'll be a big hit at Forest Lawn Cemetery."

On March 1st, Bogart underwent the 9 ½ hour operation. Dr. John Jones had removed the diseased portion of the esophagus and repositioned the stomach so that it could be re-attached to the remaining gullet. For a while he felt better, but follow up x-ray therapy nauseated him and he failed to gain weight.

Late in November, he spent five days in St. John's Hospital in Santa Monica, for what reporters were told as surgery to correct pressure caused by a nerve due to scar tissue. Nitrogen mustards were then administered in a vain attempt to keep the cancer at bay.

After this procedure he was never the same, he retreated to his home to live out the rest of his days in great pain. His only comfort was, the company of his close friends and family. They made his illness a little easier to endure.

Now weak and wheelchair bound, the only thing he looked forward to was cocktail hour. He would be dressed, and his wheelchair put in a large dumbwaiter which would be lowered downstairs to the gathering of visitors. Upon his arrival downstairs, he would be carried to his favorite chair, where he would listen to the latest gossip and relish in the comfort of his friends. Some however, were alarmed at the sight of their friend who had by now wasted away to mere skin and bones.

On Saturday, January 12th, Spencer Tracy and Katherine Hepburn dropped by to see him. They spent an evening alone with their friend watching a movie on television. As they were leaving Bogart looked up at Tracy, with a rueful smile, and said, "Goodbye, Spence;" Tracy could tell he meant it. He'd always said, "Goodnight," before, but somehow this was different. Tracy later told Hepburn, "Bogie's going to die."

That night Bogart asked his wife to lie beside him. He was terribly restless and in pain, his hands continually picked at his chest. When Dr. Brandsma came by early next morning, the dying man told him he never wanted to go through a night like that again. But there was little that the doctor could do for him.

Bogart's last words to his wife were, "Goodbye kid. Hurry back." When Bacall returned after picking up their two children from Sunday school, she noticed he was in a very deep sleep that later turned into unconsciousness.

At midnight the nurses suggested she rest in the little nap room next to their bedroom. They awoke her at 2:10am, Monday with the news that Bogie had died. In his final moments his pulse raised and his temperature shot up; he then breathed what seemed like a sigh of relief and was gone. He was 56 years old.

JAMES F. CAGNEY
1899 - 1986

FRANCES W. CAGNEY
1899 - 1994

Gate of Heaven Cemetery, Hawthorne, New York

Bogart wanted to have his ashes scattered in the Pacific, but back then it was illegal to scatter ashes in the ocean. Instead Bacall made provisions to have him interred in a simple niche in Forest Lawn. It is also rumored that she placed a silver whistle along with his ashes, symbolic to the movie in which the two had made together.

Services for Bogart were held at All Saints Episcopal Church. Since he had been immediately cremated, there was no casket present. In it's place, was a glass enclosed model of his beloved yacht, Santana.

Forest Lawn Cemetery - Glendale
1712 S. Glendale Avenue
Glendale, California
For directions to the cemetery see Jean Harlow in the Glamour Girls Chapter. Get a map, but don't ask for any celebrity locations or they will throw you out. Without a map, just follow the signs to the Freedom Mausoleum. Drive towards the "Garden of Ascension" and park at the "Court of the Christas." I believe there is a giant naked statue of "David" right around there. You will see a sign for the "Court of the Christas," on your right side if you are coming from the direction of the Freedom Mausoleum. Go to the "Garden of Memory" (the one to your left as you face the court). Sometimes it is locked and sometimes it's not. If you luck out go in and walk all the way down to the end. You will see a little room in the corner, closest to the road, called the Columbarium of Eternal Light, Bogie's in here. He's in the back wall to the left of the statue.

James Cagney
July 17, 1899 - March 30, 1986
Cagney was born in a small apartment on the top floor of a conventional brownstone on East Eighth Avenue in New York City. His family was financially poor; but rich with love. Both parents were jovial people who indulged their kids with plenty of love.

James unlike most of the characters he played, did well in school and was a pretty good citizen. Eventually he earned a scholarship via ROTC to Columbia University, where the acting bug bit. His first gig was at the B.F. Keith's 86th Street Theatre. There he earned thirty-five dollars a week for a little singing and dancing.

Eventually Cagney graduated to bigger roles like *"The Public Enemy," "Yankee Doodle Dandy,"* and *"Mr Roberts."* His prolific career lasted from 1930 to 1984, in which he made 64 feature films, 13 short films, 27 radio shows and 5 television shows.

After 1984, bad health caused him to retire to his farm in upstate New York. He was plagued by diabetes and had to follow a strict diet. The diabetes had robbed him of his sight in one eye and the other was beginning to fail as well. He was now eighty-something, and this brought him great sadness, because he knew his days were numbered.

In the second week of March, 1986, he had a heart attack. He was taken to Lenox Hill Hospital for some tests and doctors told his wife, Willie, that he perhaps had only two weeks to live. They recommended that James remain in the hospital. Instead, against doctor's order and per her husband's wishes, Willie brought him home where he wanted to be.

On Saturday, March 29th, James ate a good meal and went to sleep. He was awakened the next day, Easter morning, by his nurse; who had come to take him to breakfast. As they were on their way, Jim mumbled something to the her. As she strained forward to hear what he had said, which presumably was a joke, he winked and smiled. Then suddenly his head dropped to his chest and he was gone.

His funeral was held on April 1st, at St. Francis de Sales, his parish church that he attended. Cardinal John J. O'Connor offered St. Patrick's Cathedral, but Willie adhered to her husband's wishes and kept the services small.

James Cagney once said when Jack Warner died, "Jack made it to eighty-six. I'll be happy with that." Well he got his wish, with eight months to spare.

Mr Cagney shares his final resting place with gangster Dutch Schultz, Sal Mineo, and baseball legend Babe Ruth.

Gate of Heaven Cemetery
10 W. Stevens Avenue (Stevens and Bradhurst)
Hawthorne, New York
For directions to the cemetery see Sal Mineo in Rebels Without a Cause Chapter. Get a celebrity map and then from the main office go back to the entrance. From the direction of the gate walk directly in the direction of the mausoleum, he's right there. Usually there are American flags adorning his grave.

Al Capone
January 17, 1899 - January 25, 1947
　　　Born in a section of Brooklyn that spawned thugs the way Detroit produces cars, this barber's son learned to cut corners early by bending the law. He joined a youth gang affiliated with the notorious "Five Points" mob, whose other members were Lucky Luciano and Frankie Yale.

　　　Capone caught the attention of Johnny Torrio a "Five Points" veteran, 17 years his senior. Although Torrio was soon moving west to Chicago, he never forgot his protégée. In 1919, Al was feeling heat over a murder and Johnny needed a hitter. Capone relocated immediately and set up shop in the windy city. Neither man nor the city of Chicago would ever be the same again.

　　　When Capone was still a minor mobster in New York, he and wife, Mae raised their only child, Alphonse Jr. in a brick row house at 38 Garfield Place, Brooklyn. The supportive Mae rarely asked questions about her husband's occupation and made the spur of the moment move to the Midwest with the cheerful readiness of a corporate wife.

　　　Just 11 years after he landed on Chicago's South Side, he had wreaked enough mayhem to land on the cover of "Time." The magazine reported on his vice industries, was well as his penchant for grandstand plays, such as shelling out $3500 a day to support a Depression era soup kitchen.

　　　The editors allowed themselves to make sport of Capone's lavish threads and to take the liberty of openly calling him Scarface. The gangster was notoriously touchy about the broad gash across his left cheek, claiming it was an old World War I wound. Most likely, it had be inflicted by a Sicilian gangster instead.

　　　Capone's willingness to grant "Time" an interview was a sign of self-confidence that bordered on and sometimes crossed over into megalomania.

　　　He was unforgiving to enemies real and imagined, and also controlled his 1,000 thug gang with an iron fist. Though safe in the city, whose officials he virtually owned, Capone was hounded for years by the feds, T-man Eliot Ness, and while in his Florida hideaway, agents.

　　　What finally brought him down of course, were the bean counters. Capone never paid taxes on his income, estimated at $20 millions a year. By the time the feds obtained his books and charged him with tax evasion in 1920, he was clearly apprehensive. Rightly so, Capone was convicted and after a stint in an Atlanta penitentiary, he transferred to Alcatraz.

　　　On November 16, 1939, Capone was finally released from serving seven years, six months and fifteen days in prison. He also paid all fines and any back taxes that he owed. Prior to his prison stint he had contracted syphilis, that could have been easily controlled by penicillin. Refusing to take any medication, he developed paresis, which caused him to deteriorate gradually during his confinement.

　　　Once released he entered a Baltimore hospital for brain treatment, and then went on to his Florida home, an estate on Palm Island in Biscayne Bay near Miami. He never publicly returned to Chicago again, he had become mentally incapable of returning to gangland politics.

　　　In 1946, his physician and a Baltimore psychiatrist, both concluded after an examination, that he had developed the mentality of a 12 year old child. He remained in the secluded atmosphere of Palm Island with his wife and immediate family until his death. His actual cause of death was a stroke followed by pneumonia.

Mount Carmel Cemetery, Hillside, Illinois

He was returned to Chicago for burial, in the family plot located in Mount Carmel Cemetery. For some reason, gangsters like to grow huge bushes to hide their lavish graves. The inscription, "CAPONE," is located behind a hedge. Despite that, everyone knows where they are located. Also it is always decorated with momentos left behind by Capone fans.

By the way, he too likes to move around when dead. This is not the original burial site, the original site is located in Mt. Olivet Cemetery also in Chicago. When I called, they were extremely tight-lipped about any information concerning Big Al. The tombstone is still there; apparently he was buried with two other family members.

Formally interred at:

Mount Olivet Cemetery
Chicago, Illinois
Sec. 35,
moved to:
Mount Carmel Cemetery
1400 S. Wold Road
Hillside, Illinois
Sec. 52

Directions: I-90 exit at the Lee Street Exit, go north to Touhy Avenue make a left to Wolf Road make a right the take it to the cemetery. As you enter the front entrance make the first right and stop. He's right there.

Sam Giancana
May 24, 1908 - June 19, 1975

Sam got his start as a hit man for Al Capone during the roaring years of Prohibition. He participated in the Valentine's Day Massacre and had killed more than dozens of men before he was twenty years old.

His shrewdness made him a major Hollywood financier, who was constantly flanked by a stable of Hollywood starlets. Sam served as friend and benefactor to stars like Sammy Davis Jr., Dean Martin, Frank Sinatra as well as the rest of the "Rat Pack."

Politically he was instrumental in covert missions in Cuba, the Vatican, the Middle East and Southeast Asia. Which also included the several unsuccessful assassination attempts on Castro as well as others that netted hundreds of millions of dollars in drug revenue.

It is hard not to mention the liaison between Giancana and ex-bootlegger, Joseph P. Kennedy that lasted for decades. And Sam's role in buying votes and otherwise manipulated the 1960 presidential election so that Kennedy's son would win. In contrast to helping the Kennedys, he was the mobster responsible for wiring certain hotel rooms for sound and successfully recording the extramarital affairs of JFK. Some say he was ultimately responsible for the deaths of Marilyn Monroe, John Kennedy and Robert Kennedy.

The end came for Sam on one night in Oak Park a suburb of Chicago. He was in his home cooking Italian sausage when his assailant entered his house. The killer was no stranger and had known Sam for over thirty years. Sam must have known it was coming because he showed no fear. He turned his back and continued cooking his meal. The killer pulled out a .22, put it at the base of Sam's skull and pulled the trigger. A sharp crack rang out and his victim fell backwards, falling face up on the floor. The killer watched Sam struggle for air as he slowly drowned in his own blood. The assassin then placed the gun into his mouth and fired again. By now he was dead but just to be sure, he then put the gun under Sam's chin and fired five more bullets into whatever was left of his skull.

Mount Carmel Cemetery, Hillside, Illinois

Two days later, Chuck Giancana attended his brother's wake. There were thousands of reporters, curious onlookers, FBI agents, and police officers who crowded the chapel parking lot. Chicago's Montclair Chapel was no stranger to many mafia soldiers who had been laid out within these walls. Sam's funeral was the greatest to date. There were wreaths of beautiful flowers stacked upon one another. And in the middle of them all was his casket, dwafted by the array of floral arrangements.

The casket believe it or not, was open. Sam's face was somehow put together with mortician's wax to make it presentable to the mourners. After the funeral he was then taken to the family crypt were he his now entombed.

Mt Carmel
1400 S. Wolf Road
Hillside , Illinois
Directions: I-90 exit at the Lee Street exit go north to Touhy Ave. make a left on Wolf Rd and then turn into the cemetery and head towards section 39 his rather large family mausoleum is located on the SE corner across from section 42.

Meyer Lansky
The precise date of birth is not known
August 28, 1902 - January 15, 1983

A Jewish immigrant form Russia, Lansky (Suchowljansky) broke into a life of crime running crap games and acting as a strong arm man for Jewish and Italian gamblers on the Lower East Side of New York. Teaming up with his pals Lucky Luciano and Bugsy Siegel, he graduated to bootlegging. Clever Meyer became the master of the "share-out," keeping all the figures in his head and dividing up the spoils from smuggled liquor shipments.

In the thirties and forties, he moved on to illegal gambling, running the classiest casinos around. He invested in modern Las Vegas even though he never really liked the place and became the gambling consultant to President Batista during Havana's glory days.

During World War II, he even acted as a go between for U.S. Naval Intelligence, by paving the way for gangsters help to the Allied invasion of Sicily. Then in 1951, Estes Kefauver's Senate Crime Committee named Lansky as one of the leaders of organized crime in America, fueling the legend that would eventually destroy the gangster.

In 1960, he was expelled from Cuba as Fidel Castro's reign of power took hold. His attempts to go into legitimate business and later to settle in Israel were frustrated by the shadows of his past. His every step was dogged by the FBI and the IRS, as the family crumbled and his health declined.

In February 1980, while at a meal with his family he announced that he had been coughing up blood and that he was going to Mount Sinai to see what the doctors could do. The surgeons ended up cutting out half a lung, hoping that the procedure would stop the cancer from spreading. The surgery did little but left Meyer frail and weak, only postponing the inevitable.

By the summer of 1982, Meyer flew to the Mayo Clinic in Rochester, Minnesota, for a second opinion, which re-confirmed the prior diagnosis. Lansky was told he only had any where from three to six months to live. The cancer had spread down from the lung into the diaphragm, and into various almost inaccessible spots close to the kidney and the spine. Radiation treatment might slow the cancer somewhat, but the doctor could not hold out for much hope.

On December 31, 1982, Lansky entered into the hospital for the last time. He complained that the radiation was burning him, and that it hurt his throat. He could scarcely speak, and he did not want to eat much.

MEYER LANSKY

1902 ✡ 1983

FOREVER IN OUR HEARTS

Mt. Nebo Cemetery, Miami, Florida

In Mount Sinai, they gave him an injection to make him comfortable. There was not much more they could do. Meyer laid in bed, with tubes going in and out of his body, in considerable distress. Though he was sedated with regular injections, he would pick away at the tubes, and on the morning of Friday, January 14th, he managed to pull out the tube that ran down his throat. His wife was there as the doctor and nurses struggled to force the tube back down again. Meyer Lansky fought them off, screaming. Later that evening he suffered a nose bleed which nurses could not stem. In the end, they could do no more than pack the nostril, and leave him lying there, exhausted but conscious enough to recognize his wife.

Then he cried out to her, "Let me go!"

Heavily sedated, Lansky fell into a deep sleep from which he never awoke. He died in Mount Sinai Hospital in the wee hours of Saturday, January 15, 1983.

To the disappointment of the press there was no gangland funeral. There were no limousines, exotic wreaths, or broad shouldered ushers. The casket was not even particularly grand, Meyer's was what you would call, a low budget send off.

Mt Nebo Cemetery
5900 SW 77th Ave.
Miami, Florida

Directions: I-95 to SR 836/ W. Dolphin Expressway to Palmetto Expressway S., towards Coral Way Merge FL-826S., take SW 56th Street/ Miller Dr. exit. Keep right at fork in the ramp, merge on SW 56th Street, left on 77th Court then left into the cemetery. Don't ask for his location because they won't tell you. Go to the northwest corner of the cemetery. He is easily visible from the road. You might see the names Schiff, Bloom, Wexler, and Applestein nearby.

Charles "Lucky" Luciano
November 11, 1896 or November 24, 1897 - January 26, 1962

Salvatore Lucania was 14 when he took his first job as a $5 a week clerk, but after winning $250 in a floating crap game, he soon turned to crime and eventually became head of the U.S. Mafia.

When young Sal began running up a yellow sheet, he tried to spare his family's shame by taking the name of Charles Luciano. But most folks called him Lucky in tribute to his survival skills. Once Moe Sedway said, "When we were young we found Lucky beat up so bad, his head was nearly cut off, decapitated." Later the injury left Lucky with a big scar on his lower lip.

Luciano controlled prostitution, narcotics and gambling rings. He was also a partner in Murder Inc., and took over most of Al Capone's operations. Arrested 25 times, Luciano went to prison only twice, but was eventually deported from the United States in 1946.

Even from behind bars, he still ran the New York harbor. In 1942, the Navy sailed the "Normadie" up the Hudson to refit the luxury liner as a troopship. It mysteriously sank on February 11, 1942, allowing Luciano to patriotically "guarantee" that no further sabotage would occur. The shakedown worked. At the end of the war, Luciano was pardoned, but deported to Italy. Not even deportation could stop Luciano from operating as he continued to run a highly profitable drug ring from Italy.

The end came from not a typical assassination attempt, but simply a heart attack. He was on his way to discuss plans with a Hollywood producer for a movie about his life, when he collapsed at the Capodichino Airport. He was 65.

St. John Cemetery
80-01 Metropolitan Avenue
Queens, New York

Directions: Take the I-495 (Long Island Expressway) to Woodhaven Blvd exit. Go south to Metropolitan Avenue make a right the cemetery is right there. As you enter the cemetery you'll see Section 1 on your left and Section 2 on your right continue until you get to the 1st intersection his very large mausoleum is on the corner of Section 3. Above the doorway is inscribed, "LUCANIA" his real family name.

St. John Cemetery, Queens, New York

Lee Harvey Oswald
October 18, 1919 - November 24, 1963

Everyone was straining to see Oswald as he exited through the door and then someone shouted, "Here he comes!" Along with Captain Fritz and the four detectives, Oswald walked through the door toward the car that was waiting for him. At 11:21 am, Jack Ruby stepped out of the crowd and fired a single, point-blank shot into Oswald's abdomen. As the shot echoed through the building, a policeman who knew Ruby shouted, "Jack, you son of a bitch." Millions witnessed the murder on televison and many wondered if Ruby acted to keep Oswald from talking.

Oswald's wife, Marina, was told initially that he was shot, but his condition wasn't grave. Then things changed as she was now told that it was much more serious than they had originally thought and that he was on his way to Parkland Hospital. Finally she was told he was dead.

The first thing she wanted to do was to see her husband. At first she was advised not to go, because of the angry mob that had formed at the hospital making it an unsafe situation for her. Marina was not going allow them to talk her out of her decision and went anyway. When she arrived the hospital, the staff gave her a hard time about seeing her husband. She insisted and they finally yielded to her wishes.

Lee looked terrible. His face was yellow and unshaven. Marina wanted to see the wound that had killed him and attempted to lift the sheet that covered his body. Someone grabbed her arm preventing her from moving the sheet. So she kissed his face and touched his hand which was by now cold as ice.

The Oswald family was in real danger of some nut retaliating in behalf of President Kennedy. Everywhere they went they encountered angry crowds and something had to be done to protect them. Word had come from Attorney General Robert F. Kennedy who ordered that the Secret Service be sent out to protect Oswald's family. Within an hour the inn at which they were staying, suddenly turned into an camp, with men patrolling outside armed with carbines. "All we need is to have one more of you killed, " one of the agents said, "and we're in real trouble."

The responsibility for arranging the funeral became Robert Oswald's priority. This was not going to be an easy task. One cemetery after another refused to sell Robert a plot for his brother's body. A funeral director took up the search and finally found a cemetery in Fort Worth.

The same thing happened with ministers. Four of them turned Robert down. The office of the National Council of Churches in Dallas asked two Lutheran ministers to go to the inn and offer help. Only one dared to visit Robert in person. The funeral was arranged for 4:00, Monday afternoon, and the minister reluctantly agreed to officiate.

The Oswalds arrived at Rose Hill Cemetery in Fort Worth to find it also heavily guarded, with policemen stationed all along the fence that surrounded the burial ground. They drove to the chapel, expecting to have a religious ceremony. They found an empty and unprepared chapel. They were only able to have a quick service.

During all the commotion, Robert had forgotten to select pallbearers. A group of reporters who were covering the funeral volunteered. It was they who, even before the Oswalds arrived, had carried Lee's body down from the chapel to its grave.

Word arrived that the Lutheran minister who had promised to officiate would not be there after all. But a minister named Louis Saunders of the Council of Churches in Fort Worth had driven out on his own to Rose Hill Cemetery to see if he could help the family. It was also the Reverend Saunders who performed the funeral ceremony for Lee, when no one else would come.

Rose Hill Memorial Park
7301 E. Lancaster
Dallas, Texas

Directions: I-20 to S. Lancaster Road go north and you will bump right into the cemetery. Don't bother asking for the directions to his grave because they won't give it out. Some of the caretakers are pretty cooperative, so you could ask them.

OSWALD

Rose Hill Memorial Park, Dallas, Texas

Jack Ruby
March 25, 1911 - January 3, 1967

At 11:05 am, Ruby parked his car, with his dog Sheba inside and walked into the Western union office on Main Street in Dallas to wire $25.00 to Karen Carlin, one of his strippers. The Western Union office was only one block from the Dallas Police Headquarters.

Everyone within headquarters were told that Oswald would be moved shortly after 11 am. But in an office, Oswald began to fuss about his clothes and said he needed a sweater. A police officer in charge handed him a couple of sweaters and he tried on a beige sweater and decided he didn't like it and then he put on a black one. All this took five minutes, postponing the transfer. Perhaps if Oswald hadn't made such as fuss over the sweaters, he would have been out of the police station and out of Ruby's life.

Ruby who apparently knew nothing about the delay, walked over to the police station and saw that the crowd was still there. The rest is history.

Two days after JFK's assassination, a national TV audience watched in black and white, Lee Harvey Oswald's intended transfer to the county jail. Viewers were then horrified, when suddenly a pudgy man stepped forward from a line of onlookers and shot the prisoner in the gut, leaving the world with now another unanswered question.

Soon after he said, "Well, you guys couldn't do it. Someone had to do it. That son of a bitch killed my president... I guess I just had to tell the world that a Jew has guts..."

Still many questioned Ruby's motive, because he seemed to be the most unlikely avenger for President Kennedy. Prior to his "heroic" deed, Ruby was an ex-Chicago hustler who later became co-owner to the Carousel Club, a local Dallas strip club. Many who knew him thought he was an enigma, who earned a reputation for flying off the handle at the smallest thing. Former Colony Club owner, Abe Weinstein, described him as an odd person, "He was always jealous of my club. If he liked you, he would do anything for you. But if he didn't like you, he would stick a knife in you. He was a Dr. Jekyll and Mr. Hyde."

Many conspiracy theorists feel that he had been hired to silence the assassin, before he was able to go to trial. He was then "framed" where he spent the rest of his life in prison.

On January 3, 1967, Ruby succumbed to an extensive cancer that left his body weak and his mind filled with violent hallucinations.

Ruby's only accomplice a .38 caliber Colt Cobra, that he had bought in 1961 at a Dallas pawnshop was the focus of a legal struggle between Dallas attorney Jules F. Mayer and Ruby's two brothers, two sisters and a nephew. By the late 60's, the gun's value had increased to as much as $250,000. The case was heard in a Dallas probate court where the legitimacy of a will that Ruby dictated, but did not sign prior to going into a coma was in question. Apparently Jules Mayer also had a will that Ruby had given him, but Ruby later told him to rip it up after a falling out.

The courts ruled that the family could keep the gun if they would post a bond to ensure that all claims against the estate would be paid. Among those claims were $40,000 in back taxes and $60,000 in legal fees owed to Mayer.

In 1988, the gun was purchased at an auction for a cool $225,000. Today, it is worth around $300,000 and belongs to an anonymous Florida collector.

Westlawn Cemetery
7801 W. Montrose Avenue
Chicago. Illinois

Directions: From I-90 get off at Harlem Road (Hwy. 43) south make a right on Montrose Avenue the cemetery is on the left. Don't bother asking for any directions because this cemetery has changed it's policy. You can however obtain a map on the many displays located throughout the cemetery. Go to the Violet Section, then look for a #2 on the street. Walk all the way to the fence, then count 4 rows from the fence and there he is along with his family.

BELOVED
SON AND BROTHER
JACK RUBY
APRIL 25, 1911
—
JAN. 3, 1967

Westlawn Cemetery, Chicago, Illinois

Benjamin "Bugsy" Siegel
February 28, 1906 - June 20, 1947

His thrill for killing earned him the nickname, "Bugsy," a name that no one would ever call Benjamin Siegel, to his face. He was a tough kid from Manhattan's Lower East Side, who showed a tendency for violence at an early age. His first racket began as a youth, torching the pushcart of any Orchard Street peddler who refused to pay protection money. His ally was childhood friend, Meyer Lansky who joined him as a key player in the birth of the modern Mob.

Contrary to the movie, "Bugsy," Siegel's Flamingo was not the only casino in town. Las Vegas was on the verge of a major tourist explosion and on its way to becoming a resort town when Siegel first began to lay out his plans for his own venture. By the time Ben had finished the Flamingo, there were already ten major casinos in operation.

While building his "jewel in the desert," the initial projected investment quadrupled. This was not only due to Bugsy's stealing and exorbitant spending, but by others who chose to swindle a buck here and there by padding their expenses. He flew in carpenters, plasterers, electricians and decorators from all over the country and paid them outrageous amounts of money for their suggestions. He then designed the building with Del Webb Construction, only to abruptly change the plans which cost investors an additional $75,000.

Siegel was too busy building his empire to notice that it was crumbling beneath his feet. The bills skyrocketed as the investors saw their shares in the debacle dwindle into oblivion.

When the Flamingo finally opened it's doors on December 26th, each of his celebrity friends who had promised to attend, backed out of their invitations. The Christmas holiday it seems, was the last holiday anyone would want to be away from home, especially when it meant traveling to a desert town to help a notorious gangster save face.

When the first opening turned out to be a flop, Siegel scheduled another Grand Opening for December 28th. Siegel chartered the TWA Constellation plane, which was supposed to be crammed with stars, newspaper reporters from across the country, and fan magazine photographers. It was scheduled to arrive Saturday and leave on Sunday, the 29th. With that Ben thought he had Hollywood sewn up, the underworld bamboozled, Virginia intimidated, and the city gawking at his garish monstrosity. The only one he did not have in his pocket was Mother Nature. On Christmas Day, it poured several feet of rain, washing out roads, and making lakes in the sand. The specially built airport that Siegel commissioned had become a massive mound of mud, making it unusable and causing the flight to be canceled. He was forced to instead lease a fourteen car Union Pacific train to bring in his guests. Most of the stars who promised they'd come again canceled.

On opening day, the rain finally stopped. However, his troubles were not over, as he discovered one disaster after another. The roof leaked, the wiring was defective, and the rooms were not ready for either guests or performers. And that was only the beginning. It is strongly believed that the Mafia rivals and professional gamblers sabotaged the Flamingo to eliminate their new competitor. If they could drive Bugsy out of business, they could seize the venture for themselves. Being too preoccupied with the casino's appearance he entrusted the hiring to unscrupulous thieves. They rigged the tables, double dealt the cards and ripped off Siegel for a cool $250,000.

The Flamingo was the only casino on the strip that did not show a profit. It lost more than half a million dollars that first holiday week. Not only that, when word got around town that it was being run by gangsters, honest citizens feared that they would end up in a shoot out if they went there. His volatile temper became well known as did Bugsy's mistress, Virginia Hill's questionable moral behavior. The locals avoided the place. Bugsy's dream had turned into a disaster and the mob bosses needed to do something about it.

Hollywood Forever Cemetery, Hollywood, California

IN LOVING
MEMORY

FROM THE FAMILY

✡

BENJAMIN
SIEGEL

FEB. 28, 1906
JUNE 20, 1947

A meeting took place at the home of a Beverly Hills attorney that was tied to the Chicago mob. It was decided that it was time to "relieve" Bugsy of his duties with the casino. All, including Siegel, knew that the mafia doesn't vote someone out of power and into early retirement: they are simply eliminated, when they cease to function within their positions. Siegel knew his days were numbered, but still maintained an arrogance that prevented him from accepting the truth.

Now that Bugsy's fate was sealed, it was only a matter of time before the task would be carried out. The first thing to do was to decide whether Virginia Hill, who knew too much, should live or die as well. Joey Adonis, her ex-lover, voted to spare her and assumed full responsibility, a decision he would later live to regret. Next, they put her on a plane and shipped her to Paris on June 16th, to get her out of the way.

On June 19th Siegel and a friend, Swifty Morgan, returned to Los Angeles. Their plane touched down at approximately 2:30 am. From there they took a cab to Virginia's home on Linden Drive. Waiting at the house for Bugsy's arrival were Virginia's brother Chick Hill, and his girlfriend Jerri Mason. It was there that he spent the night.

The next morning Siegel conducted business over the phone and then left the house shortly before 10:00 am. Later that evening, Ben met friend Allen Smiley at Virginia's home. Together along with Chick and Jerri, they all went to a local restaurant called "Jack's." After dinner they made a few stops and then returned to the Linden Drive home.

There are rumors that circulated saying that Chick claimed he smelled carnations when he opened the front door of the house; a southern symbol of death or doom. Nevertheless, the four went inside and Chick and Jerri retired for the night. Siegel and Smiley stayed up and chatted.

While the four were out dinning, Jack Dragna put the final phase of his assassination plot into motion. Dragna phoned Eddie Cannazero, whom he had used as a triggerman on a number of occasions, including the failed attempt on the life of Mickey Cohen. Cannazero apparently already knew exactly where Siegel would be at any given time . He only needed the final go ahead from the boss, Dragna. At approximately 9 pm, Cannazero and four other men got into their black sedans and slowly made their way from Hollywood to Beverly Hills.

Cannazero rode in the first car with two men. The second car, which was called the crash car, a vehicle that would if needed divert police or any suspicious cars if the caravan was being followed. Unobserved, the caravan arrived at approximately at 10 pm. One car parked around the corner from the Linden Drive home; the other car parked across the street.

Cannazero loaded a .30-30 carbine and positioned himself behind a lattice divider on the neighbor's property. He was concealed, but he had a clear view of the large plate glass front window of the Hill home.

When everyone entered the home earlier, no one noticed or chose to ignore the car parked across the street. By then Cannazero had already had the carbine poised and ready.

At approximately 10:30pm, Smiley opened the front drapes which allowed Cannazero a clear view of the living room where Siegel and Smiley were talking. Siegel sat down on the couch and picked up a copy of the Los Angeles Times. He appeared edgy and quickly became bored with the paper, at that time Smiley suggested that he get them a drink and left the room. It was now 10:45pm.

At precisely the moment Smiley had distanced himself from Siegel, nine shots rang out in rapid fire, shattering the front window, smashing the white marble statue that many assumed was a figurine of Virginia, ripping apart several paintings, and drilling holes in the wall. One round melted Siegel's left eye and the other drove his right eye through the back of his skull and onto the dining room floor. Moments later, there were the sounds of screeching tires and it was over. The Mob had exterminated the"Bug."

At approximately 11:00 pm, Jack Dragna received a phone call. The voice at the other end said the words he waited to hear, "The insect was killed." Adonis received a call only minutes later in New York with the same news. Virginia was not informed immediately of her boyfriend's sudden demise. What she did not suspect, was how close she came to sitting next to him, on that sofa, on that fateful night.

The bullet ridden body of the former Las Vegas playboy lay in the Los Angeles County morgue unclaimed, with an identification tag strapped to his left big toe marked with, "B. Siegal, crypt 6." It was just another indignity that this monumental gangster incurred; the misspelling of his name on his toe tag. Another was, the fact that no one ever showed up to view the body or claim it. The official cause of death given was "cerebral hemorrhage due to a gunshot wound of the head inflicted by person or persons unknown."

His personal effects that were recovered from his body were a gold key, which Siegel had made for himself, and $108 in cash.

In contrast to the frenzied hype that surrounded Siegel's murder, his funeral was not the typical mob affair, it was extremely quiet. There were no sightseers and only seven mourners. Virginia remained exiled in Paris, putting on a teary performance each time she was asked any questions about her deceased beau. Despite all her tears, she didn't even send flowers.

The first to arrive for the 9:00 am service was Allen Smiley, who showed up in a black limousine. Then ex-wife Esta and her two daughters, Millicent and Barbara; Ben's brother, Dr. Maurice Siegel: and Dr Max Kert, who was a rabbi at the Olympic Jewish Center on Olympic Boulevard. Siegel's sister, Mrs Bessie Soloway arrived last.

Siegel was laid out in a blue suit, white shirt, and a blue tie with a white handkerchief tucked into his coat pocket He wore no jewelry. The coffin was sealed and lit by two amber lights. Dr Kert read the twenty third Psalm and a Hebrew prayer. There was no eulogy, no comments and the entire service lasted only five minutes. The underworld who usually turned out in droves, and who always competed on who has the better floral arrangements, turned their backs on the man who was later dubbed "The Man Who Invented Las Vegas."

Siegel's body was taken to what is now known as the Hollywood Forever Cemetery where he is entombed in a crypt that was purchased for him by his brother. Rabbi Kert also conducted the gravesite service. The only person who attended that was Ben's brother.

Hollywood Forever Cemetery (Beth Olam Mausoleum is closed on Saturday)
6000 Santa Monica Blvd.
Hollywood, California

Directions: For directions to the cemetery see Janet Gaynor in the Glamour Girls Chapter.If you want to buy the cemetery map for $5.00 or follow my directions for free. As you enter the cemetery go straight until you reach the first intersection which will be Maple Ave., make a right and go to the end. Make a left and follow that to the end until you reach the Beth Olam Mausoleum go inside and walk to your right until you reach the M2 section. He's on the left wall of crypts in #3087 third row up from the floor.

★ ★ ★ ★ ★

AMERICA'S FAVORITE COWBOY

ORVON GENE AUTRY

SEPTEMBER 29, 1907 – OCTOBER 2, 1998

AMERICAN HERO
PHILANTHROPIST
PATRIOT AND VETERAN
MOVIE STAR
SINGER
COMPOSER
BASEBALL FAN AND OWNER
33RD DEGREE MASON
MEDIA ENTREPRENEUR

LOVING HUSBAND

GENTLEMAN

A BELIEVER IN OUR WESTERN HERITAGE

Forest Lawn Memorial Park, Hollywood Hills, California

Quaker Cemetery-Prospect Park, Brooklyn, New York

Chapter 10: The Last Roundup
Gene Autry
September 29, 1907 - October 2, 1998

Orvon Gene Autry was born in Tioga, Texas, a small town with a population fewer than 500. His education consisted of high school, newspapers, and life's experience. Often he read two or three newspapers a day, all the way through to the classified ads.

He began singing in the church choir at age 5 and was taught to play guitar by his mother when he was 12. In 1927, Will Rogers stopped by the telegraph office in Chelsea, Oklahoma and overheard Autry playing his guitar. Autry sang a few songs for Rogers, and the humorist advised him to go to New York and get a job on the radio.

After one unsuccessful audition there, Autry took a job at a Tulsa, Oklahoma radio station and became known as Oklahoman's "Yodelin Cowboy." He was signed to a record contract in 1929. Two years later, Autry made his first marketable record, "*That Silver-Haired Daddy of Mine.*" It was a tune that he co-wrote with Jimmy Long and it sold more than 1 million copies. A record executive devised a special award for an artist that broke the million dollar mark in sales, that became an industry standard -the gold record. Later, the platinum record had to be invented for Autry's "*Rudolph the Red-Nosed Reindeer,*" which sold over 25 million copies. And remains the third biggest selling single in history.

Autry was the only entertainer to have five stars on the Hollywood Walk of Fame, one for his films (more than 90), recordings (635), television (91 episodes of "*The Gene Autry Show*") and radio (16 seasons of "*Melody Ranch*") and one for his live performances.

He was enormously successful at almost anything he tried: radio, records, song writing, television, real estate and business, as well as museums and movies. He was ranked in Forbes' magazine as one of the 400 richest American's for several years and in 1990 was the elite groups' only entertainer. By 1995, he had slipped into the "near miss" category with an estimated net worth of $320 million.

His death came just three days after his 91st birthday and just three months after fellow cowboy and friend, Roy Rogers' death. He died after a long illness at his home in Studio City.

Forest Lawn Memorial Park - Hollywood Hills
6300 Forest Lawn Drive
Los Angeles, California

For directions to the cemetery see Bette Davis in the Glamour Girls Chapter. Ask for a map, but don't ask for any directions. Park at the Sheltering Hills Section which is the 1st section to your right. There are only two statues in that section, that can be seen from the road. Look for the "WONG" statue, walk to the tree next to the right of the this statue than go 4 down and there he is.

Montgomery Clift
October 17, 1921 - July 23, 1966

He was known to be intense and melancholy. As Marilyn Monroe once said, "he's the only person I know who is in worse shape than I am." A serious car crash added to his mental problems as it transformed the handsome young actor into a haggard individual that appeared older than his years.

On May 1956, Montgomery was filming "*Raintree County*" with Elizatbeth Taylor. The two were very close friends and often socialized. On the night of the 16th Taylor invited Clift to dinner along with guests Rock Hudson and wife Phyllis Gates. During dinner it was reported that Clift had only one glass of wine and no other intoxicants. According to Taylor, Clift drove down the steep hill that led from her Coldwater Canyon home, lost control of his car and slammed into a phone pole. She said his car went up the pole like an accordian. Another guest, Kevin McCarthy, who had been following Clift, turned around and rushed back to Taylor's house to call for help.

Taylor ran down the drive to Clift's car and attempted to open the badly crushed door. Realizing that she would have to have the jaws-of-life to get it opened, she entered a rear door and climbed over the seat. Clift was crushed beneath the steering wheel and his face was a bloody pulp of flesh. As he was regaining consciousness he began to choke; some of his teeth had become lodged in his throat. Liz reached in and pulled out the teeth, perhaps saving his life. Another thing she remembers is that when he opened his eyes to look at her they were bright red, like a rose.

He was taken to Cedars of Lebanon and they operated on his broken nose, fractured jaw, and many facial lacerations. In addition to the facial injuries, he suffered a severe cerebral concussion and was put in traction for back injuries. It took nine months to recover; but his face would never be the same. This sent him into drug and booze induced depression that would last for the rest of his life.

To organize and store his extensive stock of pills he collected.Clift had a fourteen foot medicine cabinet made in his Brownstone duplex   Some were obtained legitimately, others from the local Manhattan drug runner named "Bird."

His home on East 61st Street became a hangout for druggies, drunks, and homosexuals. Clift who was a known bi-sexual allowed the traffic to continue until he hired Lorenzo James to take care of him in 1963. Lorenzo ejected the drifters, bought a new lock for the door and attempted to get the house running smoothly.

On July, 1966, Monty spent the day secluded in his bedroom. He and Lorenzo barely spoke to each other. Clift had a goose liver sandwich and at 1:00 am Lorenzo came up to his bedroom to say goodnight. "*The Misfits*" was on TV that night and Lorenzo asked if Monty wanted to watch it and his reply was, "Absolutely NOT!" Those were his last words.

At 6:00 am Lorenzo went to wake him, but the bedroom door was locked. He tried to break it down, to no avail. He ran down to the garden and climbed up a ladder into the bedroom window. There he found Monty lying face up in bed, wearing nothing but his eyeglasses. His fists were clenched and rigor mortis had already set in. He was only 45.

Lorenzo phoned Dr Howard Klein who came over immediately, to examine the body. After a brief examination, Monty's body was taken to the City Morgue, were an autopsy was performed. No evidence of foul play or suicide was detected. The official cause of death was occlusive coronary arteriosclerosis with pulmonary edema from many years of alcohol and drug abuse.

Monty was put in a mahogany coffin at the Frank E. Campbell Funeral Home. The 15 minute funeral service was held in St. James Church. In attendance were only 150 invited guests, while many more waited outside. After the services, his body was taken to the Quaker Cemetery in Brooklyn's Prospect Park.

It is said that Monty haunts the Hollywood Roosevelt Hotel. He lived there for three months while filming "*From Here to Eternity.*" Maids claim that they often feel a something cold brush past them, while others have felt a presence watching them or walking beside them. On November 1992, an overnight guest who stayed in his former room, felt a hand patting her shoulder while she lay in bed reading. When she turned to her husband, he was sound asleep. Another guest claimed he was shoved in the middle of the night. Something to ponder....

Quaker Cemetery - Prospect Park
9th Street and Prospect Park West
Brooklyn, New York
NOTE: Don't even think about making the trip until you call the Brooklyn Rangers at 718-438-0100 or you'll end up seeing the grave as I did. Once a year they give a tour of the Quaker Cemetery and this is the only way you can get in. Also don't even think about climbing the locked fence, because the park is crawling with cops, seeing Monty is not worth the trespassing charge. If you do go on the tour, DO NOT mention Monty or they will throw you out. Just discretely look for him on your own. Also in that same cemetery if you are interested is the MOTT family, as in MOTT Applesauce.

Directions: Take the Brooklyn Queens Expressway and get off at the 4th Avenue exit. Continue on 4th Avenue to Union Street make a right on to Prospect Park, make a right and then a left onto Prospect Park SW and park at 9th Street or as close to it as possible.

Chuck Connors
April 10, 1921 - November 10, 1992

This all American cowboy was born in Brooklyn, New York in 1921. He is best known for his role on *"The Rifleman,"* as Lucas McCain; a moralistic widowed rancher who lived alone with his young son.

He was strongly identified in the series because he carried a rifle instead of a pistol. For all you gun lovers, it was a .44-40 modified Winchester, custom fitted to fire eight shots in 2.5 seconds. At the beginning of each show, he would fire off ten shots, with an extra one dubbed in to match the music. The Winchester was also modified with a special lever to enable Connors to cock it by twirling it in a circular motion.

Prior to becoming one of TV's most popular western figures of the 1950's, he had a less successful sports career. He was a ball player for the Brooklyn Dodgers and the Chicago Cubs. In addition to that, he played professional basketball for the Boston Celtics.

A week prior to his death, Connors checked into Cedar-Sinai Medical Center. Chuck, who had been a heavy smoker for most of his life, died on November 10, 1992, at 2pm, of lung cancer. He was 71.

Connors is buried at the San Fernando Mission Cemetery in Missions Hills, California. He shares it with at least two other 50's icons: Fred Mertz (a.k.a. William Frawley) and La Bamba King, Ritchie Valens.

As I was looking around for Chuck's grave (despite the fact that the office gives you a map with the graves numbered; most are numbered incorrectly), I was getting frustrated because I just could not find it. Finally I saw his face. On his grave stone, he has a photo that was taken as the Rifleman, holding his famous rifle. Also are the icons from the teams he proudly played on, the Cubs, Dodgers and Celtics. Most of all, it indicates that he was the Rifleman. I like that. I hate when actors try to divorce themselves from the role that made them famous, just because they want to be considered as "serious actors." Chuck Connors was proud of all his accomplishments and it shows.

San Fernando Mission Cemetery
11160 Stranwood Avenue
Mission Hills, California
Section J

For directions to the cemetery see Scott Beckett in "The Little Rascals" Chapter. Get a celebrity map at the office and then proceed to the J Section. Park at the 120 which is marked on the curb. Estimate what would be 125 which is approximately 5 tombstones to the right. Then walk up 20 rows, he's right there.

Alan Ladd
September 3, 1913 - January 29, 1964

Most thought that the five foot, five inch actor could not cut it in a Hollywood world of six footers that included the likes of Wayne and Gable. He had a different look accompanied by a deep voice that helped him to succeed as a cowboy. He also appealed to his agent who was his wife Carol Ladd.

His first job was as a grip at Warner Brothers, which later led to some acting in local theatrical productions, radio shows and small film roles. He rose quickly through the ranks to top star with *"A Gun For Sale," "Paper Bullets"* and *"Captain Caution."* Alan appeared in war dramas, crime films but mostly western movies.

OUR BELOVED FATHER

KEVIN "CHUCK" CONNORS

The Rifleman

APR.10.1921 ✝ NOV.10.1992

San Fernando Mission Cemetery, Mission, California

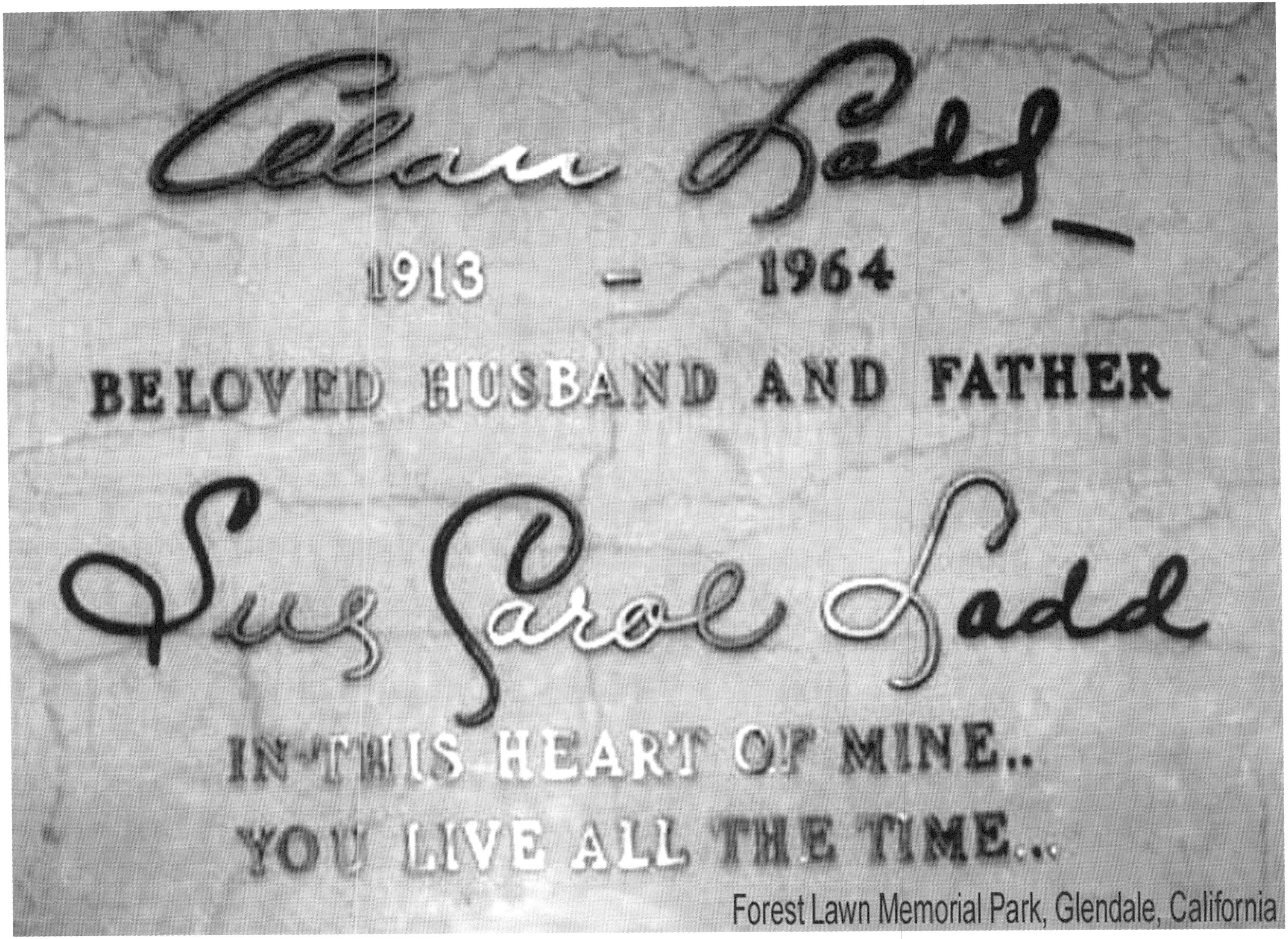

Clair Dale

1913 – 1964

BELOVED HUSBAND AND FATHER

Sus Carol Dale

IN THIS HEART OF MINE..
YOU LIVE ALL THE TIME..

Forest Lawn Memorial Park, Glendale, California

Ladd lived the last years of his life in Palm Springs. While there during the 1950's, he opened a fashionable gift and hardware store that still bears his name to this day. He was an ordinary guy who could be seen in his front yard waving to his friends as they passed by.

Most would think that a successful career and devoted family would be all anyone would need for happiness. But for Alan that was not enough. Perhaps the battle of depression obscured all the good things life had to offer. Alan's depression caused him to make two attempts at suicide. His first attempt on his life was a self inflicted gunshot wound that failed to kill him. A second attempt 14 months later, did the trick as he overdosed on sedatives and alcohol.

Forest Lawn Memorial Park
1712 S. Glendale Avenue
Glendale, California

For directions to the cemetery see Jean Harlow in the Glamour Girls chapter. Get a map but don't ask for any celebrity locations. Drive to the Freedom Mausoleum, if you get lost follow the signs there are many to guide you. Go inside and go right to the Sanctuary of Heritage. You'll see many celebrities in that area. The Ladds are on the right hand wall as you enter.

Roy Roger and Dale Evans
November 5, 1911 - July 6, 1998

For years during the 1950's, Roy Rogers and his real life wife, Dale Evans entertained youngsters with wholesome programming. Each week they would teach a moral lesson through their many adventures. Roy and Dale were one of the few stars in Hollywood that actually lived the wholesome life they portrayed. There were no scandals about them. And so what, if his horse, Trigger, received top billing over Dale, she didn't seem to mind.

Inevitably after suffering a long illness, Roy went to his final roundup. He died from congestive heart failure. He was 86. A couple of years later, Francis Octavia Smith who was better known as Dale Evans died on February 7th, 2001 at the age of 89. She was surrounded by her family as she peacefully slipped away from congestive heart failure. (Born October 31, 1912)

Roy and Dale lived in a small town in California, called Apple Valley. It should be renamed Roy Rogers and Dale Evansville. Everything in this very small rural town, has some sort of tribute to their heros.

Their plot practically takes up the whole cemetery. It is really far from the highway and any major roads. But once you get there, it is a sight to see. The Sunset Hills Memorial Park is nestled in the middle of mountains in a desert. It seems like an appropriate resting place for one of Hollywood's finest cowboys.

It is amazing, their plot is at the entrance of this very small cemetery, so you can't miss it. His gravesite is enclosed in an area with a little fence. It has a beautiful pond with a Frederick Remington like eagle right in the middle of it. Then there are two tombs in white marble, one for Roy and the other for Dale. Before you walk into the gate, you'll notice two sets of horse shoe prints on the ground. There is also bench with the name of Alice Van Springsteen, who by the way is very much alive, she was Dale Evans stunt double. Roy and Dale have included her in their family plot when she dies, I was told she will be cremated. The grave, I'm told was designed by Roy, Dale and their son, Dusty (Roy Jr.). On the wall are two plaques that have a cowboy's prayer and a psalm for Dale. The whole grave has a western motif, which I guess reflects their lifestyle. If you stand there facing the west you can see the snow capped mountains. It is really a very nice spot.

Sunset Hills Memorial Park
24000 Waalew Road
Apple Valley, California

Directions: From I-15 get off at Hwy 18 head east into Apple Valley make a left at Corwin Road and then right on Waalew. Drive to the end, the cemetery is on your left. This is such a small cemetery and Roy and Dale are to your left in a very large section near the entrance. It is the only section there with a lake. It is a must see, because it is one of the prettiest gravesite I have ever seen.

Sunset Memorial Park, Apple Valley, California

Trigger

Trigger retired from show business when Roy and Dale stopped shooting the TV show. Some years before that, he was beginning to show his age and was referred to as "the Old Man." As he got on in years Roy and Dale had no choice but to put him out to pasture. He lived his final years in a real big stall near their home.

Early one morning in 1965, Roy was awakened with the news that his pal had died. Danny the stable manager, said that Trigger had finished his breakfast and was turned out into the pasture as always. He lied down to take a nap. After awhile Danny went out to check on him, but Trigger was dead. The old horse passed away gently, as he slept in the field. He was 33.

When news of his death was released, the Smithsonian Institution in Washington D.C. asked if they could have his remains for their collection of historical Americana. But Roy didn't want his pal so far away. Nor could he bare to see him put into the cold ground. So he came up with a plan to preserve his companion so both he and Trigger's fans could always enjoy seeing him.

Mr. Bischoff, a famous taxidermist in Los Angeles mounted Trigger forever where he is on display in the Roy Rogers and Dale Evans Western Museum.

John Wayne
May 26, 1907 - June 11, 1979

It is not often that an actor can transcend a role, to become that of an American icon. One role in particular goes hand in hand with the name of John Wayne and that is the role of a cowboy. He staggered into this world as Marion Michael Morrison in Winterset, Iowa. He was attending the University of Southern California on a football scholarship when he stumbled into acting by virtue of a summer job as a laborer at Fox. On the studio lot, he met and befriended director John Ford and occasionally Wayne would appear as an extra in some of his films.

In the late 20's, he was billed as Duke Morrison and eventually he was entrusted with several larger, but still insignificant assignments in some of Ford's films.

In 1930, he was recommended for a lead role in Raoul Walsh's epic, *"The Big Trail."* This was his big chance for some recognition. But it wasn't until 1939, that Wayne's performance as Ringo Kid in *"Stagecoach,"* would propel him into overnight star status.

By the late 40's and 50's, he was considered a monumental star, that was recognized worldwide for many cowboy and military films. As time went by, Wayne's status as an American hero grew even greater. He became politically active in many conservative causes, including support for the Vietnam War. Despite adverse reactions from politically liberals audiences, his films still continued to please mainstream America.

His final film, *"The Shootist,"* (1976) he played a gunslinger who is dying of cancer, that must come to terms with his life. This mirrored real life for Wayne, because he too would die three years later from cancer. Aside from the fact that he made some people uncomfortable with his strong beliefs, he still left a nation in mourning. On June 11th, Wayne lost the well publicized battle with lung and stomach cancer. He was 72.

Pacific View Memorial Park, Newport Beach, California

JOHN WAYNE

1907-1979

"TOMORROW IS THE MOST IMPORTANT THING IN LIFE.
COMES INTO US AT MIDNIGHT VERY CLEAN.
IT'S PERFECT WHEN IT ARRIVES AND IT PUTS ITSELF IN OUR HANDS.
IT HOPES WE'VE LEARNED SOMETHING FROM YESTERDAY."

On A&E's John Wayne biography, his daughter said the family was hesitant in erecting any kind of marker on the Duke's grave. They were afraid that some manic would desecrate his tombstone, due to his controversial beliefs. Finally, almost twenty years later, they put a tombstone on his grave. It was something that he wanted.

He is buried high up on a hill, by a shade tree overlooking a reservoir. The cemetery is very small, but peaceful.

The City of Newport Beach, California is dedicated to Wayne's memory. They have memorialized him by changing the name of the Orange County Airport to the John Wayne Airport. Inside there is a nine foot statue of "The Duke," citing the long time Newport Beach resident's distinguished film career and reputation as a true American patriot.

Pacific View Memorial Park

3500 Pacific View Dr

Newport Beach, California

Directions: Take the 405 south to Newport Beach Blvd. To U.S. 1 to Corona Del Mar. Drive to the top of the hill by the wall of crypts. John is located across the street by a huge tree.

✝

LOUIS FRANCIS CRISTILLO

1906 — 1959

BELOVED HUSBAND AND FATHER

Calvary Cemetery, Los Angeles, California

Chapter 12: Dynamic Duos
Bud Abbot and Lou Costello
Lou
March 6, 1906 - February 27, 1959

Louis Francis Cristillo was born in Paterson, New Jersey the son of a large Italian family. Along with his parents and siblings he shared his loving home with his grandfather, Uncle Pete, Aunt Alma, Aunt May and Aunt Eva.

Once in high school he participated in sports, basketball and boxing. Due to his small stature, five feet, four inches, he realized that he'd never be a success. Boxing was also short lived because he felt that the punishment didn't equal his potential for prosperity. The only thing left for him was Vaudeville, there he could display his comedic talents.

Reared in an immigrant community, he was instilled with the idea of the American dream. He believed that you could do anything or be anyone if you tried hard enough. Charlie Chaplin was his biggest influence and perhaps responsible for his desire to pursue a career in comedy.

Lou's older brother, Anthony, had joined the Navy during the war, but grew tired of a lifestyle that offered nothing more than mopping decks. He opted for an easier gig, ship orchestra. Once discharged, he went into the music business in New York. That's when his girlfriend dubbed him 'Pat' because he was from Paterson. 'Cristillo' was not easy to remember, so he took the name 'Costello.' Lou followed suit and became Lou Costello.

Eventually Lou moved to Hollywood to seek his fortune in films. His first gig for MGM was not in the movies as desired; it was building sets. There he graduated from set building to stuntman. He got a lot of work as stuntman until he landed in the hospital. After his broken bones healed he realized that perhaps this was not an ideal career choice for him. He was now out of work and broke, so he headed back home.

Finally in 1934 he got a break he was hired to play the burlesque circuit in New York. There he met his wife Anne Battler and his other future partner, Bud Abbott.

The new team of Abbott and Costello found approval with the Burlesque houses. From there they ventured to Hollywood achieving more success than Lou had ever experienced on his own. Their union reaped many movies and engagements that would last for the next twenty-two years.

All was well for the pair with exception to Bud's apparent problem with alcohol. Abbott was an epileptic that drank to compensate for his affliction. Unfortunately for both, his problem became so bad that it sometimes interfered with the show. It had happened one too many times and Lou was fed up

Their last engagement together was in the Sahara in Las Vegas. Between shows Bud played the crap table. Apparently his luck changed from good to bad, and with that Bud's attitude. To keep him happy, the pit boss placated Bud with one drink after another.

The midnight show was packed with people and NBC had some executives in the audience scouting Bud and Lou for a new series. The Bud half of the team was missing and the show was about to go on. Everyone scoured the casino looking for him. When they finally found him, they hurried him backstage and put him into his costume. As they got on stage, Lou realized that something was wrong, Bud was smashed out of his mind and not responding. Lou, not wanting to miss an opportunity with the NBC big wigs, made a feeble attempt to proceed with the show. After several tries, he gave up and pushed Bud off stage. The show was over and so was their relationship as a team.

Two years later, Lou was making the movie *"The Thirty-Foot Bride of Candy Rock."* It was a B-movie, and a fantasy about a little man with a giantess bride. One late afternoon, while shooting, Lou asked to go home because he was tired. After the film was complete, he didn't attend the 'wrap party,' because he his health was beginning to fail him.

On February 26, 1959, Lou began to feel pain. That night, he attempted to go to sleep but the pain worsened. His wife, Anne, became alarmed and called Lou's sister, Marie. Marie rushed over to see her brother, only to find him lying on his stomach in intense pain. They called Dr Stanley Imerman, who ordered a prescription for the pain. He was no better; so he was taken to Doctor's Hospital in Beverly Hills. His wishes were to tell no one, not even his old partner Bud.

A specialist was flown in from San Francisco to see Lou. His prognosis was not good; his weakened heart was not responding to treatment. His breathing was labored and the his face turned from the ruddy complexion he had all his life to grey. At one point, Anne was told that he would not survive the night. A priest came for last rites and Lou gestured him away saying that he wasn't ready for that yet and that he was going to beat this and be alright.

The next morning, Lou looked better. The color had returned to his face and he was sitting up in bed.

"I feel marvelous!" Lou said as he spoke with manager Eddie Sherman for fifteen minutes. Then suddenly he felt nauseous. He breathed through his oxygen mask for a little bit and the nausea disappeared. Then he did the unthinkable; he asked for an ice cream soda. Eddie came back with a two scoop strawberry ice cream soda.

As he drank the soda he felt livelier than ever and talked about the prospects of doing some movies. Eddie said that he could do as many pictures as he wanted, after he got the rest needed to regain his health. His last words were: "Don't worry, I will," he took the last sip and said, "That was the best ice cream soda I ever tasted." He put the container on the bedside table and died.

A shocked Bud heard the news and said weeping, "But if only I had known. I could have brightened him up, made him laugh."

Lou's funeral was on March 7th, four days after his fifty-third birthday. Four hundred people piled into Costello's parish church, St. Francis de Sales. Bud who was one of the pallbearers, medicated his grief with scotch. Instead of holding his own, he leaned against the bronze casket that carried his former partner, adding to the burden of the other pallbearers.

FRED ASTAIRE

I WILL ALWAYS LOVE YOU MY DARLING

THANK YOU

Oakwood Memorial Park, Chatsworth, California

ROGERS

LELA
1890–1977

GINGER
1911–1995

Oakwood Memorial Park, Chatsworth, California

The limousine took Lou to his final resting place, The Calvary Cemetery. He was placed in a crypt in the mausoleum chapel. A few steps away is a small marker that bears the name of Lou Costello Jr., Butch, who had drowned in a swimming pool as a baby. A bracelet that had reminded Lou of his son, remained on his wrist. Before the year's end, Lou's wife joined her husband, the official cause was heart attack.

Calvary Cemetery (Mausoleum)

4201 Whittier Blvd.

Los Angeles, California

Directions: Take the 710 to 60W get off at 3rd Avenue exit travel south to Whittier make a right and look for the gates. Don't ask for a map; this cemetery runs hot and cold when it comes to sharing information with the public. Go to the main mausoleum, once inside walk up stairs. At the top of the stairs you'll notice a chapel. Bear right to the hallway go to the 2nd doorway look to you left in the 1st row. He's on the top row.

Bud

October 2, 1895 - April 24, 1974

Bud lived for another fifteen years after his partners death. He did not live the opulent life as most would expect; he spend his final years in poverty and misery. He had lost everything to delinquent taxes and poor management.

He suffered a stroke which left him paralyzed. Prostate surgery left him weak and two years later he suffered another stroke. His health declined and he needed to be hospitalized. Since he had no money he would have to go to the Country Hospital which was operated by the Motion Picture Relief Fund.

Bud didn't stay there long; he wanted to go home. He went to live with niece, Betty, who set up a room within her home as a hospital room and cared for Bud until the day he died. They spent their time watching old movies as they had their nightly cocktail. After some time Bud lost his taste for alcohol and in the last year of his life gave up drinking entirely.

The night he died he made a familiar noise from his throat. It was the same noise his mother had made just before she died. At seven the next morning, Bud had died. His funeral was at the First Christian Church of Reseda, which Bud had never attended. Two hundred people were in attendance, after which his body was cremated and the ashes scattered on the ocean.

Fred Astaire and Ginger Rogers

Fred

May 10, 1901 - June 22, 1987

Born Frederick Austerlitz in Omaha, Nebraska he started performing at age seven and hoofed his way to stardom. His greatest success came when he teamed up with Ginger Rogers in such romantic movies as *"Top Hat," (*1935) and *"Shall We Dance"* (1937).

On June 12th he had been admitted to a Los Angeles hospital with a severe cold that soon settled into pneumonia. Ten days later, at 4:25 am, as his strength ebbed, his wife, former Jockey Robyn Smith, lay down beside him and held him. "He died in my arms," she said, "the way he wanted it. He died holding on to me."

At his funeral he was eulogized by President Ronald Reagan, "the ultimate dancer who made it all look so easy." He was buried coincidently in the same cemetery as his former dance partner Ginger. For directions to his grave, read on.

Ginger
July 16, 1911-April 25, 1995

Born Virginia Katherine McMath she made a total of 73 movies during a period of 40 years. Surprisingly enough she only made 10 with Fred.

Near the end of her life she would have friends over, and screen videos of her movies. She would let guests choose the film they wanted to see, but insisted on quiet once the film began.

Ginger was a devout Christian Scientist and only consulted one of the church's practitioners for spiritual healing, whenever she was ill. On the day of her death her assistant, Roberta Olden was with her until the end. She passed away at home as she had wished. Her last words were, "I've had a wonderful life. God's will, will now be done. Praise to God." She was 83.

Despite the fact that she was 83 and of poor health, authorities performed an autopsy. Reason being, that in the State of California if a person dies without having been under a doctor's care for the past 40 days, it becomes an automatic coroner case. Their findings were that she died of natural causes combined with heart disease.

Oakwood Memorial Park
22601 Lassen Street
Chatsworth, California

For directions to the cemetery, see Bob Crane in the Season's Finales' Chapter.For directions to Fred get a celebrity map and proceed to Oakwood Drive and make a right on to Cresent Lane park at the corner at Section G, on your left side, walk maybe 4 spaces and he's there (Section G, Lot 82, Space 4). From Fred, continue down Cresent Lane to Valley Road make a left. Look for a path on your left and park. Follow that path and you will bump right into Ginger and her mom (Section E, Lot 303, Space 1).

Edgar Bergen and Charlie McCarthy
February 16, 1903 - September 30, 1978

It is amazing how time effects how one perceives a name. If you were to mention the name "Bergen" in the 1950's and 60's, the first thing that you would think of would be Edgar Bergen and Charlie McCarthy. But today you'd get a very different concept, you think of his daughter "Candice."

Edgar Berggren was born in 1903 to Swedish parents who immigrated to the U.S. to seek a better life. They settled in the Midwest, bought a dairy farm and raised two boys.

The only entertainment available to middle America during that era, was Vaudeville. Edgar and his brother would sometimes sneak under the canvas of the tent or if they had the money, they'd pay a nickel to sit on a splintered wooden bench to see the many acts offered.

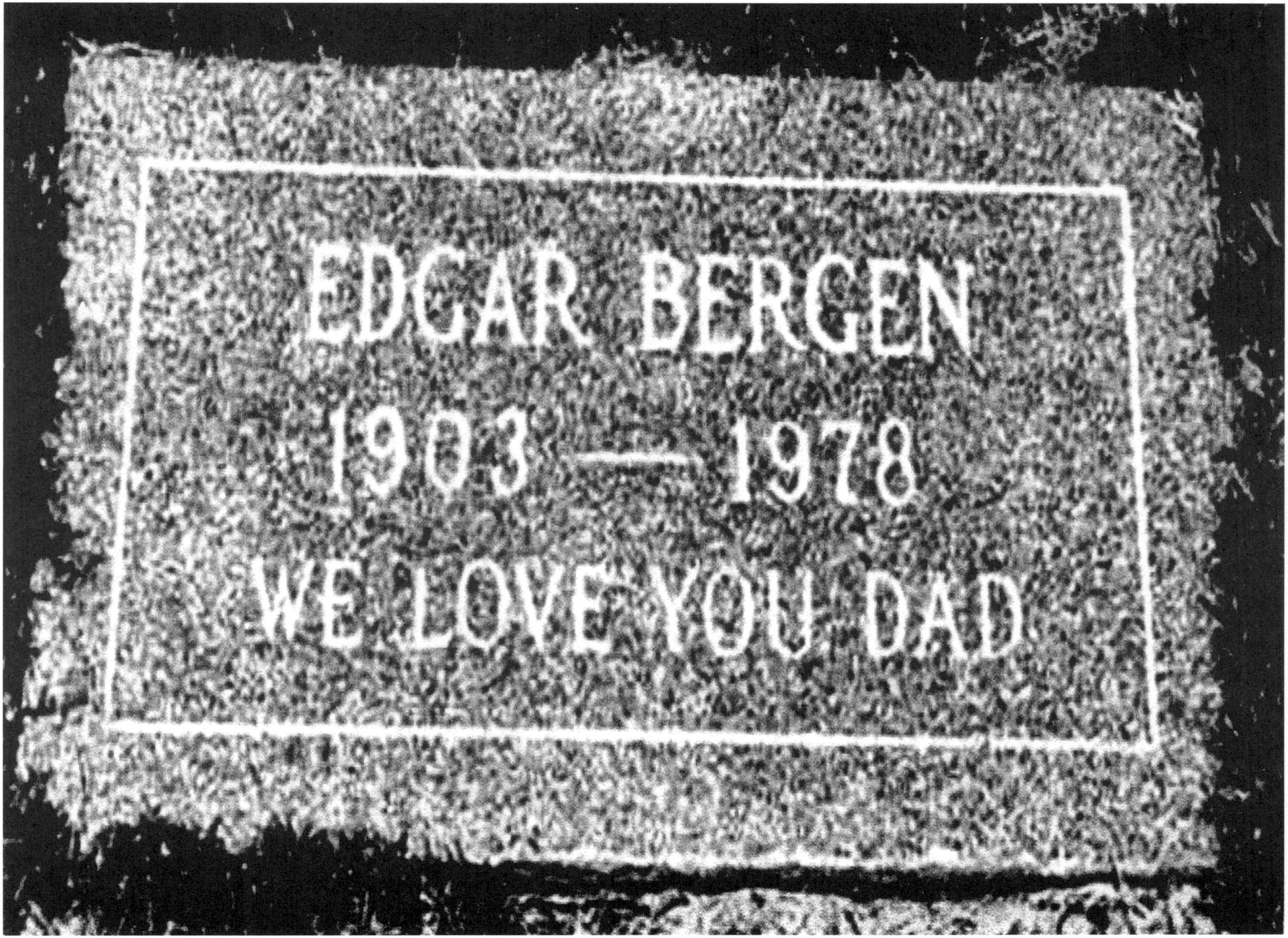
EDGAR BERGEN
1903 — 1978
WE LOVE YOU DAD

The life of a Vaudevillian was something that many others like Bergen, wished to aspire to. But there was one major problem: he was painfully shy and self-conscious. Nevertheless he was spellbound. At eleven, he thought he could perhaps do magic tricks. He ordered "The Wizard's Manual" that he found in a magazine ad. His quarter investment was the beginning of a life long career. One of the things that the book taught was ventriloquism. This was something that captivated the young boy's interest; so he began to practice his new found craft diligently.

He began by throwing his voice into an apple pie that his mother was taking from the oven. The pie, in a tiny, high pitched voice, shrieked, "Help, help! Let me out! Oh, thank you, thank you." Soon as he became more proficient, he needed a partner, preferably a wooden partner, to exhibit his skills.

The character, with whom he would share the spotlight, was based on a quick witted, redheaded Irish boy, close to his age by the name of Charlie. Charlie had sold newspapers on the corner in their town of Decatur. As Edgar would pass the boy each day, he would make sketches. Eventually he gave these sketches to a barkeeper called Mack who was also a woodcarver. They first worked on a clay head which served as a model. Then Mack went to work carving the little 'dummy' which Edgar christened "Charlie McCarthy." The "McCarthy" was named after Mack.

The dummy and Edgar became inseparable. Charlie would accompany him to school and there he would answer the roll call for any absent students. He first real public appearance was at an amateur show that paid five dollars a night. There he 'neatened' up his name by removing a 'g' and a 'r,' now becoming "Edgar Bergen: Voice Illusionist."

After traveling the second circuit, Edgar switched from Vaudeville to become a freshman at Northwestern, something that pleased his mother. Show biz however, was in his blood, so he abandoned his mother's dream for him to become a doctor and returned to the road. For ten years Edgar and Charlie traveled 'the Sawdust Trail" by rail entertaining his way across the country.

Eventually by 1930, his popularity earned him a spot in the big time, playing the 'Palace.' There he rubbed shoulders with great performers such as Jack Benny, Al Jolson, The Barrymores, Houdini, the Marx Brothers, Will Rogers, and Fred Astaire. Each time he played the Palace, it would ring with laughter, and at the end of each show the audience would beg for more.

In 1932 the Palace closed, symbolizing the death of Vaudeville. The thing that would replace it would be silent pictures and the birth of the Golden Age of radio.

Surprisingly enough in 1936, Edgar found himself in Hollywood with his own radio show. The Chase and Sanborn Hour" which was listened to on Sunday evenings at 8pm. Personally speaking, how does a ventriloquism act fly on the radio? Don't you need to see it to appreciate it? I guess their amazing success answers those questions.

Their new found fame became very marketable selling everything from Charlie McCarthy dolls to coloring books and many other toys.

One Charlie McCarthy doll was given to Francis Westerman, 14, who was recovering from a skull fracture she had received in an automobile accident. Later this girl would become Mrs. Edgar Bergen, mother of Candice.

GRACIE ALLEN
1902 - 1964

AND

TOGETHER AGAIN

GEORGE BURNS
1896 - 1996

Forest Lawn Memorial Park, Glendale, California

Edgar and Charlie enjoyed great success until the 1960's arrived, in which he began to work less. Television eclipsed radio and for some reason Edgar and Charlie never quite found a home in that medium. They appeared in a number of movies with W.C. Fields; but still there was little appeal for their act in that era. Despite this, Edgar still loved to perform and found himself playing country fairs and benefits or taking third billing at Las Vegas.

By 1978 at the age of seventy-five, Edgar had grown old over night. He had developed a host of health problems: high blood pressure, memory loss, deep fatigue, but worst of all his heart was in bad shape. He had been hospitalized for an episode and was now prescribed a mulitude of medications. All this made him short tempered and distracted. For the better part of the year, his health continued to deteriorate.

In the summer of 1978, Edgar and Charlie reluctantly called a press conference at the Brown Derby in Beverly Hills to announce their retirement. His final engagement was at the Caesars Palace in Las Vegas on a bill with Andy Williams. The engagement was a serious health risk to him; since he had just been hospitalized six months earlier in the coronary intensive care unit.

That night's performance went well and Edgar and his wife went to bed in good spirits. As Frances got up the next morning to open the window blinds, she called out to Edgar softly. Several minutes had passed before she realized that he had died. His heart had stopped as he slept peacefully.

The services were held at the All Saints Church in Beverly Hills. Ronald Reagan, Rams owner Carroll Rosenbloom, Johnny Carson, and Jim Henson along with Kermit the frog all gave the eulogies. Charlie's final resting place is the Smithsonian Museum, in Washington D.C. and Edgar's is that of Ingelwood Park Cemetery in Los Angeles.

Ingelwood Park Cemetery
720 E. Florence Avenue
City of Ingelwood, California
For directions to the cemetery see William Thomas (Buckwheat) in the The Little Rascals Chapter.Get a map and proceed to the Miramar Section. This is a very small section and you should n't have a problem finding it. Look for an upright tombstone with the name "Berggeren" on it. His grave marker is in front of it, lot #131, grave #2.

George Burns   and   Gracie Allen
January 20, 1896 - March 9, 1996   July 26, 1895 - August 27, 1964
Nathan Birnbaum grew up on the Lower East Side of New York City. By the age of seven, he knew that singing, soft shoe dancing and telling jokes was what he wanted to do with his life. He dropped out of school in the fourth grade and at the age of 13, he bombed with his first vaudeville act. At 16, George took up cigar smoking as part of his act, and it became his trademark.

In 1922, while on the road in Union City, New Jersey, he met a jobless seventeen year old dramatic artist named Grace Ethel Cecile Rosalie Allen. They formed an act where in their first routine, Burns had Gracie feed him straight lines so he could tell the jokes, but nobody laughed. Instead, they broke up over Gracie's straight lines. From that first day on, George became the straight man, Gracie did the jokes and got the laughs:

George: "Did the nurse ever drop you on your head when you were a baby?"

Gracie: "Oh, we couldn't afford a nurse. My mother had to do it."

George and Gracie married on January 7,1926 and began a love affair that continued beyond her death and for the rest of his life. Together they worked on stage, in radio and on their TV show, until Gracie's health had begun to deteriorate.

In the late 1950's Allen began to suffer migraine headaches brought on by the constant strain of the intense rehearsals required for live television. In addition to that Gracie suffered chronic heart problems and by the third season, she was finding it harder and harder to have the show go on. In the early 1950's, she suffered her first coronary, and within a few years the heart problem had become a daily burden. A bottle of nitroglycerine tablets were always close by, to relieve her frequent chest pains. Burn's later admitted that he never really knew how serious the extent of her heart problems were.

In 1958, after eight seasons, Gracie announced her retirement without divulging that she was leaving upon her doctor's orders. Burns attempted to do a show on his own, changing the name to, "*The George Burns Show,*" unfortunately without Gracie it only lasted a season.

Gracie would live only a few more years after that. On August 26, 1964, she entered the Cedars of Lebanon Hospital in Hollywood after suffering a massive heart attack. She died the next day. Her death left Burns devastated and alone; he would never marry again. He visited Gracie's grave monthly without fail until his health prohibited the trip.

As for George, he had another 32 years left on this earth. Despite his two martinis and countless cigars he consumed daily, he would live a century. In fact, Burns had two jokes about his longevity: "I'm going to stay in show business until I'm the only one left." or "I can't die, I'm booked."

Two years prior to his death, he slipped in the bathtub hitting his head, an injury that might have triggered his final decline. On March 9th, he died quietly at his home in Beverly Hills.

George and his lovely wife are entombed in Forest Lawn Cemetery, located in Glendale. They are in the Freedom Mausoleum, not far from Nat King Cole, Clara Bow, Alan Ladd and Jeanette MacDonald.

The epitaph says it all, "Together Again."

Forest Lawn Cemetery - Glendale

1712 S. Glendale Avenue

Glendale, California

Freedom Mausoleum - Sanctuary of Heritage

For directions to the cemetery see Jean Harlow in the Glamour Girls Chapter.Get a map of the cemetery but DO NOT ask for any celebrity locations or you will be thrown out. Follow the signs to the Freedom Mausoleum, go right after entering and look for the Sanctuary of Heritage. Their crypt is on the right wall, you can't miss it.

Clark Gable and Carole Lombard

Clark

February 1, 1901 - November 16, 1960

Forest Lawn Memorial Park, Glendale, California

Photograph by Anne Parisi

Born into a transient family, his father was a wild cat oil driller. Gable dropped out of school and worked with him in the Oklahoma oil fields for several years as a young man. Working outdoors appealed to Gable, however acting seemed to fill a void that no other profession ever could. He grabbed the first opportunity into show business by joining a touring stock company.

Having lost his mother at ten months, he married two women many years his senior who were helpful in getting him started in his new found profession. Later thanks to them and his talent, he became Hollywood's most popular male lead for the next three decades, starring in films like *"Red Dust"* (1932), *"Mutiny on the Bounty"* (1935) and of course as Rhett Butler in *"Gone With the Wind"* (1939).

Ironically, he reluctantly accepted the role that would make him known to many as *"Rhett Butler."* The thing that persuaded him most, was not the potential fame that this once in a lifetime part would bring; it was his love for Carole Lombard. Clark and Carole had begun seeing one another soon after she divorced William Powell. They fell madly in love.and couldn't wait to marry. Clark needed the extra money for a quicky divorce from then wife Ria, ASAP. Carole and Clark were perfect together, he called her Ma and she called him Pa. Also they both enjoyed practical jokes and outdoor activities such as hunting and fishing.

After she was killed, Clark was inconsolable and did everything he could to take his mind off his grief. In 1942, he joined the Air Force and served with distinction, participating in several bombing raids over Nazi Germany, achieving the rank of Major and ultimately receiving the Distinguished Flying Cross. He returned to Hollywood still very despondent.

He made his last movie in 1961, Arthur Miller's *"The Misfits."* It was rumored that this film was responsible for the heart attack that would later kill him. Most people focused on the fact that it was Marilyn Monroe's constant lateness and mental frailties that caused the excessive stress that wore on him

It was most likely that if anything, his heart attack was provoked by the arduous stunts Gable insisted on doing himself. This included being pulled along the ground by a wild mustang (which was really a truck, that pulled him over four hundred feet at 35 m.p.h). Despite his protective clothing he was cut and bruised.

Gable told his wife that John Huston's demands on his stuntmen were beyond the call of duty, that he didn't seem to care if they lived or died. As long as Huston achieved his objective in the film that was all that he was concerned with, not the stuntmen's safety. It was Gable's belief in the film, that kept him going, believing that this was the best picture he had ever done.

So after the film was done shooting, Clark was working around his ranch when he began to experience severe chest pains These were confirmed as a coronary thrombosis and his prospects for recovery appeared pretty grim at first. Over the next few days, however, Gable seemed to rally. He enjoyed a telegram from President Eisenhower that read: "Be a good boy, Clark, and do as the doctors tell you to do."

By now he was married once more and expecting his first child. He lived long enough to hear his baby's heartbeat, but not long enough to see him born. On November 16th at 10:50pm, Gable turned the page of a magazine he was reading, suddenly fell back into his pillows and died. He was only 59. The cause was a massive heart attack.

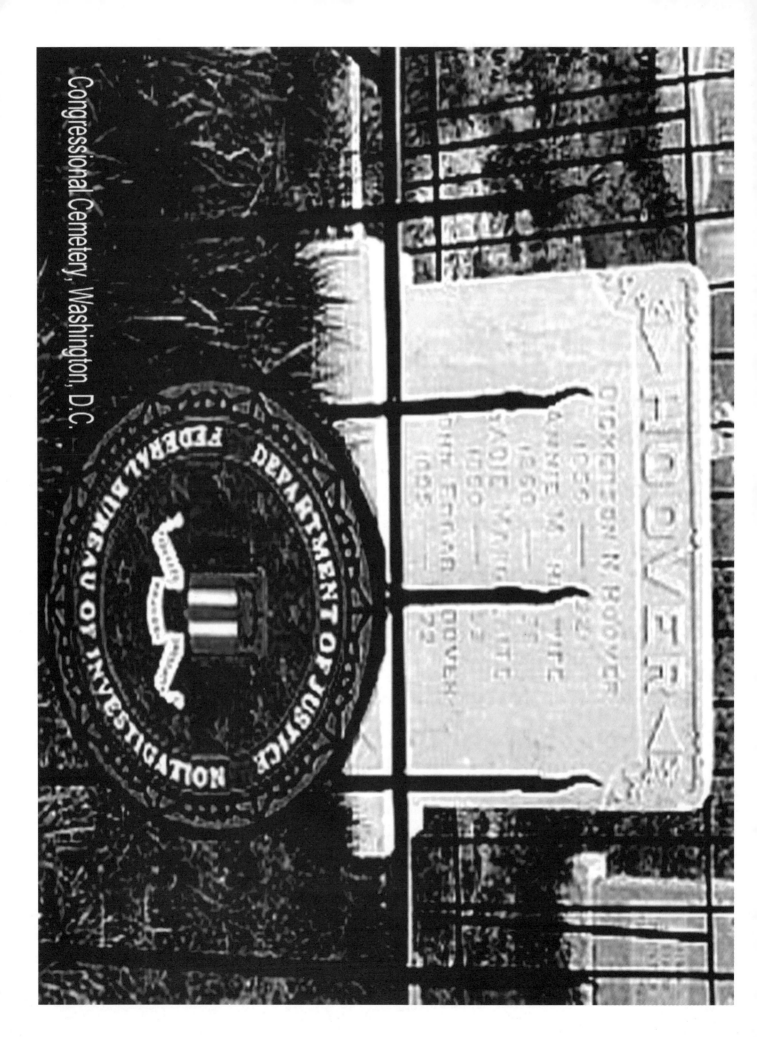

Carol
October 6, 1908 - January 16, 1942

Carole first appeared in the movies at the age of 13, where she evolved into a saucy, fast talking, blonde who appeared in many successful, tailor made for her vehicles. By the 1930's she became Hollywood's top comedic actress.

Eventually she married again and became Mrs.Clark Gable. It was during their marriage that she interrupted her busy Hollywood film career to go on a World War II bond drive in Indiana. Despite her mother's psychic predictions of a pending disaster, she booked a flight on a TWA DC-3, instead of using her already purchased train tickets. Apparently she couldn't wait to see Clark and didn't want to endure a long train ride. At first her mother declined to accompany her anxious daughter, in hopes to discourage her travel plans. But when she realized how much her daughter wanted to return to Clark, she reluctantly boarded the plane with her

Unfortunately her mother's premonition came true as the plane crashed into a mountain killing all on board. Gable was on the scene almost immediately, and watched as they brought his wife's charred body down from the snow capped mountain on a stretcher pulled by mules.

Carole had written a will just two years earlier, requested that she be buried at Forest Lawn in a modestly priced crypt; dressed in her best color, white. Both requests were granted. Although burned almost beyond recognition, her gown was pure white. She is laid to rest in a crypt along side of Clark's.

Forest Lawn Memorial Park
1712 S. Glendale Avenue
Glendale, California

For directions see Jean Harlow in the Glamour Girls Chapter. Get a map of the cemetery but don't ask for any directions to celebrity graves. Head over to the Great Mausoleum (if you don't get a map just follow the signs). The is a locked area and closed to the general public. If you are invited in by a property owner or cemetery personnel, go to the Sanctuary of Trust. Both Carole and Clark are side by side on the left wall.

J.Edgar Hoover and Clyde Tolson
J. Edgar
January 1, 1895 - May 2, 1972

J. Edgar Hoover and Clyde Tolson called one another cute little nicknames like, "Speed" and "Junior." The pair flew to Miami for vacations and spent their weekends together at home in Washington D.C. Forever unmarried they went everywhere together; they even dressed the same. And finally they were buried within yards of one another.

Rumors of Hoover being homosexual swirled around him all of his adult life. However, if anyone was to suggest such a thing he would go nuts, hunt the perpetrator down and make their lives a living hell.

CLYDE ANDERSON
TOLSON
MAY 22 1900 APRIL 14 1975

Congressional Cemetery, Washington, D.C.

Hoover reigned as F.B.I. king for 48 years, where he made it the pride and admiration for all Americans. As long as his G-men were on the job, everyone rested just a little easier. During his tenure the bureau was responsible for arresting a number of famous criminals, adding to it's already brilliant reputation.

Assistant, James Crawford arrived early Tuesday morning to help the Director plant some rose bushes that he had ordered eariler that week. He parked out front of the two story colonial brick home at 4936 Thirtieth Place NW, behind the shiny black bulletproof Cadillac. Since the Boss wasn't up yet, Crawford went around the back and started to unpack the rosebushes.

Not long after that, Annie the housekeeper asked Crawford if he would go upstairs and check on Hoover. It wasn't like him to sleep so late. Anne wanted to avoid going up there because he had a habit of sleeping in the nude.

Crawford went up and knocked on the door and there was no answer. Again he knocked and there was still no answer. He slowly opened the door to the darkened room and saw Hoover's body on the carpet next to the bed. He rushed over to him and picked up one of his hands. One of the most powerful men in the world was dead.

Anne called his personal physician and then Clyde Tolson, Hoover's closet friend and confidante. Tolson was shocked. His life had changed forever. Decades of protecting the Director from every conceivable kind of harm had suddenly come to an end, yet there were final orders yet to execute.

First he called Helen Gandy, Hoover's secretary for fifty four years. Hoover's death was not formally announced for more than two hours after the discovery of his body. The reason for the delay was because everyone was not sure on how to proceed. This resulted from the frantic efforts of official Washington to answer the three questions he had successfully evaded during life: What was in his personal files, who in government had authority over him and finally who would be the appropriate person to announce his death.

When his physician arrived, he examined Hoover's body and determined that he had died of hypertensive cardiovascular disease. It was not an uncommon scenario for an overweight man of 77 years to keel over from a heart attack. No autopsy was ever performed to coincide or refute the attending physician's opinion.

The Director was known for his unwavering punctuality, until recent months. The morning he died brought on much whispering from fellow employees at the bureau, due to the fact that he had not yet arrived for work The next ritual always closely scrutinized was the Bureau's nurse's regular visit to Hoover's office to administer an injection of "vitamins." Whether or not the injections were really vitamins was purely a matter of conjecture. The visits that were a daily event, were not to take place on this day or on any other day ever again.

Upon hearing the sad news, President Nixon ordered a full state funeral with all of its pomp and ceremony. Hoover's body was taken to the Capitol's Rotunda in a lead lined coffin weighting over a thousand pounds to lay in state.

On the morning of May 4th , Hoover's body was moved to the National Presbyterian Church for the funeral. Supreme Court Justice Warren E. Burger (who Hoover had supported as a court nominee), spoke at the services, calling Hoover a man who did not abandon his principles to "popular clamor." Over 2000 invited guests were in attendance and all the television networks carried the services live. For directions to his grave read on....

Clyde Tolson
May 22, 1900 - April 14, 1972

Tolson was a tall, handsome man from Missouri who was five years younger than Hoover. In addition to that, he received his law degree from Hoover's alma mater, George Washington University. Upon graduation in 1927, Tolson applied at the FBI only to be turned down. The following year he applied again, but this time his application and photo was seen by J. Edgar who promptly hired him.

He joined the Bureau in April, 1928 and quickly became Hoover's closest personal friend and business associate, replacing Frank Baughman who had gotten married. Tolson's promotions within the Bureau was unprecedented, within three short years he became the second most powerful man in the Bureau. Whenever Hover was invited to a social event, so was Tolson.

The two maintained a spousal relationship where they rode to work together, ate their lunches together and vacationed together. People secretly referred to the two as "J. Edna and Mother Tolson." It is alleged that Mafia boss, Meyer Lansky, had obtained photographic evidence of Hoover's homosexuality and was able to use this to stop the FBI from looking too closely into his criminal affairs.

Hoover became very dependent on Tolson. He told friends that, "Clyde Tolson is my alter ego. He can read my mind." Tolson was a smarter man than Hoover, unfortunately he slavishly followed Hoover's every dictate therefore never realizing his own potential.

When Hoover died, he left virtually his whole estate to Tolson, which included his considerable secret files. Soon after Hoover's death Tolson retired and never left the house with exception to visit his boss' grave.

Citing ill health, Tolson submitted his resignation on May 3, 1972 the day after Hoover's death. He appeared that day, feeble and bewildered after attending services for Hoover. Near the end of his life he lived in the $100,000 Georgetown home bequeathed to him by Hoover. Tolson was admitted to Doctors Hospital in Washington where he later died of apparent natural causes. He was 74.

Funeral services were held at 2 pm, two days after his death at the Joseph Gawlec's and Sons Funeral Home. Officiating at the service was Dr. Edward L.R. Elson, chaplain of the Senate, who also officiated at the funeral of Hoover.

Congressional Cemetery
1801 East Street SE
Washington, D.C.

Directions: Go through the main entrance, past the "Latrobe Cenotaphs", then bear left about 100 feet. Hoover's family plot is fenced in with a Department of Justice shield welded to it. Clyde is buried about 20 feet away.

Westwood Memorial Park, Los Angeles, California

WALTER MATTHAU

OCTOBER 1, 1920 – JULY 1, 2000

Westwood Memorial Park, Los Angeles, California

Jack Lemmon and Walter Matthau The Odd Couple
Jack Lemmon
February 8, 1925 - June 27, 2001

Jack's entrance into this world was quite unique, as he was born in an elevator at a Newton, Massachusetts' hospital. He grew up in an upper middle class environment due to his father's position as the president of a doughnut company.

Lemmon's education was made up of a series of prep schools before entering Harvard, where he joined the Dramatic Club. At a young age, Jack desired a career in show business which was strictly against his father's wishes His father finally relented and his last dying words to his son were: "Spread a little sunshine."

Forty years and many movies later, we have enjoyed him in a range of parts that have been challenging and unpredictable. Most would have been intimated by playing with many of Hollywood's major actors, he had an ability to hold his own.

During the 1960's and 1970's he was teamed up with Walter Matthau in several films. Most remembered are *"The Odd Couple"* (1968) and then *"Grumpy Old Men"* in 1993.

Jack admitted to having a serious drinking problem at one time in his life. The one positive thing he reaped from this bleak chapter in his life was that it enabled him to do so well in the Oscar winning role as Harry Stoner in *"Save the Tiger"* (1973). This performance, he felt, was the most gratifying, emotionally fulfilling performance of his career.

In 1999, Lemmon was diagnosed with cancer and had three surgeries in an attempt to rid himself of the disease. All seemed well until May of 2001 when his condition started to deteriorate. Physicians discovered his colorectal cancer had spread and operated to remove his bladder. After that procedure, he was given just weeks to live.

Despite his gloomy prognosis his spirits rallied as he regaled the nurses with stories of what it was like to work with Marilyn Monroe in *"Some Like It Hot,"* and he also talked candidly about the days when buddy Matthau and him pulled many a prank while making many films together.

After his bladder was removed his condition worsened almost immediately. He was hooked up to IV's and pain medication to make his final days comfortable. Soon he began sleeping frequently. The 5' 9" actor rapidly dwindled to a mere 100 pounds and nurses shaved his head bald because the cancer treatment left him with bald patches.

Finally just four days shy of the one year anniversary of pal, Walter Matthau's death, Lemmon succumbed to cancer.

It is said that he now inhabits the crypt that once belonged to Peter Lawford. Having shared many films with Matthau; he also shares the same cemetery with him.

Westwood Memorial Park
1218 Glendon Avenue
Los Angeles, California

For directions to the cemetery see Marilyn Monroe in Glamour Girls As you enter the cemetery look to your left and you will see a wall of crypts. There are three columns of crypts on that wall, counting from the bushes count three over and three up from the ground. That's him. At the time that this book was written, there was no marker on his crypt.

Walter Matthau

Born Walter Matuschanskayasky (and you thought Matthau was hard to spell), he was the son of Russian-Jewish immigrants. He grew up on New York's Lower East Side and sold soft drinks and three flavored ice bricks during intermission at Yiddish theaters on 2nd Avenue.

Playing bit roles for 50 cents a performance didn't immediately lead to a life in the theater. Matthau performed a series of jobs before hitting the big time. He was a filing clerk, boxing instructor, basketball coach, floor scrubber and cement bag handler, all of which might have given him the experience he needed in order to play the different roles he would encounter as an actor.

After World War II he enrolled at the renowned Dramatic Workshop of New School for Social Research and began appearing in summer stock productions. His first professional job was in 1946, where he played in *"Three Men on a Horse"* at the Erie County Playhouse, which was soon followed by bigger and better roles.

One of the few actors in Hollywood to successfully move from supporting roles to heavies and ethnic types to leading men, Matthau excelled at both comedy and drama in his career of more than 50 years.He is best known for the comic persona perfected in such movies as Neil Simon's *"The Odd Couple,"* opposite his frequent foil Jack Lemmon. Most recently he was paired up again with Lemmon in *"Grumpy Old Men"* in 1993, *"Grumpier Old Men"* in 1995, *"Out to Sea"* in 1997 and a sequel to *"The Odd Couple"* in 1998 in which Madison and Unger reunite after 30 years to travel to the wedding of their children.

Matthau had been plagued with heart problems since his 30's and suffered a very serious heart attack that prompted him to abandon his several pack a day habit of smoking.

On July 1st, Matthau was rushed to St John's Hospital in Santa Monica in full cardiac arrest. He was pronounced dead at 1:42am that Saturday at the age of 79.

Westwood Memorial Park
1218 Glendon Avenue
Los Angeles, California

For directions to the cemetery see Marilyn Monroe in the Glamour Girls Chapter. As you enter the cemetery from where you are standing (I assume you're at the entrance)walk towards the left rear of the cemetery. There you will see a little new area with a few gardens, niches, and a little fountain. Walk to the other side opposite the fountain towards a family mausoleum. You will then see a locked fenced in area. Look over the little locked gate and you will see several garden type graves, his is the first one without any name. If you look at the photo it seems that there is a large tree in your way, it is deceptive the tree is only about 4 inches in diameter.

PATRICIA E. BOYER
BELOVED WIFE & DEVOTED MOTHER
1910 — 1978

CHARLES BOYER
BELOVED HUSBAND & DEVOTED FATHER
1899 — 1978

Holy Cross Cemetery, Culver City, California

Chapter 12 - Song, Dance and Comedy
Charles Boyer
August 28, 1899 - August 26, 1978

Boyer arrived in Hollywood in 1929 and became the quintessential Frenchman, retaining his accent and charm to the end of his life. He appeared in more than 65 films, including *"The Garden of Allah," "All this and Heaven Too"* and *"Gaslight."* It was in the film *"Algiers"* that Boyer was widely quoted as saying, "Come with me to the Casbah." They were words that were never actually used in the picture. His final film was *"Barefoot in the Park"* in 1969, where he appeared with Jane Fonda and Robert Redford.

Two terrible tragedies led Boyer to take his own life, the death of his wife from cancer and their son's suicide from a self-inflicted gunshot wound. All this was was too much for him to bear, so he overdosed on Seconal tablets at the age of 79.

Holy Cross Cemetery
5835 W. Slauson Avenue
Culver City, California

For directions to the cemetery see Audrey Meadows in the Season Finales Chapter. Get a celebrity map and head towards the grotto. Even though the map says that he's in St. Anne's, which is supposed to be Section F, he's more in the grotto. Walk towards the bushes and he's right there next to his wife in #L186.

Bing Crosby
May 2, 1904 - October 14, 1977

Harry Lillis "Bing" Crosby was born in Tacoma, Washington in 1904. As a child he was dubbed "Bing" from his favorite "Bingville Bugle" comic strip character, *"Bingo."*

In 1920 he entered Gonzaga University in Spokane to become a lawyer, but found much more pleasure and money in playing the drums for a local band. Later he joined Al Rinker whose sister was jazz singer, Mildred Bailey. She helped them break into the big time.

They started in Vaudeville and sang in theaters throughout California. Bing and Al recorded their first song, *"I've Got the Girl,"* in October, 1926. Bing and Al achieved modest success, but Al fired him as grew weary of Bing's drinking and carousing.

In 1931, Mack Sennet was impressed with Bing's performance and signed him to do a short musical comedy film titled, *"I Surrender Dear."* This led to five more films with Sennet. Then in 1932, Bing teamed up with Bob Hope and Dorothy Lamour in what would be called "Road films." Bing received an Academy Award for Best Actor as a priest in *"Going My Way."*

On the screen he was perceived as saintly and wholesome, his personal life however, was filled with controversy and rumor. Depending on which family member you listen to, he was either a loving father and faithful husband or an abusive father and a cheating husband. Son Gary wrote a scathing novel entitled, *"Going My Way, "* which painted a gruesome picture of his father. In public Bing maintained a sparkling image as an all American husband and father. His second wife, Kathryn portrayed Bing as an all around great guy in her book, *"My Life With Bing."* She remembers him as a man who swept her off her feet and was too soft to discipline their three children

BELOVED BY ALL
HARRY LILLIS
BING
CROSBY
1904 — 1977
IHS

Holy Cross Cemetery, Culver City, California

In early 1974, Bing fell ill and feared the worst, that it was perhaps lung cancer. But on January 13th, the doctors found and removed a large benign tumor in his left lung. As he slowly recovered, he was able to record albums and perform live concerts again.

In March 1977, Bing was injured while doing a televised celebration for his 50th anniversary in show business. He fell from the stage into the orchestra pit 25 feet below, rupturing a disc in his back. After recuperating in the hospital for several months, he returned to his hectic schedule. While in Europe doing concerts, he flew to Spain to play golf to relax.

While playing a round of golf at the La Moraleja golf course near Madrid, a happy and autograph signing Bing showed no sign of fatigue. He and a friend finished 18 holes of golf, defeating two Spanish golf pros. After making his last putt, his last words were, "It was a great game," as he bowed to the applause of several fans. As the four golfers walked back to the clubhouse, Bing suddenly collapsed from a massive heart attack. His companions carried him to the clubhouse where a physician made a feeble attempt at administering oxygen and adrenaline.

Bing was flown back home to California where he was laid to rest in Holy Cross Cemetery. His will specified that he have a private family funeral, Kathryn however, invited Bing's siblings, friends and the media. He is buried next to first wife Dixie Lee and nine feet deep so second wife, Kathryn can be buried with him.

Holy Cross Cemetery
5835 W. Slauson Avenue
Culver City, California

For directions to the cemetery see Audrey Meadows in the Season's Finales Chapter. If you are facing the grotto (the actual cave-like structure) turn around and walk four rows, he is grave #L119 the markers are easy to read in this area.

Al Jolson
May 26, 1886 - October 23, 1950

Known as Jolie to his friends, Jolson used black face and white chalk on his lips to accent his famous rolling eyes. Jolson became famous as a jazz singer and immortalized many tunes such as *"Mammy,"* *"Rock-a-bye Your Baby with a Dixie Melody"* and his theme song, *"You Ain't Heard Nothing' Yet."*

His father was a stern, humorless rabbi named Moshe Joelson, who had little use for his son's show business ambitions. By the age of 12, Jolson was in vaudeville, singing and telling jokes, with little initial success for nearly eight years. That is, until he came up with his famous black face trademark. Always a nervous performer, the black face acted as a mask where he could hide his stage fright.

He soon caught the attention of the Schubert brothers, who began featuring him in their Broadway shows, where he starred on the New York stage from 1911 to 1937. *"The Jazz Singer,"* released in 1927, was the first talkie and an instant success for Jolson. He quickly followed up with *"The Singing Fool,"* in 1928, *"Say It with Songs,"* in 1929, *"Big Boy,"* in 1930, and *"Hallelujah, I'm a Bum,"* in 1933.

Hillside Memorial Park, Culver City, California

Jolson who was never much of an actor, and saw his career begin to decline in 1937. Soon he was given little parts here and there. To add insult to injury, when it came time to make *"The Jolson Story"* in 1945, the producer hired young actor Larry Parks to play Jolson and lip sync his songs.

Al Jolson once said these words in the latter part of the 40's, just prior to his death: "Hey, don't look so sad. I'm gonna be around for a long time. My father lived to be ninety-five years old." Unfortunately, Jolie didn't inherit his dad's genes.

On October 23, 1950, after taking a flight from Los Angeles, Al Jolson arrived in San Francisco at 3:45pm. He registered at the St. Francis Hotel, and decided to go to the hotel's Turkish bath. After that, "Jolie" and some friends had decided to get some dinner at a local restaurant. Their first choice was Amelio's, but upon arriving there, they were disappointed to find that it was closed. So they went to Tarantino's instead, a famous seafood restaurant located on Fisherman's Wharf. Even though it was crowded, there would always be a table for Jolie and his friends.

They arrived back at the St. Francis at 8:45, after eating a huge meal. Jolie invited his friend up to his suite 1220-21, to play cards. A few minutes later, Jolie requested that one of his friends go downstairs to get some bicarbonate of soda, because he was having chest pains which he thought might be indigestion from that excessive meal he had just finished. In the back of Jolie's mind he feared the worse, and told his friend to call a doctor as well. The two doctors that the hotel had were on other calls, so they sent a nurse. Meanwhile, he told his friend to call Dr Kerr, a cardiologist, that his personal doctor had recommended.

Jolie drank the bicarbonate of soda, and received no relief from his pain. He kept tapping his chest and said to his friend, "I'm not going to last." His friend tried to comfort him by saying, "Al, don't talk that way, it'll pass. It's nothing but indigestion."

When the nurse, Anne Murchison, arrived she took Jolie's pulse and reassured him that he would be alright. One of Jolie's friends took her aside and asked if she thought it was a heart attack and she said, "Definitely not." Jolie's friend persisted, "How do you know?" She responded that usually a heart attack is accompanied by an ashy grey pallor, which Jolie did not have. But then again he was all tanned from a recent trip to Palm Springs.

Finally at 10:00pm, two doctors, Dr Kerr and the hotel physician arrived. Jolie apologized for having them come out to see him. As they prepared to examine him, they began by asking him questions on what he had done that day. Then suddenly, without warning, Al reached for his pulse or to raise himself up. His last words were, "Oh, I'm going." as he sank into the pillow.

They tried to revive him by giving him stimulants and massaging his heart for a half an hour. But their efforts had failed, and at 10:35, Jolie was pronounced dead from a massive coronary occlusion. He was only 64. Unlike his father, he did not live 95 years as he predicted..

Jolie's funeral was held at 2:00 on October 26th, at the Temple Israel at 7300 Hollywood Boulevard. Early that morning, despite the rain, crowds of people began to converge on the temple. It is estimated that more than 20,000 people filed past Jolie's body, until they had to close the temple doors by 11:30, leaving thousands of disappointed fans, who did not get to walk by his body

He was buried in a blue suit, and was draped in a white fringed tallis. Some thought that this was hypocritical, because Jolie was never a religious Jew. Others believed that this was a nice way for him to reaffirm his religious beliefs.

Although Jolie had told his wife, Erle that he did not want George Jessel to eulogize him, Jessel did anyway.

The first time that Jolie was buried he was buried in the Beth Olam Cemetery in Los Angeles. But Erle was determined to erect a monument that would also act as his final resting place.

She withdrew $84,000 from the estate to build this massive memorial. It cost $9000 for a plot in the Hillside Memorial Park in Culver City. The structure cost $75,000, which by today's standards would be worth millions.

For the reburial, they had another much smaller service. He was this time, eulogized by friend, Jack Benny (who now is interred just several feet away from Jolson). His is by far the most spectacular monument that I have ever seen. You can see it from the San Diego Freeway as you drive by. He is up on a hill beneath a dome supported by six towering marble pillars. On the ceiling of the monument, is a mosaic of Moses holding the Ten Commandments. Next to his tomb is a life size statue of him in his famous, "down-on-one-knee-with-his-arms- outstretched-pose." And if that isn't enough, as you enter the cemetery gate, you'll immediately see a 120 foot waterfall cascading down a hill, which was provided by the Hillside management, this too is part of his gravesite. Jolie had told Erle that he wanted to be buried near a waterfall. A waterfall in the middle of Los Angeles? What was he thinking?

Hillside Memorial

6000 W. Centinela Avenue

Los Angeles, California

Jolson Memorial

For directions to the cemetery see Moe Howard in the Five Stooges? Chapter. If you can't find this one, just close this book and go home because your hopeless. This waterfalled structure is the first thing you see as you enter the cemetery.

Abel's Hill Cemetery, Martha's Vineyard, Chilmark, Mass.

IN LOVING MEMORY OF
1949   OUR SON   1982
JOHN A. BELUSHI
"HE GAVE US LAUGHTER"
BELUSHI
FATHER   MOTHER
ADAM   AGNES
MAR. 23, 1922 – DEC. 21, 1989

Elmwood Cemetery, Rivergrove, Illinois (Cenotaph)

Chapter 13 - Last Laughs
John Belushi
January 24, 1949 - March 5, 1982

Born in Wheaton, Illinois in 1949, John's interest in show biz was sparked by his high scholl drama club. Ironically, while in high school, he shunned all drugs and alcohol and led a very clean cut life. His tenure in the "*Second City Comedy Troupe*" would later change his philosophy.

Belushi was largely popular from the late 70's until his death in 1982. He had won an Emmy award for his comic routines on the show, "*Saturday Night Live.*"

In one skit, entitled, *"Don't Look Back in Anger,"* he performs in a most ironic and perhaps now the most eerie skit he has ever done. It shows John as a lonely old man walking through a cemetery in the snow. He comes to a group of tombstones, that turns out to be his former cast members from SNL,: Radner, Aykroyd, Murray, Curtain, Chase, etc. He explains how each member died, and then after he is done recounting their stories, he looks into the camera and says,"They all thought I'd be the first to go. I was one of those live fast die young, leave a good looking corpse types, you know. But I guess they were wrong. Why me, why did I live so long? (pauses) Do you know why? " After he questions fate, he comes up with an answer for his longevity, "Cause, I'm a dancer!" The camera then shows a distant shot of Belushi dancing a jig on everyone's grave. Well in real life, he danced his way right into an early death.

During his very short life he starred in many movies: *"Animal House," "1941," "The Blues Brothers," "Continental Divide," "Neighbors," "Goin South"* and *"Old Boyfriends,"* His movies sometimes reflected his wild character that was fueled by the use of excessive alcohol and drugs, something he mimicked in real life. Unfortunately these things did not contribute to a long healthy life for John.

On March, 1982, he was found dead in the Chateau Marmont Hotel in Hollywood from an overdose of heroin and cocaine. Close friends and family were surprised when they found out that he had died from an intravenous drug, because John was petrified of needles. So petrified of the obigatory blood test, that it almost prevented him from getting married.

On the night of his death, he met former backup singer for SNL, Cindy Smith, at the Roxy, a trendy Hollywood nightclub. After scoring some drugs she accompanied John to his bungalow and the two partied into the night. Cindy, according to her story that she had told to a tabloid, she was the one who administered twenty "speed balls" to Belushi within the last 24 hours of his life. She claims that she fell asleep on the couch and a very alive John also went to bed. Around 7:30 the next morning, she tried to wake John but he wanted to sleep. So before leaving, she cleaned up all the drug paraphernalia.

The next morning, John was suppose to be at the studio for a meeting for an upcoming movie he was trying to sell. Friends became concerned when John did not show up for his appointment. After many failed attempts to call him, his friends were sent to rouse the sleepy John from his slumber. When they arrived sometime around noon, they discovered that he was dead. He had died from an overdose of heroin and cocaine: a speedball. He was only 33. Close friend, Danny Aykroyd, was the one who had to tell John's wife of his death.

John's body was flown back to Martha's Vineyard where he and his wife had a vacation house. The funeral was simple and just prior to closing his coffin, a close friend slipped three joints in John's pocket and a Grateful Dead sticker under him. After the funeral, John's wife had a huge garage sale to sell all of John's belongings. Everything was sold within hours.

Not only did he live excessively in life, he was also excessive in death. John has two tombstones. His body is buried in Martha's Vineyard, and a Cenotaph is located in his hometown of Chicago, within the family plot.

I first visited the real gravesite in Martha's Vineyard. According to *"The Tombstone Tourist,"* by Scott Stanton, Belushi's body is not where this tombstone is either. Stanton claims that it is located in an unmarked grave to the rear of the cemetery. He also said, that it is the only unmarked area where there are flowers placed.

I called the head caretaker of the cemetery to verify this, he told me that although he was not working for the cemetery at the time of John's burial, he does know for a fact that he is indeed buried at the tombstoned site. He said that originally Belushi was buried elsewhere in that cemetery, he was then uninterred and re-buried at the site he now inhabits. The head caretaker gave me the name of the retired caretaker who was present at the second burial. He confirmed the story of the first caretaker I spoke with. The reason for the switch was so that his wife could be buried along side of him, this new location unlike the first, is a double plot.

The tombstone where he is buried, is in a small fenced in area to your left as you drive in through the gate. You could easily drive right past him, if you do not know what to look for. He is all by himself in a fenced in area surrounded by a lot of trees and bushes. The tombstone is a rock that simply says, "BELUSHI." Once you see the grave, you'll notice all the junk that people leave behind in his honor. The day I visited his grave, it was pretty clean. My impression is that the people on the island are not too crazy with the fact that he is there, because he attracts groups of rowdy people who do weird things at his grave. The island residents tried to discourage his burial there, but since the Belushi's were property owners; it was their right to be buried on the island.

The second grave (cenotaph), I visited was located in River Grove, Illinois. The tombstone there, is where his mother and father are buried. John is also mentioned on the tombstone along with a cameo photo that frequently goes missing. But the grave is neatly kept, no beer cans, female undergarments, condoms, or any other type of John Belushi offerings.

Abel's Hill Cemetery

(Martha's Vineyard) Chilmark, Massachusetts

Once on the island head towards Chilmark which is on the southwest part of the island. The cemetery is on your right side. John's grave is the big rock with "Belushi" on it. It is located near the entrance.

Cenotaph located in family plot:

Elmwood Cemetery

2905 Thatcher Avenue

Rivergrove, Illinois

LENNY "BRUCE" SCHNEIDER
BELOVED FATHER · DEVOTED SON
1925 ✡ 1966
PEACE AT LAST

Eden Memorial Park, Mission Hills, California

Lenny Bruce

October 13, 1926 - August 3, 1966

In the late 50's and early 60's, many comedians focused on clean humor, while Bruce explored the darker side of comedy. He dealt with controversial topics such as nuclear testing, racism, illegal drugs, homosexuality, back-alley abortions and the death penalty.

He wanted the ability to talk on stage with the same freedom he exercised in his living room. But instead he ended up having many encounters with the law. Soon he became paranoid and ended up at the FBI headquarters in San Francisco to complain that there was a conspiracy between the courts of New York and California to violate his rights.

Lenny was arrested 15 times within two years for obscenity. The constant arrests combined with his excessive drug intake and what he viewed as harassment turned him into a delusional, and bitter comedian who did nothing but read from legal briefs on stage. All this plus the fact that audience attendance began to dwindle,.made club owners wary of hiring him. He carried law books in his suitcase and his hotel rooms were littered with tapes, transcripts, photostats, law journals and legal briefs.

Little did Lenny realize that his quest for free speech would open the doors to future comedians who would then abuse that freedom. Although it is doubtful he would be offended by today's liberal use of speech on stage, radio and television. It is no doubt that he would feel that despite it's offensiveness, it is the risk one must take to maintain one's freedom of speech.

On August 3rd, Bruce was discovered naked on his bathroom floor, with the needle still protruding from his arm, dead from an overdose of heroin. Four years after Lenny's death, the New York Court of Appeals upheld a lower court's reversal of his guilty verdict.

Eden Memorial Park (Closed Saturday)

11500 Spulveda Blvd.

Mission Hills, California

For directions to the cemetery see Groucho Marx in the Famous Brothers Chapter. Don't bother asking for any directions to anyone here, this cemetery has had too many incidents and is very protective of its residents. Drive around to the Mt. Nebo Section, which is located above the crypts. Park at the sign Find the "HAMMOND" and count 6 down and there he is.

John Candy

October 31, 1950 - March 4, 1994

A loveable big guy from Canada, who will be remembered best for his comedic roles. John got his start with the famous "Second City Comedy Troupe" and ended with forty plus movies to his credit.

Unfortunately, due to a family history of obesity and heart disease, (that was exacerbated by excessive food consumption, drinking, and smoking) he had a heart attack that would end both his career and his life.

At age five, Candy lost his father to a heart attack; he was only thirty-five. This plus the fact that his brother also had a heart attack, should have cautioned John to take better care of himself. But like an addict he found it hard to give up his excessive lifestyle. Though several attempts to lose weight hoped to prove successful, John sometimes ballooned to a massive 400 pounds.

JOHN F. CANDY

OCTOBER 31, 1950 — MARCH 4, 1994

IN LOVING MEMORY

"ONE HEART AND ONE SOUL"

WE MISS YOU DEARLY

Holy Cross Cemetery, Culver City, California

Whenever John experienced any emotional upheavals, he would neglect himself by smoking, drinking and staying up late partying. Despite all this, one of his biggest fears was, that he too would die before the age of forty.

Once at a small party at his Brentwood home, a friend remembers John's staff bringing in several pizzas, cases of beer, and everything else you could think of that was fattening. He sat there eating huge amounts of pizzas and washing them down with gallons of beer. Many of his closest friends were shocked and would warn the rotund actor about his weight, suggesting that perhaps he should shed a few pounds. He would either politely ignore them or sever the relationship all together.

Despite the fact that Candy consumed tons of food, he was very sensitive about his weight problem. Once in an interview he was asked about his weight, "My metabolism is slow, so exercise is very important. I can eat a normal 2000-calorie diet and put on weight. I know what I have to do if I want to lose weight and stay healthy; eat a proper diet and exercise. All I've got to do is apply it." Easier said than done.

His final movie was "*Wagons East*", which was filmed in Durango, Mexico. Most people would think that a man who was at least one hundred pounds overweight along with a history of heart trouble, would be barred from work in a place noted for its high altitude. Some of John's colleagues who worked on the film with him, recalled that he often had trouble catching his breath while he was there. Not only that, Candy gained an enormous amount of weight while in Mexico.

He was obviously self conscious about his weight, because he would make a show of bringing diet drinks and carrot sticks to his trailer. But in the meantime he would be discretely stocking up on beer, candy, chips and cookies. He claimed they were for people who visited him.

John even brought his personal chef, to cook him calorie conscious meals. But unfortunately, he would frequently fall off the food wagon. He would eat the meals that his chef would make for him, only to secretly order several pizzas later.

His appetite was as enormous as he was, once at a small gathering of ten people, John ordered thirty pizzas, putting aside several for his own consumption. Another time, John was seen eating, in one sitting six chickens and five pounds of ham at another. Also he consumed large quantities of tacos, burritos and fried chicken, while on location.

At one of his favorite restaurants in Mexico, the *Fonda do la Tia Chona*, John would order enough to feed three people with healthy appetites. According to one of the workers there, "He started with a combination platter: a tostada, enchilada, sope (chicken and cheese tortillas) and chonita (fried turnover with cheese inside). He liked the chonita so much, he ordered eight more. Then he ordered a sope dinner, washing that down with three large margaritas."

Morning meant having his maid make him an "eye opener," consisting of ten pieces of buttered toast to prep him for his regular breakfast. All this eating was taking a toll on John, he was gaining weight at an alarming rate. The wardrobe people had to let out his clothes, because he gained two inches in one month. Not only that, a special horse had to be flown in to accommodate his excessive weight and it took two burly men to push him up a step ladder to get onto the poor horse's back.

The movie's producers feared that Candy might not be able to finish the movie. Many times the script called for him to be on a horse, but his hips were in such bad shape, that a stand in had to be used. Due to his excessive weight, his knees and hips caused him a lot of trouble. John flew to Los Angeles, to consult a doctor about his problems. The recommendation was hip replacement, a procedure that could not be performed until John lost a substantial amount of weight.

On the evening of March 3rd, John cooked a pasta dinner for his assistants. He then phoned his co-star, Richard Lewis, around midnight to tell him how pleased he was with the day's scene. The next morning he was going to fly to Los Angeles to be with his family. He then went to bed, and that was the last time anyone ever saw John alive again.

The next morning at 8 am. Candy's bodyguard Gustavo Populus phoned the house to wake him up. There was no reply. So at 8:15, he got the keys and let himself in, disclosed Alejandro Castillo, whose family owns the house.

Gustavo banged on John's bedroom door for two minutes, upon getting no response he opened it and looked in. There, lying in the bed, half in and half out, was John Candy obviously dead. He had been dead for several hours. By the position of his body, it looked as if he had tried to get out of bed and then had fallen backwards. He was wearing a long red and black checkered nightshirt. His mouth and fingertips were purple which is a classic sign of death by heart attack.

According to the official reports, Candy's weight at the time of his death was 330 pounds. It took a group of four workmen to move his body out of the house. When the pilots arrived to carry his body back to the states, they had a hard time finding a body bag large enough to hold him.

John's body was returned to California for burial. Two hundred mourners attended the funeral, which was held at St. Martin of Tour Roman Catholic Church in Brentwood. Security officers surrounded the church, only allowing those, "that were on the list," to attend. Prior to the service the hearse pulled up to the rear of the church and his coffin was covered with a plastic tarp, to prevent photographers from getting a picture. After the service, police closed a section of the San Diego Freeway to make way for the procession of fifty cars that followed the hearse to the cemetery.

Candy is buried in a very large Catholic Cemetery located in Culver City, California. He is located in the top crypt above Fred MacMurray. Don't get me wrong, I adored John Candy, and I don't mean any disrespect, but I couldn't help but think, if he isn't cremated, poor Fred!

Holy Cross Cemetery
5835 W. Slauson Avenue
Culver City, California
Mausoleum
For directions to the cemetery see Audrey Meadows in the Season's Finales Chapter. Get a celebrity map and head to the mausoleum. Go into the main entrance and go right to room #7 which is the third room on your right. His crypt is way up top, on the left wall.

Chris Farley
February 15, 1964 - December 18, 1997
His idol was fellow *SNL* cast member John Belushi, a poor role model that would end up costing him his life. Another thought is that, perhaps he was another victim to fall prey to the *"Saturday Night Live"* curse, or just another overindulgent cast member who pushed his luck a little too far. Nevertheless, he will be remembered best for poking fun at his weight problem as a Chippendale dancer or as the motivational speaker that lived in a van by the lake.

CHRISTOPHER CROSBY FARLEY

FEBRUARY 15 1964   DECEMBER 18 1997

Resurrection Cemetery, Madison, Wisconsin

Chris had purchased an apartment on the 60th floor of the John Hancock Building, on Michigan Avenue in downtown Chicago. It was there were he partied with local prostitutes on a regular basis and it was also there where he spent his final moments.

His last day was spent primarily with a hooker called Heidi. She had been hired by one of Chris' friends for the entire day, at a cost of $2000. The two later met at a party in Lincoln Park, Chicago. A typical party for Chris was one that had unlimited drugs and prostitutes. And this party was no exception; complete with a pre-paid hooker to fulfill his every need or attempt to do so, and more drugs than one human could consume. The two eventually wanted to be alone, so Heidi invited him to her apartment where they continued to smoke crack and snort heroin. They attempted to have sex, but Chris couldn't.

Chris told her casually that he'd been up for four days partying without any sleep. The drugs were beginning to have a bad effect on Farley, where not only he couldn't sleep but also he couldn't perform sexually.

After spending some time at her apartment doing drugs, they decided to go back to his place. Once at his apartment, a dispute broke out over payment. When she demanded that Chris pay her, he refused saying that his friend had already "taken care of it." Finally, after he calmed her down they attempted to have sex again, unsuccessfully. At 3:00 am, she decided to leave, by then Chris who was clearly inebriated, tried to follow her but collapsed ten feet from the front door. Heide claimed that she could hear that he was having difficulty breathing. His last words were, "Don't leave me." She figured that he had finally passed out, she snapped a photograph of him lying there and then left.

The next day his brother John found him. Chris was still lying in the same place wearing sweat pants and an open button down shirt. He was supposedly clutching a baseball cap and rosary beads. There was a blood tinged fluid coming from his nose, and a white, frothy fluid coming from his mouth. John called 911 after 2 pm and the Chicago Fire Fighters responded. Farley was pronounced dead at the scene. He like his idol Belushi, was only 33 years old.

There were two stories as to what was found at his apartment. One story said that no illegal drugs were found at the scene, just prescription drugs. Another version was that the apartment was littered with empty liquor bottles and several bags of a white powdered substance.

Chris' body was taken to the medical examiner for an autopsy. The samples that were sent out, came back with the finding that he died accidentally from an overdose of opiate and cocaine. The other things found in his system that might have contributed to his death were, Prozac, morphine, and marijuana. A major cause of his death was due to his excessive weight of 296 pounds which created a narrowing of three coronary arteries, this combined with the vasoconstrictor, cocaine. Even at his young age his liver had taken a beating, it showed fatty changes consistent with heavy drinking and drug abuse.

"IN ANOTHER TIME AND PLACE
HE WOULD HAVE BEEN CALLED PROPHET"

SAMUEL BURL KINISON

DEC. 8, 1953
APRIL 10, 1992

Memorial Park Mausoleum, Tulsa, Oklahoma

His body was taken to the McKeon Funeral Home where he was later taken to the Johnson Williams Funeral Service in Madison, Wisconsin where a private funeral was held. Then on Tuesday, December 23rd, another funeral was held at Our Lady Queen of Peace Roman Catholic Church for his close friends. Over 500 were in attendance including: Lorne Michaels, Dan Aykroyd (wearing the same leather jacket over his suit that he wore for buddy, John Belushi), John Goodman, Tom Arnold, Chris Rock, Adam Sandler, George Wendt and Rob Schneider. Good friend David Spade was too distraught to attend. The funeral program contained the serenity prayer, from Alcoholics Anonymous and the Clown's prayer.

Resurrection Cemetery
2705 Regent Street
Madison, Wisconsin

Directions: Take I-90 to 12S to Mineral Point Road to Regents Road. Go to the mausoleum (if you go on Saturday be sure to get there before noon, because that's when they close it.) Walk in the first thing you will see is an alter, walk towards it and enter the doorway to your right. As soon as you do you'll see the Bishop to your immediate right a few more steps will take you to Chris. He's on the left wall at the very top.

Sam Kinison
December 8, 1953 - April 10, 1992

A former Pentecostal preacher, turned hard drinking, loud mouthed wild man comedian, had looked as though he was finally going to turn his life around. He had just returned from his Hawaiian honeymoon with wife Malika, a 26 year old Las Vegas dancer and Kinison wanted to settle down and sober up.

Close friends described Kinison as a warm, generous man, something that seemed to vastly contrast his on stage persona. In the early years of his career, the rotund comic was the "king of shock" comedy, tackling topics that most comics would avoid. He held court with another "king of shock," Howard Stern, where he often appeared very drunk and very loud.

When other comedians joked about sex, Kinison screamed about carnal relations among lepers and homosexual necrophilia. Other favorite targets included televangelists, women, and Andrew Dice Clay.

Unfortunately his life was cut short by a tragic auto accident. A 1974 Chevrolet truck, with two teenagers, was seen earlier swerving into oncoming traffic as they tore down U.S. Highway 95, near the Nevada-California border. Moments later the two hit Kinison's Pontiac Trans-Am head on. At the moment of impact, beer cans flew out of the pickup, scattering all over the highway.

Immediately after the crash, which occurred near Needles at about 7:30 pm., Kinison appeared to be fine, said friends who watched the crash from a second car. He had some cuts on his lips and forehead, and wrenched himself free from his mangled vehicle. He lied down only after friends begged him to suddenly he took a turn for the worse.

He said, "I don't want to die, I don't want to die." said Carl LaBove, Kinison's best friend, who held the comedian's bleeding head in his hands. Then Kinison paused, as if listening to a voice that LaBove could not hear.

"But why?" asked Kinison. It sounded as if he was having a conversation, talking to somebody else. "He was talking upstairs," said his friend. "Then I heard him say, 'Ok, Ok, Ok, ' The last 'Ok' was so soft and at peace.Whatever voice was talking to him gave him the right answer and he just relaxed with it. He said it so sweet, like he was talking to someone he loved."

Kinison, who was on his way to a sold out show in Laughlin, Nevada, died at the scene from internal injuries. He was only 38.

His wife was knocked unconscious and taken to Needles Desert Community Hospital were she was listed in serious condition. It was there that she was told the terrible news of her husband's death. It was later rumored in the tabloids that she was pregnant, but lost Kinison's baby in the accident.

The driver, who sustained moderate injuries, according to witnesses jumped out of his truck and yelled, "God! Look at my truck!" He was taken to Juvenile Hall in San Bernardino, where at the time of the accident, he was being held on suspicion of felony manslaughter. He went on to boast about being, "the dude who killed Kinison." His companion was more seriously injured and also taken to the same hospital as Malika.

Those in Kinison's party speculated that the youths had been drinking. There was beer in the truck's bed and cab.

Memorial Park Mausoleum

5111 S. Memorial

Tulsa, Oklahoma

Directions: Take I-44 east/turnpike exit, exit 138A,towards Tulsa. Merge onto I-44E (Portions Toll). Take the US-64/OK-51 exit, exit number 231, towards Muskogee/Broken Arrow. Keep right at the fork in the ramp. Merge onto US-64E/OK-51E. Take the Memorial Dr. exit. Take the Memorial Dr ramp. Turn right onto S. Memorial Dr/S81st Ave. E. Once in the cemetery go to the rear, soon you will see many "Kinisons" he is buried there. If you have any trouble ask a cemetery worker they are quite helpful. Also his grave is usually adorned with gifts from fans.

✝

CHARLES ATLAS

1892 — 1972

St. John's Cemetery, Queens, New York

Chapter 14: The Great Showmen
Charles Atlas
October 30, 1893 - December 24, 1972

Born in Acri, Italy, this barrel chested man with amazing strength and physique had actually been a skinny teenager by the name of Angelo Sicilano. Later he would aspire to being called the "World's Most Perfectly Developed Man."

During his hey day, three generations of pulp comics carried his advertisement: a strong man with a big smile that seemed amused at flabbiness. He would pose in what is now accepted as the popular bikini type, legs planted apart in hot white sand asking only a five day trial to turn a skinny man into a tower of strength.

In 1938, weighting 178 pounds Atlas towed a 145,000 pound railroad car through the Sunnyside yards of the Pennsylvania Railroad. Using one rope, he moved the heavy car 122 feet along the rails. Even as he approached the years of middle age his chest measured 47 inches in normal position. He had biceps that measured 17 inches and a 32 inch waist.

Despite his yen for fitness he suffered a heart attack as he walked on the beach. He later died at a Long Beach Hospital. He was 79.

St. John's Cemetery
80-01 Metropolitan Avenue
Middlevillage, New York

For directions to the cemetery see "Lucky" Luciano in the Crime and Punishment Chapter. As you enter the cemetery, you can get a map or follow my directions. Head towards the mausoleum. Atlas is in the main one in the middle, go to the third floor, and look for the St. John's cloister, he's on the right side wall crypt. Section 001, Crypt 1A/3A single broadside.

Harry Houdini
March 24, 1874 or April 6, 1874 - October 31, 1926

There have been many rumors as to how Houdini died, but the most accurate and most plausible story was the told by Ruth Brandon, author of his biography, *"The Life and Many Deaths of Harry Houdini."*

While touring in Canada and the northern United States, he had broken his ankle and it was causing him a lot of pain. As he was sitting around backstage nursing his foot, some students decided to visit him. One of the guys asked if it were true that he, Houdini, could resist any blow to his body. Houdini, who was writing a letter at the time and really not paying attention to the student, said "Yes." So he, started punching Houdini in the stomach. After four very hard blows, Houdini told him to stop. Later that evening he told his wife that he had a bad pain in his stomach, but nevertheless refused to do anything about it. He always had this exaggerated idea about his own mortality; that he thought he was above pain, injury and death.

Machpelah Cemetery, Flushing, New York

He was in Detroit doing a show. As the evening progressed so did the pain, up to the point where he had to do the unthinkable: stop the show. His wife, realizing the seriousness of the problem, insisted that he see a doctor. He was diagnosed with acute appendicitis and the doctor told him that he had to go to the hospital at once. Once again, Houdini ignored his doctor's advice and called his own doctor in New York for advice. After alot of convincing from his doctor in New York, he entered the hospital. When they performed the surgery, his appendicitis had progress to something far worse, acute peritonitis. A few days later Houdini was dead.

It has always been suspect, that the blows to his stomach ruptured his appendix. But according to doctors, this is impossible. Besides there were many newspaper clippings that suggested that he had been complaining of stomach problems for a long time prior to his hospitalization.

One of the tricks Houdini was famous for, was the escape from a coffin which was suspended in water. In Detroit, while he was in the hospital, it was clear that the show would not continue. His assistant sent twenty four cases of his props back to New York on the train and he was notified after Houdini had died, that one of the cases had been left behind by mistake. It happened to be the case containing the coffin. So that was the one that he was buried in.

Harry Houdini is buried in the Machpelah Cemetery, I couldn't really tell how big this cemetery was because I didn't go beyond Houdini's grave. He greets you right at the gate. and is buried in the family plot, "Weiss" "Houdini," which is pretty large. It has a nun type figure kneeling at the base of the monument and at one time above the family name was a bust of Houdini. It has since been stolen.

The Machpelah Cemetery, as most Jewish cemeteries, has been victimized by vandalism. One year the entire Houdini gravesite had been desecrated. Its Gothic benches and ornate headstones were destroyed.

During Houdini's lifetime he was known to pay homage to fellow magicians of the past by spending time and money to fix up what was often long neglected grave sites. Now the tables were turned and Houdini's grave was in bad shape. David Copperfield carried on the Houdini tradition and donated $10,000 to help repair the damage to his hero's grave. The gravesite was fully restored, (with exception to Houdini's bust), just in time for the anniversary of his death, October 31st.

For 68 years, on every Halloween, Houdini admirers gather at the gravesite to pay homage to him. Standing in a semicircle around his grave, they read excerpts from his 1926 burial service. A wooden wand is snapped in two, over the gravesite, a symbol of the death of a magician and the loss of his power. Then a Conservative rabbi says Kaddish.

On October 20, 1995, chief operating officer of the cemetery, David Jacobson, decided it would be best if he padlocked the gate on Halloween. He felt that the publicity behind the event had attracted too many unwanted guests to the grounds, leading to vandalism. He said the problem has gotten out of hand and that he has a responsibility to protect the people who are buried there. The Society of American Magicians have a different opinion, they fought to keep the gates open, and enlisting the help of the Governor of New York, George Pataki. Mr. Jacobson says he has no problem with them visiting the cemetery, just don't do it on Halloween.

Finally an alternative date for the ceremony was agreed upon, November 16th, the anniversary of Houdini's death on the Jewish calendar.

Machpelah Cemetery
8230 Cypress Hills Street
Flushing, New York

Directions: Take the Interboro Pkwy to Cypress Hill Street exit. Continue down Cypress Hills and on your left you should see this cemetery prior to Cooper Avenue. Houdini is right at the entrance.

Ernie Kovacs
January 23, 1919 - January 13, 1962

"*The Ernie Kovacs Show*" which ran from 1956-57, consisted mostly of mime, and the incorporation of a surrealistic world that he used as a foil for his humor. It was a smash hit, and he was besieged with offers from Hollywood. He was on his way to stardom. Soon he would make several films, and TV specials. There were both very popular and attracted large audiences. As a workaholic; his epitaph states it clearly, "Nothing in moderation."

An avid poker player, his trademarks were his large moustache and an even larger cigar. Unfortunately his comedy was cut short due to a freak auto accident. In the case of Kovacs: those who lived by the cigar, die by the cigar. On Saturday, January 13th, Kovacs put in his usual long day and met his wife at a christening party at Milton Berle's house. After the party, he told his wife he'd meet her at home and that he was going to stop at PJ's in Hollywood for a nightcap. When attempting to light yet another cigar, he lost control of his car on the wet road and smashed into some telephone poles. He died almost instantly.

Forest Lawn Memorial Park
6300 Forest Lawn Drive
Los Angeles, California

For directions to the cemetery see Bette Davis in the Glamour Girls Chapter. Get a map, but don't ask for any celebrity directions. Proceed to the Court of Remembrance and circle around Vista Lane look for "NAZIRA HAYIKIAN" by the street, then count 13 in and there he is along with his daughter.

Liberace
May 16, 1919 - February 4, 1987

Liberace lived almost a fantasy life both in real life and on stage. Although this flamboyant star leaves no question in our minds that he was gay, he himself tried desperately to keep that a well-guarded secret, and really believed that no one suspected a thing. In fact, when a British tabloid had published an article saying that Liberace was gay, he sued and won the libel suit. It is a bit of sad irony that Liberace would contract AIDS, a disease that was then termed the "gayplague."

Friends began to notice that he was losing weight and becoming easily tired. Finally, a local Las Vegas newspaper broke the news that Liberace was diagnosed with AIDS.

In November, a Palm Springs acquaintance, scarcely recognized him when he spoke to her. He had lost 70 pounds, was chalk white, and all his hair was gone. She had never seen a man so thin, and still have the ability to stand on his own.

Forest Lawn Memorial Park, Hollywood Hills, California

FRANCES
OUR BELOVED MOM
1891 – 1960

GEORGE
SON BROTHER HUSBAND OF DORA
1911 – 1983

LIBERACE
SON AND BROTHER
1919 – 1987

Ernie

(ERNIE KOVACS)

1919 — 1962

-"NOTHING IN MODERATION".-
- WE ALL LOVED HIM -

Forest Lawn Memorial Park, Hollywood Hills, California

On Sunday, February 1st, Liberace slipped in and out of a coma. The end came three days later. A lifetime chain-smoker who suffered from advanced emphysema and heart disease, he was weakened by these conditions and apparently was unable to stave off the deadly syndrome. He died with both his sister Angie and his adored Shar-pei, Wrinkles at his side. Despite the family's vain efforts to cover up Liberace's disease, the results of an autopsy was announced, that he had died from complications of AIDS.

Liberace rests in Forest Lawn Cemetery in Hollywood Hills. His grave is located inside the Court of Remembrance. You can't miss it. It's really beautiful, it's white marble with a classic statue on top. On the outside is his classic signature with a piano and candelabra. He is interred with his mother and brother, George. Also there looks as though there was another name on the crypt, but it was removed. I don't know who this could have been.

In Las Vegas, Liberace has a fabulous museum, a must see for any Liberace fan. I am told it is the third most visited attraction in Las Vegas.

Forest Lawn Cemetery - Hollywood Hills

6300 Forest Lawn Drive

Los Angeles, California

For directions to the cemetery see Bette Davis in the Glamour Girls Chapter. As you enter the gate you can ask for a map, but NOT directions to any celebrity graves. They WILL throw you out. Follow the signs to the Court of Remembrance. Once there park and walk into the entrance. You'll pass Bette Davis and go inside to the first courtyard, keep going to the next and you'll see Liberace in the right hand corner. Grave# L120

Chapter 17: Matinee Men
Lee J. Cobb
December 8, 1911 - February 11, 1976

Born Leo Jacoby he was best known for his role as Willy Loman in *"Death of a Salesman"* in 1949. In between these famous roles he made movies like *"On the Waterfront"* with Hollywood new comer Marlon Brando. In the 60's he made the transition to television in the role of Judge Garth in *"The Virginian."* This series lasted from 1962 to 1966.

In 1955, due to a period of extreme stress, Cobb had suffered a heart attack that almost killed him. It was his friend Frank Sinatra, who rescued him. Sinatra paid Cobb's hospital bills, set him up with servants in the singer's Palm Springs home and would accept neither thanks nor public acknowledgment by Cobb for his kindness. "I couldn't believe it, I hadn't seen Frank since we worked together in '*Miracle of the Bells*' and he wouldn't even let me say thank you." said Cobb. His health, and his personal and professional lives showed improvement almost at once. He married Mary Hirsch, a school teacher and began to work again.

In 1976, Cobb had been in good health when he died suddenly of a heart attack at his San Fernando Valley home. By the time the paramedics arrived, Cobb was already dead. At the time of his death he was considering a return to stage work. He was 64.

Mt. Sinai Memorial Park (Closed Saturday)
5950 Forest Lawn Drive
Los Angeles, California

For directions to the cemetery see Phil Silvers in the Season's Finales Chapter. Get a map and head to Shemot 1, which is across the street from the Courts of TaNaCH. It is not a very large area so you shouldn't have a tough time finding him. He's in space#4, tombstone #421. If I remember correctly he's under a tree.

Peter Finch
September 28, 1916 - January 14, 1977

He grew up in a well to do family in both France and India. Later he returned with his family to Australia, where he found work in the legitimate theater. He became the protégée of Sir Laurence Olivier who invited Finch to work with him in London. There he received good reviews and won British Film Academy awards for his work in *"A Town Like Alice"* and *"The Trials of Oscar Wilde."* He was Oscar nominated for his work in the British-U.S. production of *"Sunday Bloody Sunday."*

This Australian was most famous for his role as the crazed newsman who yelled, "I'm mad as hell and I'm not going to take it anymore." in the 1976 movie, *"Network."* His performance in that film remains one of the best remembered by movie goers, and unfortunately he had to be awarded posthumously for his efforts.

The end came for Finch as he was standing in the lobby of the Beverly Hills Hotel, when suddenly he collapsed of a massive heart attack. He was 61.

Hollywood Forever Cemetery, Hollywood, California

(The new marker with the new birthday).

PETER FINCH

DISTINGUISHED ACTOR

LOVING HUSBAND AND FATHER

SEPT. 28, 1912 ∞ JAN. 14, 1977

FOREVER IN OUR HEARTS

Mt. Sinai Memorial Park, Los Angeles, California

Hollywood Forever Memorial Park
6000 Santa Monica Blvd.
Hollywood, California

For directions to the cemetery see Janet Gaynor in the Glamour Girls Chapter. From the main entrance make an immediate left onto Lakeview Avenue. Follow that all the way around until you get to the mausoleum. From the entrance walk down to the second corridor on the left, then walk all the way in and on your right you will see his crypt, #1244.

Bela Lugosi
October 20, 1882 - August 16, 1956

Bela Ferenc Dezso Blasko was born in believe it or not, Transylvania. Many in Hollywood questioned the true origin of his birth place, because it seemed too coincidental that the man who played Dracula would actually be born in such a fictitious sounding city associated with monsters..

As a young child he loved the theater and was encouraged by his parents to write, produce and star in his own homespun plays. His teachers however, felt that he was only wasting his time with nonsense and tried to discourage his efforts.

These plays were performed in a vacant warehouse near his home and seldom did he play to less than standing room only crowds. His shows became very popular in town for two reasons: one, they were the only entertainment available and two, they were free.

In spite of Lugosi's local success in the theater, he chose to leave Europe for an uncertain future in America. But travel to the. U.S. was an expensive venture that poor Bela could not afford. So in order to get to the States he took a job as a seaman. When the ship he was working on docked, he claimed himsfas as a political refugee and requested asylum in America.

He quickly blended into the sizeable Hungarian community in New York City and established a contact in which he could find work in the local theater. Quickly he had discovered that his reputation as an actor had proceeded him to New York. Local Hungarians were very loyal to their countrymen and followed his career back home very closely.

In 1931, he played in his most famous role, Dracula. It was released on February 14th , a planned "coincidence" that billed the movie as the strangest love story ever told. Although Bela had done many other roles on stage, studios perceived him as nothing more than a ghoul. Hollywood had done to Bela, as they had done to so many, they typecasted him. So when audiences saw his face or heard his voice he was instantly connected to Dracula.

Bela being from the old school did not resist this and did all he could to perpetuate the image. Unfortunately for him, roles dwindled in the forties and finally to an abrupt end in 1948. His last legitimate film was *"Abbott and Costello Meet Frankenstein."* This was Universal Studios' swan song to horror flicks.

Forced retirement, years of alcoholism and drug abuse all took their toll on Bela. His health was failing rapidly and he needed to be hospitalized in order to save his life. While there he obsessed with the fear of going insane. Sometimes he would go into deep depression expressing the desire to die. Normally, Bela never talked about death unless it was a role. He was getting to an age where forever ended and death was becoming more of a reality. He never went to the funerals of friends and always refused to talk about them after they were gone.

BELA LUGOSI
BELOVED FATHER
1882 — 1956

Hollywood Forever Cemetery, Hollywood, California

After Bela's release from the hospital he vowed to change his life. Apparently as most close to him thought, he gave up booze and drugs. He even entered a hospital to 'dry out.' When he emerged drug free, he religiously attended Alcoholics Anonymous meetings with friend, Ed Wood.

After one meeting, his friend noticed Bela sipping something from his coat. Once outside, Ed confronted his friend and Bela denied the allegations. Ed ripped opened his friend's coat and discovered that Bela had sewn little pockets into the lining. Each little pocket contained a little bottle of scotch in it.

Despite his drinking, his friend, Ed, realized that the best therapy would be work. He had given Bela a script for an upcoming movie, *"The Final Curtain."* As Lugosi sat down to read it, his wife Hope went out shopping. He was very excited at the prospect of making a come back.

When Hope returned, she noticed an unusual stillness in their apartment. She called out to her husband, but received no reply. Alarmed she rushed into the bedroom only to find him lying motionless on the bed, his fingers still clutching a copy of the script his friend had given him to read. Lugosi had died of a heart attack.

Bela's will stipulated that he be buried in his Dracula cape and after his viewing, cremated. Hope made plans to inter him in the Hollywood Forever Cemetery. But son, Bela Jr., vehemently objected and instead had his father buried in the Holy Cross Cemetery's Grotto. This he thought would be a more fitting resting place for a man who deserved a public monument. Ex-wife Lillian purchased the tombstone and plot. And Hope purchased the coffin. Services were held at the Utter-McKinley Mortuary on Hollywood Boulevard. He was laid out in a tuxedo and cape. A short service in the chapel was accompanied by the moody violin composition of Kerekjarto.

What took place after the services perhaps showed Bela's greatest vindication as the horror to end all horrors and an indication that his power was still very much a part of our world. After the service friends and family filed solemnly out of the side entrance and waited for the funeral procession to begin. Bela's cape was folded over his shoulder and the coffin was closed. Mr. Kranke a long-term employee of Utter-McKinley, was the driver because he was best acquainted with the route to Holy Cross Cemetery. After all he had driven it hundreds of times.

As Kranke prepared to turn right onto Hollywood Boulevard, according to strict police procession regulations, the hearse, however, sped across oncoming traffic and turned left across Hollywood and Vine. It proceeded down the magical mile, Bela considered his. Then past the news stand where he bought his paper every evening and past the tobacco shop where he had bought everything from Havanas to Tijuana ropes. When the procession finally reached La Brea Kranke turned left and drove to the cemetery without further incident. Marie Staats, Kranke's boss, was very upset by the change in route. When the procession arrived at the cemetery, she walked over to Kranke and demanded an explanation. But as she approached him, she saw by his pallid expression that the route he took was not of his choosing.

"Mr Kranke, why on earth did you ignore standard procedure?" asked Staats in a very business like tone.

"I'm really sorry, Mrs. Staats, I know about the permits. I just don't know what happened in the hearse. I was ready to turn right on Hollywood Boulevard and then..."

His face turned white at the thought of that inexplicable moment when he was no longer in control of his hearse. He walked away muttering, "I don't know what happened, I just don't know.."

Mrs. Staats had believed him, because she had worked with him for many years and he was not the type for pranks, especially when it could have cost him his job.

Is it so strange for Bela to take just one more trip down the boulevard he loved?

Holy Cross Cemetery

5835 W. Slauson Avenue

Culver City, California

For directions to the cemetery see Rita Hayworth in the Glamour Girls Chapter. When you arrive in the cemetery get a celebrity map and head towards "The Grotto," Which is just up the hill from the office. Once there you will see a cave on the left hand side of the road, park there. Walk towards the cave. With you back to the cave count approximately 4 rows down. You'll see Bing Crosby, count six to the left and there's Bela.

VICTOR "VIC" MORROW
1929 — 1982

LOVED HIM AS "DAD"

[...] FOREVERMORE [...] HE WAS
[...] SAM

Hillside Memorial Park, Culver City, California

Vic Morrow
February 14, 1932-July 23 1982

After playing a film heavy in the 1950's he made the transition to television. He became known for his part as Sgt. Chip Saunders, in the long running television show *"Combat."*

While shooting *"The Twilight Zone,"* a four segment anthology movie, Morrow and two Vietnamese children ages 6 and 7 were killed. The film footage of the ill-fated scene shows Morrow struggling to get across a river amid explosions, while holding the two children in his arms. The next thing you see is a flash of light and then a helicopter falling on top of all three.

During the filming outside Los Angeles, the tail motor of the chopper carrying a camera crew was hit by debris from explosives detonated in a Vietnam War scene. The children and Morrow, were struck and killed, by the main rotor of the helicopter as it pitched into a river on the set. Morrow, who was said to be decapitated by the accident was 51.

Later charges were filed against directors, Steven Spielberg, John Landis and Warner Bros. for possible negligence in their role in the accident. They were acquitted of all charges.

Hillside Memorial Park and Mortuary
600 W. Centinela Avenue
Culver City, California

For directions to the cemetery see Moe Howard of the Five Stooges? Chapter.First all get a celebrity map at the office. Then from the office, go to the "Mount of Olives" section. Go to section 5, look for "Anna Louise Fuchs" by the road and count 6 down that row. There he is.

Spencer Tracy
April 5, 1900 - June 10, 1967

Born Spencer Bonaventure Tracy, in Milwaukee to a strict Irish Catholic family. His childhood was tempestuous which caused him to quickly develop a reputation for fighting. He was not a stellar student and majored in expulsion and failing grades. Spencer was forced to attend the Jesuit Marquette Academy where he promptly straightened out. After two years, he became stage struck and ventured to New York for drama school. Soon he obtained bit parts on and off Broadway.

It was common for Hollywood in the 1930's to seek out talent for their films and John Ford was scouting for Fox. While looking for talent, he noticed Tracy in a performance where he played a prisoner in *"The Last Mile."* Impressed, he signed Tracy to a contract to star in a prison movie along with Humphrey Bogart, *"Up the River."* After that he slowly moved into the first ranks of stardom, capped by back to back 'Best Actor Oscars' for *"Captain Courageous"* and *"Boy's Town."*

As his star status grew so did his reputation for heavy drinking and an explosive temper. He was known to fight with photographers, breaking their cameras. Despite all this he was adored by his fans. Although married Tracy teamed up with Katherine Hepburn both professionally and romantically. She seemed the only one to calm his demons. This relationship would last for the next twenty five years until his death.

His last movie was with Hepburn in *"Guess Who's Coming to Dinner,"* (1967). By now, Tracy had been in bad health and the studio refuse to insure him. Director Stanley Kramer took full responsibility for the risk. He shortened Tracy's work day and slowly but surely the movie was finished. Unfortunately he would never live to see it on the screen.

Forest Lawn Memorial Park, Glendale, California

The night Spencer died, according to Katherine Hepburn, was nothing like the other stories that were written about that event. First of all, he died at approximately 3 am, and Hepburn was there with him the whole night, because they lived together. In those days, it was still socially unacceptable for a woman to be living with a man, let alone a married man.

That night was no different than any other night, she said she sat with him until he fell asleep. Then she crept out of the room, taking a buzzer, so he could summon her if needed. It was almost like clockwork that the buzzer would ring with some request, but for some reason that night, it never did.

Apparently he wanted a cup of tea and had gotten up to get it. She heard him walk down the hall and go into the kitchen. Kate got up to see if she could help him but before she arrived she heard a cup smash to the floor followed by a thud. It was him falling to the floor after experiencing a massive heart attack. She crouched down and took him in her arms. His eyes were closed and he no longer had a pulse. It happened so fast that he probably never felt a thing. He went out the way he wanted to, without pain or a long illness.

Kate put Spencer on a rug, until someone could help her put him back into bed. Kate said he looked happy to be done with living. Despite all his accomplishments his life had been a burden. Spencer was once quoted, "You only live once, but if you do it right that's all you need." He was 67.

Forest Lawn Memorial Park
1712 S. Glendale Avenue
Glendale, California
For directions to the cemetery see Jean Harlow in the Glamour Girls Chapter. Get a map but don't ask for any celebrity locations. Follow the map or signs to the Freedom Mausoleum, when you arrive, park. Look for the Garden of Everlasting Peace which is directly outside the mausoleum. Once inside go to your right and look for a little garden with "TRACY" that's him.

JOHN BARRYMORE

✝

1942

"GOOD NIGHT SWEET PRINCE"

Calvary Cemetery Mausoleum, Los Angeles, California

Chapter 16 - Classics
John Barrymore
February 14, 1882 - May 29, 1942

I would have to call this man, who was once recognized as the world's a leading Shakespearean actor and film idol, one who cannot rest in peace. After years of excess began to eat away at his body and mind, John Barrymore who was destitute and dying, spent his last days at his friend, Errol Flynn's house. As his health grew worse John had to be taken to Hollywood Presbyterian Hospital. He had by now developed bronchial pneumonia, congestion of the lungs, all resulting from his cirrhosis of the liver. It was not long before his prognosis would worsen and he slipped into a coma.

Surprising doctors, he awaken the next day from his coma and was extremely alert. Looking at a very plain nurse he cracked, "Well, get into bed anyway." Since his condition seemed to be improving, the doctors decided to relieve the edema in his stomach by draining twelve quarts of fluid. Soon after the procedure, he took a turn for the worse and became delirious. Attendants put white mittens on his hands to keep him from clawing his skin. Eventually he had to be fully retrained. Near the end, his breathing became labored and then finally the inevitable happened, he expired of a heart attack. Apparently his last words were: "Die? I should say not, dear fellow. No Barrymore would allow such a conventional thing to happen to him."

Errol who was saddened by the demise of his pal, Barrymore, joined some friends (including director Raoul Walsh), who had gathered at a bar to mourn their dearly departed friend. Walsh excused himself, claiming that he was too upset to remain with them and was going home to be alone. Instead he and two friends went to the Pierce Brother's Mortuary on Sunset Boulevard and bribed the caretaker into lending them Barrymore's body for $200. They transported the body to Flynn's house in Walsh's station wagon, brought it into the house and propped it up in Errol's favorite living room chair, facing the door. This is what happened according to Flynn:

"I walked in, sad and alone. As I opened the door I pressed the button. The lights went on and I stared into the face of Barrymore! His eyes were closed. He looked puffed, white, bloodless. They hadn't embalmed him yet. I let out a delirious scream."

Errol then bolted from the house, intending to flee in his car. His friends quickly caught up with him on the porch and convinced him that it was only a gag.

Although John Barrymore's last request was to be cremated and buried in the family plot in Philadelphia, his sister, Ethel, however, decided to bypass his request. So on June 2, 1942, he was entombed at the Calvary Cemetery's Mausoleum in East Los Angeles. His crypt is beside brother, Lionel Barrymore, and Lionel's wife Irene. On the crypt it is inscribed with a line from his most famous role in Shakespeare's Hamlet: "Good Night, Sweet Prince."

Well sweet prince, wake up because it's time to go, you're going to get your wish. In 1980, he was removed from his final resting place and his final wishes finally honored by son, John Barrymore Jr, (father to Drew Barrymore) who brought him to Mount Vernon Cemetery in Philadelphia.

In order to accomplish this caper John Jr., had to first get dispensation from the Catholic Church and some not so genuine family signatures before the Cemetery would agree to exhuming the body.

Finally after receiving the okay from the cemetery John Jr, along with son John III, met two grave diggers at the Mausoleum. After prying the marble slab off the front of the tomb they found that the casket had leaked gluing it to the marble slab. John Jr., who was very drunk pushed the grave diggers aside and put one foot on Irene and the other on Lionel and yanked hard until the casket was free. Before turning the casket over to the crematorium, both were compelled to look inside. Though the face was recognizable, time had not improved the corpse.

Hollywood Forever Cemetery, Hollywood, California

John's ashes were put into a book shaped urn. Penniless but yet still obsessed with their mission, John Jr had to pawn several personal items in order to make the trip to Philly. John Barrymore's new home is adorned with simple ground marker with the words: "Alas poor Yorick - Hamlet." In my opinion, I felt that the original burial spot was more appropriate for this Barrymore, it was classic, and reminiscent of a past time.

Calvary Cemetery Mausoleum
4201 Whittier Blvd
East Los Angeles, California
For directions to the cemetery see Lou Costello in the Dynamic Duos Chapter.Go to the mausoleum. Once inside go upstairs and walk to the right to the first hallway, on the right wall you'll see three Barrymores.
Cremated and moved by son John Barrymore Jr. on December 2, 1980 to
Mount Vernon Cemetery
Philadelphia, Pennsylvania

Douglas Fairbanks Sr. and Douglas Fairbanks Jr.
Douglas Sr.
May 23, 1883 - December 12, 1939
Born Douglas Ulman in 1883, he popularized the California tan with his bronzed complexion. He liked to claim that he was so dark at birth his mother refused to show him to neighbors. She would make an excuse that he was sleeping and that she didn't want to disturb him. At the age of three, he distinguished himself by climbing trees, scaling roofs, and swinging from one branch to another.

The product of his mother's third marriage, he lived with the consequences of an unhappy mother and an absent father who in later years became a heavy drinker. His father, a former lawyer, would show up backstage for handouts from his son, whom Douglas never turned away.

Fairbanks first joined the theater at 17, but then enrolled in Harvard for a semester, after receiving some bad reviews. He then worked through Europe, still momentarily absent from the theater. But Fairbanks missed the the footlights and greasepaint and returned after a brief hiatus.

There was no physical feat the exuberant actor would not attempt, from shinnying up a drainpipe to leaping into the sea from the top of a ship's mast. Nothing could stop his death defying personality.

At the age of 41, bare chested, with white teeth gleaming he had looked wonderful in *"The Thief of Baghdad."* But now doctors were warning him that he was muscle bound and if he didn't cut down on his activity he would suffer serious circulatory problems. The prospect of aging was not helped by his son, Douglas Fairbanks, Jr. who recently launched his career.

Doctors proved to be right, when suddenly Fairbanks Sr., died of a heart attack, a day after attending a U.S.C.-UCLA football game. It was a surprise to all. As he was dying they said his final words were: "I've never felt better." He died while he was in the middle of making, *"The Californian."*

As one of Hollywood's royalty, he was mourned like a king. His body lay in an ornately carved bed before a window of his Santa Monica mansion, which looked out onto the vast Pacific. Through night and day, came a procession of the Hollywood elite and the forgotten, who had worked with and known Fairbanks in his "swashbuckling" days. For hours Mr Fairbanks' 150 pound mastiff, Marco Polo, whined beside the death bed, refusing to move.

Fairbanks is interred in Hollywood Forever in a magnificent sunken garden. His final resting place was designed by William Cameron Menzies, one of the industry most creative set designers. As pictured the long reflecting pool leads you his tomb, a marble sarcophagus is surrounded on three sides by fluted columns. If you stand in front of the tomb you can see an unobstructed view of the famous Hollywood sign, that is a landmark for everyone that ever aspires to be a star. Inscribed on his tomb is: "Good night sweet prince and flights of angels sing thee to rest."

Douglas Jr.
December 9, 1909 - May 7, 2000

Born Douglas Elton Fairbanks to Douglas Sr and Anna Beth Sully. Their marriage was not a happy one and they divorced when he was 9 and young Douglas went on to live with his mother. For the next decade, he saw his father infrequently and when he did, he showed the boy "no real affection." It was not until the 1930's that the two became close friends.

The Douglas Jr., made his acting debut at the age of 13 in the movie *'Stephen Steps Out."* The 1923 film failed and he continued to struggle to earn a living, partly by writing silent film titles, acting and doubling as a cameraman or prop mover. He appeared occasionally on the Los Angeles stage in plays like *"Young Woodley'* and *"Saturday's Children."*

As an adult, he struggled to carve a distinctive acting career in the shadow of his superstar father, who was the unrivaled swashbuckler of silent films. He was not the gymnast that his father was, but he was a versatile actor who could easily play a wide variety of roles. So as to to be compared to his father, he avoided most swashbuckling roles that were offered to him.

Throughout his life he wore many hats, in addition to being an actor, he produced, and wrote. His biggest and most important role was in real life when he served during World War II under Adm. Lord Louis Mountbatten. He was the first American officer to command a British flotilla of raiding craft. Through the Admiral, Douglas was introduced to the royal family where they became close friends.

At the age of 90, Douglas entered the Mount Sinai Medical Center in Manhattan where he later died. His body was flown out to Hollywood, California where he is was entombed along with his father in the family crypt.

Hollywood Forever Cemetery
6000 Santa Monica Blvd
Hollywood, California

For directions to the cemetery see Janet Gaynor in the Glamour Girls Chapter. You can purchase a cemetery map for $5.00 if you'd like or follow my directions. As you enter the cemetery you'll make a left and follow the road around until you see the mausoleum. Park anywhere. Walk to the bridge and look to your left, there they are.

Errol Flynn
June 20, 1909 - October 14, 1959

Born in Tasmania he was educated in Paris, London, Sydney and Ireland. His extensive resume consisted of many jobs including journalist, sailor, novelist, fighter and knockabout, all of which perhaps inspired his acting abilities.

His big break came when he was discovered on his sailboat off New Guinea by a film crew. After that, some small parts preceded his successful *"Captain Blood"* in 1935 for which he was a replacement for Robert Donat. That opportunity propelled him to instant stardom. This romantic, hero, adventurer, was one star who enjoyed being typecasted.

Adventurous in films as well as in real life, he would sometimes be rebellious and unpredictable, while keeping constantly in the public's eye. It also kept him in hot water with the studios and his women. Not very discreet, he was notorious for his nonstop drinking and insatiable womanizing.

In 1941, at the height of his popularity, he escorted Peggy Satterle, a dancer from the Florentine Gardens, to his yacht, 'The Sirocca'. She accused him of rape, which prompted a lengthy scandalous trial which ultimately hurt his career. A grand jury vindicated him, but the district attorney overruled the decision and prosecuted him. He was represented by Jerry Geisler and he was finally acquitted on all counts.

Just one year later he was in trouble again, this time he was charged with statutory rape. After some legal wrangling he was fortunately acquitted. His trials were attended with the same excitement as his films. But these scandals seemed to break his spirit and he experienced a steady decline both professionally and personally.

Forest Lawn Memorial Park, Glendale, California

ERROL FLYNN
JUNE 20 1909
OCTOBER 14 1959

IN MEMORY OF OUR FATHER
FROM HIS LOVING CHILDREN

Forest Lawn Memorial Park, Glendale, California

His on-screen magic disappeared and the studios began to cast him in the roles of a drunkard, as in Hemingway's *"The Sun Also Rises"* and *"Too Much, Too Soon."*

Flynn's final years afforded him some happiness aboard his beloved yacht, 'Zaka.' During this time he worked on his autobiography, appropriately entitled "My Wicked, Wicked Ways," which ended up being published posthumously. He died in Vancouver, British Columbia, of a heart attack at the age of 50.

It is rumored that Errol took six bottles of whiskey with him to the great beyond. Such provisions, however, were probably not needed due to all that he had imbibed throughout his life. His final wishes were to be cremated and his ashes scattered at sea. But he knew this was not to be and was quoted as saying "I can tell you, I know my wishes will not be carried out." He was right, third wife, Patrice Wymore adamantly opposed his wishes saying that he would have to be buried in a manner fitting a Hollywood star. This "Hollywood star" did not acquire his grave marker until twenty years after his death in 1979.

Forest Lawn Memorial Park
1712 S. Glendale Avenue
Glendale, California
For directions to the cemetery see Jean Harlow in the Glamour Girls chapter. Get a map of the cemetery but do not ask for any celebrity directions. Follow the signs to the Freedom Mausoleum, when you get there, park. Next to the mausoleum near a statue of Washington is the Garden of Everlasting Peace go in there. You'll see a bronze statue of a woman with one hand around her waist and the other over her shoulder against the far wall. This is his grave.

Mary Pickford
April 8, 1893 - May 29, 1979
Gladys Marie Smith started acting as a small child to help support her family after the death of her father. At the age of 13, Mary took the role in a David Belasco theater production, *"The Warrens of Virginia"* in 1908. She enjoyed the part, but signed on with the movies for bigger and more profitable roles.

At Biograph Studios, Pickford made dozens of silent short features where she played scrub women, Mexican teenagers, and choir singers. Later she would become a giant voice behind, as well as in front of the camera. She was a capable dramatic actress as well as an astute businesswoman. She produced many of her pictures and negotiated some of the toughest starring contracts in silent film history. Later Mary became one of the founders of United Artists, and the Motion Picture Relief Fund.

Her marriage to Douglas Fairbanks was a well publicized part of Hollywood society. They purchased a lavish home in which they called, "Pickfair" where royalty, heads of state and other dignitaries were entertained. Not only did she grow as an actress, but so did her fortune and circle of fans.

This paradise lasted only 15 years, Fairbanks was bored and wanted to entertain a mid-life crisis with constant travel and adventure. Mary divorced him in 1935 and retired from acting and life.

She retired to bed and with exception to her clandestine nocturnal trips around the house. Her butler brought up her meals, whiskey, and a newspaper with all the disturbing stories clipped out. No visitors would be permitted upstairs to see her; all communication was done via the downstairs phones.

Despite her vegetative inactivity, she died at the old age of 86 of a stroke.

Forest Lawn Memorial Park
1712 S. Glendale Avenue
Glendale, California

Forest Lawn Memorial Park, Glendale, California

For directions to the cemetery see Jean Harlow in the Glamour Girls Chapter. Don't ask for any celebrity tombstone directions, just request a map and proceed to the Freedom Mausoleum. From the direction of the Freedom Mausoleum head towards the Court of the Christus. You'll see a sign on your right side, park there. These gardens are sometimes locked if they happen to be opened or you are invited in proceed to the Garden of Remembrance in this garden she is located against the rear wall in a very large white sarcophagus with "PICKFORD" written on it. You really can't miss it.

Tyrone Power
May 5, 1914 - November 15, 1958

Being the son of silent movie actor, Tyrone Power Sr., you could say that acting was already in his blood. He was resolved to follow in his father's footsteps, acting on stage while still a teenager and making a movie debut as a cadet in *"Tom Brown of Culver"* in 1932.

With his handsome face he quickly progressed to better roles, including three with Loretta Young, Alice Faye, Norma Shearer, Betty Grable and many more. He played roles predominately of a lover or a swashbuckler.

During World War II he entered the armed services where he served until the war's end. When he returned from the conflict, he was a changed man; more serious and grim. He resumed his career at Fox, and starred in *"The Razor's Edge,"* in 1946.

Power was a perfectionist who constantly strove to improve himself. He expanded his abilities by portraying the famous pianist and orchestra leader in *"The Eddie Duchin Story."* His last on screen performance was in *"Abandon Ship!"* where he excelled.

As time went by he became increasingly tired and nervous. He developed a heavy drinking habit and did not take care of himself. Power went overseas to shoot the Biblical epic *"Solomon and Sheba"* While filming a duel scene, he suddenly collapsed of a massive heart attack and died. He was only 44.

Power's obituary in the New York Times stated that "only 100 close friends of the actor could be accommodated in the small chapel at the cemetery." His wife, Deborah Anne Power, sat in front of his open coffin, while Cesar Romero gave the eulogy.

Hollywood Forever Cemetery
6000 Santa Monica Blvd.
Hollywood, California

For directions to the cemetery see Janet Gaynor in the Glamour Girls chapter. You can shell out $5 or follow my directions. Make your first available left onto Lakeview Avenue and drive to Section 8, the only section with a lake. Park when you get to the intersection of Rosemary and Lakeview, which is right by the mausoleum. Get out and walk towards the lake, you'll see his memorial bench to the left of the Marion Davis' mausoleum (which is marked with the name "DOURAS"). You can't miss it!

Virginia Rappe
1895 - September 9, 1921

The facts are still not clear as to what happened in the St. Francis Hotel that Labor Day weekend in 1921. A few film stars had rented three suites in the San Francisco hotel and settled in to celebrate.

Roscoe "Fatty" Arbuckle, who had just signed a $3 million contract with Paramount, was there and so was Virginia Rappe. Arbuckle was described as a slapstick buffoon who liked to drink hard. Virginia was a star whose career was on the down slide. One of her claims to fame was that she appeared on the cover of sheet music for *"Let Me Call Your Sweetheart."*

Maude Demont, who procured young women for such parties and then sometimes blackmailed the men afterward, claimed Fatty dragged Virginia into a suite and violently raped her crushing her beneath his enormous weight. One rumor stated that he violated her with a champagne bottle or a piece of ice which pierced her bladder, killing her.

Hollywood Forever Cemetery, Hollywood, California

Another rumor was that she had died from peritonitis after a botched abortion. In any case she was taken to the hospital where she slipped into a coma and died of a ruptured bladder five days later.

After that things were never the same for Arbuckle. He now had to endure three lengthy trials (two were hung juries) for 1st degree murder. It took the San Francisco jury only one minute to acquit the comedian. But the Tabloids across the country portrayed Arbuckle as a pervert thus condemning him to a sentence that would forever ruin his career. The public outcry over the affair had been so great that he was fired from Paramount and his films were withdrawn by distributors. Goodbye $3 million contract.

Film director Henry Lehrman, Virginia's sweetheart, fashioned the rest of his life around her memory. He visited her grave weekly and eventually join her in 1946.

Hollywood Forever Cemetery
6000 Santa Monica Blvd.
Hollywood, California

For directions to the cemetery see Janet Gaynor in the Glamour Girls chapter. You can shell out $5 or follow my directions. Make your first available left onto Lakeview Avenue and drive to Section 8, the only section with a lake. Park when you see Cecil B. DeMille's crypt from the street. Walk straight past him towards the lake, bear left and keep going and you'll bump in to Virginia.

Lillian Russell
December 4, 1861 - June 6, 1922

Born Helen Louise Leonard, in Clinton, Iowa. Her father was an easygoing newspaperman and her mother was a head strong woman who was perhaps one of the first feminist of her time.

Helen was discovered by Tony Pastor, a star maker of that era. After hearing her sing at the home of a friend he offered her $75 a week on the spot to sing at his variety theater. She accepted and changed her name to Lillian Russell. Who knew that she would later become the most durable sex symbol in American theatrical history. When motion pictures became popular, she left the theater to make movies..

For that era she led a highly unconventional life, in which she had more than the contemporary quotient of husbands and lovers. She campaigned strongly for the women's rights movement. And during the last several years of her life, her career took a turn that was unexpected and uncommon for women of her day. She became a politician. She was violently Republican and disagreed with Woodrow Wilson's plan to join the League of Nations.

By May, 1922 Lillian was now ill and fighting for her health. While on board a ship traveling from Europe she had slipped and fell, incurring several internal injuries for which she had dismissed as trivial. She had refused to consult a doctor due to her earnest practice of the Christian Science faith.

When she returned to her Pittsburgh home she was seriously ill and was forced to seek medical care. Unfortunately for Lillian it was too late. A month after her accident, she was dead. The cause of death was reported to the newspapers as a complication of diseases. Whatever they were she kept them a secret.

She went to her grave with the undiminished affection and gratitude of the theatrical profession. President Harding's orders were to have her buried with full military honors, and with a floral centerpiece from the White House on her coffin. There were memorial services in many American cities in her honor.

Allegheny Cemetery
4734 Butler Street
Pittsburgh, Pennsylvania

VIRGINIA RAPPE

1895 – 1921

Hollywood Forever Cemetery, Hollywood, California

Directions: Rt 19 (West Liberty Ave.) To Saw Mill Run Road for half a mile than turn right onto Liberty Tunnels this becomes Liberty Bridge. Stay straight on Crosstown Blvd. Take I-579 North ramp take PA-28N exit towards Etna. Merge PA-28N it becomes Allegheny Valley Expwy/PA28. Turn slight left to take the 40th Street Bridge ramp, turn right onto Washington Crossing Bridge/40th Street. Turn left on Butler Street and believe it or not the cemetery is right there. Once inside the office and ask for a map. I'm sorry but this is one time where I have no directions for you. Unfortunately, I arrived at the cemetery a little late and the office was closed. Thank God, I spotted a very nice lady, Suncerre, whose kids were playing in the fountain. As it turned out, lucky for me, her uncle works for the cemetery and she knew it like the back of her hand. She took me winding through all kinds of roads in this HUGE cemetery, passing perhaps many historical graves. Once again special thanks, to you Suncerre!

Rudolph Valentino
May 6, 1895 - August 23, 1926

He was born Rodolpho Alphonso Raffaelo Pierre Filibert di Valentina d'Antonguolla in Taranto, Italy in 1895. He was spoiled rotten by his mother, and by the age of 10 he was a bully and thug. The next phase of his life was spent stealing and exposing himself in church, This type of behavior was not tolerated and he was expelled from school. At 15 he sat for an exam to enter the Naval Academy but failed on physical grounds, a deep humiliation and the root cause of his future obsession with macho muscularity.

Already a confirmed homosexual, though bisexual for gain, he spent a month in Paris with his mother who had hoped he might "lose his rough edge." Instead he haunted the homosexual clubs and sold himself to rich businessmen, always trying to make enough money to fulfil his ambition: to go to America. By 1913, he finally succeeded, sailing from Hamburg to New York. His family were only too relieved to see him go.

The initial American years were as sleazy as ever. He was a gigolo to rich, aging women and was not above blackmailing a male john after performing sexual favors on them. But he learned to dance the apache and the tango with some success, this opened a few doors for him professionally

Rudolph traveled west to Hollywood, where he rose from "extra" to small part player via the homosexual Torch Club and the equivalent lesbian establishment of Alla Nazimova, two of whose protegees he later married, which suited all parties admirably. Despite his studio reputation, "that dago whore," "that damned faggot gigolo." Valentino landed the lead in *"For Horsemen of the Apocalypse,"* followed by *"The Sheik,"* which brought him stardom and mob female hysteria.

Valentino's huge success and popularity would be short lived due to the ruptured appendix and gastric ulcer that claimed his young life at the age of 31. He was rushed to Manhattan's Polyclinic Hospital where for seven days the world held it's breath as his temperature fluctuated and then soared past normal limits. Rumors grew that he had been poisoned or shot by a jealous husband. Despite these allegations, an autopsy was never performed. Instead he was laid out at the Frank E.Campbell Funeral Home and a dignified, by invitation only, funeral was planned.

His fans were outraged, and by 2:00 that afternoon, 20,000 people were outside the chapel demanding to see their star. They finally crashed in the plate glass window and trampled floral arrangements in an effort to find their idol. During the melee one hundred people were injured. When peace was finally restored, another fight broke out between a self appointed honor guard of Black Shirts and the Anti-Fascist Alliance of North America. Pola Negri added to the carnival atmosphere, insisting that she and Valentino had been engaged. She then put on a performance for the press, screaming and fainting on command.

LILLIAN RUSSELL MOORE

THE WORLD IS BETTER
FOR HER HAVING LIVED

Allegheny Cemetery, Pittsburgh, Pennsylvania

With his brother's approval, Valentino's body was brought by train to Los Angeles, where blueprints for a monument at Hollywood Memorial were drawn up by architect Matlock Price. These plans included a large statue of Valentino as *"The Sheik,"* set in a semicircle of Roman columns. At the base of each column would be bas reliefs of Valentino in his six greatest films: *"The Four Horsemen," "The Sheik," "Monsieur Beaucaire," "Blood and Sand, " "The Eagle,"* and of course *"Son of Sheik."* In the meantime, he was placed in a vault that had been purchased by June Mathis Balboni. After she died tragically in a fire and the monument was still not built, he was moved to her husband's more modest crypt. A few years later, Albert Guglielmi quietly purchased the vault from Sylvano Balboni to make sure his brother at least had a roof over his head.

At least his funeral was the mammoth production fitting for a start of his caliber. The streets were lined with thousands of weeping, screaming, fainting women laced with "gays." At home, thousands of women were sobbing next to their radios overcome by the news of his death. In his honor, one woman ordered 4,000 roses for his bier; another fan shot herself.

Valentino's grave is still considered one of the most visited graves. Since his death there have been a number of "women in black" who have mysteriously visited his grave leaving bouquets of roses behind.

Hollywood Forever
6000 Santa Monica Boulevard
Hollywood, California
For directions to the cemetery see Janet Gaynor in the Glamour Girls Chapter. From the main entrance make an immediate left onto Lakeview Avenue. Follow that all the way around until you get to the mausoleum. From the entrance walk down to the second corridor on the left, then walk all the way in and on your left you will see his crypt, #1205.

Hollywood Forever Cemetery, Hollywood, California

RODOLFO GUGLIELMI VALENTINO

1895

1926

1205

Chapter 17: And A One and A Two....
Louis "Satchmo" Armstrong
August 4, 1901 - July 6, 1971

Throughout Satchmo's entire life, July 4, 1900 has been universally recognized as his birthday. Maybe because the date reflects two important events: the birth of our nation and the start of a new century in which Armstrong would influence the creation of American art through his music.

His real birthday is August 4, 1901 a fact that was discovered recently by writer Gary Giddins who was doing research for his book *"Satchmo."* Giddins came across baptismal and census records which clearly indicates his correct date of birth.

We do know that Louis was born in New Orleans in the notorious Storyville section of town. He was raised by his grandmother after his father abandoned him. At age 10, he left his grandmother to live with his mother Mary Ann.

As a youth, he was a small time hood who stole and schemed his way through life. An event that changed his life occurred when he fired a pistol into the air to celebrate the New Year. He was arrested and put into the New Orleans Home for Colored Waifs for an indefinite sentence. It was more or less a boot camp for juvenile delinquents. Also while there they received an education. It was there where he was exposed to music for the first time..

After spending two years at the home, he was returned to the care of his mother. His first job was delivering coal. While there at the home he developed quite a love for music and wanted to continue playing. He saved up his money and purchased a used cornet. By the age of 17, Louis was playing with local bands.

In 1918, Louis left his home to travel on the river boats of the Mississippi River where he could play his music professionally. After his stint on the river boat he returned home, married a prostitute, and was off again, this time to Chicago to play in the Creole Jazz Band. From there he ventured to New York to record with Fletcher Henderson, blues giant Bessie Smith, and Sidney Becht. In 1925, he then returned to Chicago to make records.

The depression forced him to move back to New York. where the 1930's brought a transition for Louis. It was during this time that he moved from a great musician to great entertainer. It is because of this that we know him for his gravelly singing style and his improvisational technical skill he displayed on his cornet.

In 1935, he was under the management of Joe Glaser, who made sure Louis had a steady diet of concert dates, recording sessions and film appearances. During his career he played with greats like Barbara Streisand, Grace Kelly and Bing Crosby.

For the last ten years of his life he was plagued with heart and kidney problems. Against his doctor's advice, he continued to perform. Just two weeks before his last engagement he began gasping for air; his doctor told him that he would have to stop. But Louis told him that he lived for the horn and would continue to perform.

He made his last engagement at the Empire Room of the Waldorf Astoria Hotel in New York City. For two weeks, he played each night for an hour. After his obligations were met he checked back into the hospital for observation, where he was released several weeks later. Late one evening, Armstrong was feeling better so he called his manager to secure rehearsal dates for the band. Unfortunately this was a date he was going to miss because he was dead the following morning from kidney failure.

His funeral procession was covered on television and his body was laid in state at the National Guard Armory on direct order of the President. Twenty-five thousand mourners including a slew of celebrities walked past his coffin. He was finally laid to rest at the Flushing Cemetery along with another musical great, Dizzy Gillespie.

LEONARD
BERNSTEIN
1918 ⟶ 1990

Greenwood Cemetery, Brooklyn, New York

43642

Flushing Cemetery
163-03 46th Avenue
Queens, New York
Directions: Take the Long Island Expressway (I-495) to the Utopia exit and go north. Drive one mile and make a left at Hollis Court Blvd. Drive a half a mile until you see the cemetery on your left. Once inside the cemetery make a left on the first road by the office, look for section #9. You can't miss his black marker with a white cornet on top.

Leonard Bernstein
August 25, 1919 - October 14, 1990

He was born in Lawrence, Massachusetts, a musical prodigy. At the age of 10, he fell in love with his aunt's piano and insisted that his parents provide lessons. Six years later, he gave his first recital at his high school. During summer camp, when most kids were weaving baskets, or catching poison ivy, Leonard was producing his version of "*Carmen*" and singing the title role.

In 1934, he entered Harvard and began a radio series in Boston called *"Leonard Bernstein at the Piano."* Later he moved to Philadelphia, where he studied conducting under Fritz Reiner at the Curtis Institute of Music.

In 1943, at the age of 25, he was invited by Artur Rodzinski to be Assistant Conductor of the Philharmonic Symphony Society of New York. Four months later, he was given the opportunity to debut with the N.Y.P. when the guest conductor, Bruno Walter, fell ill and Rodzinski could not return to New York in time to take over. Confidently leading the orchestra, Bernstein received enthusiastic applause after each number. Since the concert was being broadcasted, the deafening applause that he received at the end of the concert could be heard nationally, which made him an overnight sensation..

Bernstein conducted the New York City Center orchestra from 1945-47 and appeared as guest conductor in the U.S., Europe and Israel. In 1953, he became the first American to conduct at La Scala in Milan, Italy. From 1958 to 1969 he continued to write music and appeared as guest conductor throughout the world.

Age did little to slow Bernstein down. Between 1985 and 1990, he conducted not less than fifteen concerts and made at least three foreign tours, including an appearance in Japan where he collapsed from exhaustion. On October 9, 1990, at the age of 72, he announced his plans to retire due to health reasons. Five days later, he died of a cardiac arrest brought on by mesothelioma. Sixteen days after his death a small private funeral was performed at his home.

Greenwood Cemetery
500 25th Street
Brooklyn, New York
For directions to the cemetery see Albert Anastasia in the "Wacked and the Rested" Chapter. Go to the office and get a celebrity map. From there turn left onto Battle Avenue and drive around the twisting road to Border Avenue. Turn left onto Border then turn right on Garland Avenue and stop about 50 feet up from Garland, there you will see a small footpath on your right. Follow the footpath into section G/H marked by a little square cement marker. Turning left in the middle of the section at the intersection of the two paths. Walk about 50 feet and on your right you will see the Bernstein bench. He's right there.

John Coltrane
September 23, 1926 - July 17, 1967

He was born in Hamlet, North Carolina, the son of a tailor. As a youngster, he developed a love for music. First on clarinet and then on the saxophone.

With the onset of World War II, Coltrane was drafted into the Navy. Stationed in Hawaii, he made the best of his situation by playing the clarinet in the U.S. Navy Band. When he was finally discharged, he was determined to return to Philadelphia to make his mark on the music world.

Pinelawn Memorial Park, Farmingdale, New York

It didn't take long for his first big break to play in the road band for blues singer, Eddie "Cleanhead" Vinson. Less than a year later, he joined Dizzy Gillespie's big band. The same band that provided invaluable training for Charlie Parker and a number of other jazz musicians.

Unfortunately like most musicians, he was sidetracked from his music by drugs. During the 1950's Coltrane developed an increased dependancy on heroin, which caused him to be kicked out of the band he was playing in. The habit that compromised the thing he loved best, would last for the next five years.

When Miles Davis needed a replacement for Sonny Rollins, he did not hesitate on calling Coltrane. In their first year together they made five albums for the Prestige Label. At the time, the band was often being referred to as "The J & B (Junk and Booze) Band" by insiders, who knew the illicit habits of it's members. Despite their various addictions. Coltrane pushed the music to the limits of conventional jazz. Miles, considered an enlightened bandleader, was given the freedom to develop his "sheets of sounds." Unfortunately once more Coltrane was asked to leave yet another band, because of his drug problem.

By 1966, Coltrane traded the road for religion and a wife and tried to lead a quiet life in Dix Hills, New York.. It was a little too late because he was now suffering from serious liver disease. He was brought to Huntington Hospital where he died at the age of 41.

Pinelawn Memorial Park
Pinelawn Drive
Farmingdale, New York
Directions: Take the LIE (I-495) to Wellwood Avenue exit and go south, keep going Pinelawn Cemetery is on your right. Get a map from the office and travel up the main road and make your first left. Go to the next road and make a right. Go all the way up and just before you see a division in the road by some trees make a left, then at the first road make another right. Go all the way up to an island and park. Okay as you can see it is set up like a square. Walk up the path and you'll come to a planter on your right, look for "Koesslinger" and count 20 (you'll pass over a mini path, keep counting) and he's right there.

Miles Davis
May 25, 1926 - September 28. 1991
Born in St Louis, Missouri. he played his first trumpet at age thirteen. After a brief two week engagement with the Billy Eckstine orchestra, Miles headed to New York to attend the Julliard School of Music. After a semester, he became a member of Charlie Parker's quartet and moved in with him. For the next several years, Miles performed and recorded with Benny Carter, Coleman Hawkins, and Billy Eckstine. Eckstine had once said, earlier in Miles' career that "..he sounded terrible, he couldn't play at all." Later he noted his improvement and praised him.

In the 40's, Miles became involved in drugs and was arrested in 1948 for the first time. If it had not been for his drug addiction he could have enjoyed living large. Frequently he led a pathetic existance often without money, ending up in the streets or at a friend's apartment.

Miles found himself hopelessly addicted to drugs for four years. Finally he broke free of his habit cold turkey only to find himself plagued by a number of illnesses. His voice was reduced to an often imitated whisper that became chronic.

In 1970's, Davis' music was less of a concern to the press, as they focused attention more often on his contradictory cliches regarding race, women and other musicians. He was described as bitter, hostile, and arrogant. In interviews he seemed obsessed with analyzing everything in terms of race, which sometimes was detrimental to his popularity.

His health and strength slowly disappeared in his last year of life. Despite this he continued to tour and record. His final concert was performed at the Hollywood Bowl. Two weeks later he was admitted to a hospital in Santa Monica, California. He died there from complications from pneumonia and a stroke.

Sir Miles Davis
In Memory Of
1926 — 1991

Woodlawn Cemetery, Bronx, New York

Miles' funeral was a private service which was held at the Woodlawn Cemetery where he is buried.

Woodlawn Cemetery
Webster Ave and E. 233rd Street
Bronx, New York
Directions: Take the Bronx River Parkway north and exit at 233rd Street. Turn left and Woodlawn Cemetery is right there. Go to the office and get a map of this cemetery because it is very large and filled with notable people. Go to the Intersection of Heather, Fir and Knollwood Avenue you'll see the large billboard type black onyx headstone on the corner.

Tommy Dorsey
November 19, 1905 - November 26, 1956
    Determined not to see his sons follow in his professional footsteps as a coal miner, the elder Dorsey taught both sons the fundamentals of music. As a teenager along with his brother, Tommy formed *"Dorsey's Novelty Six"* and later *"Dorsey's Wild Canaries."* By the 1920's Tommy was in big demand by such prominent dance orchestras as those led by Jean Goldkette and Paul Whiteman.
    Dorsey moved from his Pennsylvania hometown to New York where he was successful in both the studio and pit orchestras. He teamed up with his brother to form the *"Dorsey Brothers Orchestra."*
    In a highly publicized fight at the Astor Hotel, the two brothers ended a successful union, that would deprive many of their combined talent. After Tommy's last set was done, Jimmy and Tommy exchanged a few snide remarks. Then, suddenly Tommy whacked Jimmy in the face and knocked him to the floor. Jimmy immediately jumped up, chairs went flying, and the two world famous millionaire bandleaders were in a full blown fist fight like a pair of adolescent school boys. The problem was, that the room was filled with reporters at the time of the incident, and the fallout became front page news. It would take the death of their father, fifteen years later before the two would talk again.
    In the 1950's, despite the decline in popularity for big bands, the brothers resurrected the *"Dorsey Brothers Orchestra"* which was particulary successful.
    In November of 1956, Tommy returned to his Greenwich, Connecticut estate on Flagler Drive after a concert at the Statler Hotel. After playing with his children, Stephen and Susan, the bandleader had dinner with his wife and mother, Later that night, he took several sleeping tablets and fell into a deep sleep. The following morning a servant discovered his body. He drowned in his own vomit, failing to awaken after he became ill.
    His funeral was attended by many celebrities who adored his music. The coffin was covered with purple orchids and golden chrysanthemums sent by Jackie Gleason. Over it hung a wreath of flowers circling a brass trombone, a fitting tribute from Louis Armstrong.
    After the service, pallbearers Gleason, Tex Benecke, Guy Lombardo and Joe Venuti accompanied the casket to historic Kensico Cemetery in Valhalla, New York.

Kensico Cemetery
273 Lakeview Avenue
Valhalla, New York
Directions: Take the Taconic Parkway to Tarrytown Rd exit the cemetery is right there.Get the cemetery's beautiful celebrity map. Then travel up Tecumseh Avenue, drive past the lake and turn left onto Cherokee Avenue. Park just past the intersection of Ossippee and Cherokee. On the right, just off the road you'll see a headstone with Dorsey and then a flat marker with a trombone, that's him.

THOMAS F. DORSEY JR.
"TOMMY"

NOVEMBER 19, 1905
NOVEMBER 26, 1956

The Sentimental Gentleman

Kensico Cemetery, Valhalla, New York

Benny Goodman
May 30, 1909- June 13, 1986

Born in abject poverty in Chicago's immigrant district, Benjamin David Goodman began his career with the Hull House Band. Although the musical repertoire was limited to marches and popular American tunes, Benny was more inspired by the jazz sounds of the King Oliver Band, Bix Beiderbecke and Dixieland from New Orleans.

He made his first recordings at age 19 for the Victor label. Though considered a dance orchestra the music allowed for solo improvisation. In 1935, Benny played in New York as a freelance studio player. This finally allowed him to attain the success with his brand of hot swing jazz.

A two month concert engagement in Los Angeles developed into a national tour that caused riots, crowd control problems, and the then unheard of dancing in the aisles. For the next ten years Benny had the hottest band in the nation. Despite the Depression and World War II, Goodman was touring the U.S. and Europe, playing 300 days a year, sometimes doing up to six performances a day, and making over a million dollars a year.

By the 1950's Benny was making records for Columbia, RCA and Capital and even had his own TV show. In the late 60's, he began to play classical music in addition to jazz and was the featured soloist with many symphonies for six to ten dates a year.

Although his role as an influential musician was over, his status as an elder statesman of jazz was intact. However, the years of touring and the lifestyle took their toll on his health. By now, he was suffering from arthritis in the hands, chronic knee problems, and a weakened heart, which required a pace maker. Benny continued to play selected dates and even scheduled a tour for the West coast for late 1986. Unfortunately he never made the tour.

After spending some time relaxing at his home in St. Maarten in the Caribbean, Benny came back to his home in New York that summer. Later that day, while practicing his clarinet, he died of a heart attack. He was discovered by a friend with his clarinet and the Brahms Sonata opus #120 on the music stand beside him.

Long Ridge Cemetery
Long Ridge Road
Stamford, Connecticut

From: From I-95 to exit 8, Atlantic Street turns into Bedford Street continue until split in the road Long Ridge Road and High Ridge, bear left and take Long Ridge. Keep going until you see a flashing light Erskind Road make a left and go about two miles Long Ridge Cemetery is on the left side. From the third drive look for "SIDAWAY" stop and get out. Walk past a boulder on your From the center road you should see "SKINNER" on your left and "ROWLAND" on your right. Start walking to the rear of the cemetery, stop where it begins to curve and go right, you should see a collapsed looking bench under a tree. Right next to that some cement squirrels and three "GOODMANS." Ben is the middle one.

Gene Krupa
January 15, 1909 - October 16, 1973

The youngest of nine kids he was born on Chicago's south side. As a boy he worked in his older brother's record store. Showing some musical ability at an early age. Gene first started on alto jazz but quickly moved to the drums. At age 13, he was already playing in several speakeasies and gin joints that flourished during Prohibition.

In 1936, Gene hooked up with Goodman and Teddy Wilson for the first incarnation of the Benny Goodman Trio. Two year later the group played Carnegie Hall in a highly acclaimed jazz concert. The concert, featuring the Benny Goodman Quartet with an appearance by Jass Stacey and members of Duke Ellington's band, initially had a rough start. However, by the time Gene started the jungle rhythm on his tom-tom to signal the start of "Sing, Sing, Sing," the crowd was already joyously applauding the arrival of the Swing Era.

BENJAMIN DAVID GOODMAN

1903

1986

Long Ridge Cemetery, Stamford, Connecticut

The Swing Era lasted about ten years, but unfortunately for Gene, he didn't get to enjoy it's popularity. He was dismissed from the group because the others did not want to share the spotlight. Musicians being the hams that they are, found Gene's rising popularity unsettling. By the time of the Carnegie Hall concert, Benny was forced by Gene's fans to allow him several lengthy drumsolos in each performance. Benny in an attempt to cut off his nose to spite his face, fired Gene. It didn't matter that they were receiving great reviews and money, the bottom line was that Benny had to be number one at all costs.

However Gene was good natured about his dismissal and once remarked to another fired musician, "Just remember, baby, he's fired the best." Within weeks of his departure, he had his own band and was touring the U.S. to great acclaim. At the same time he was voted top drummer by several magazines and made his move west to play and star in several feature films. He even reunited with Benny for short tour and later played for bandleader Tommy Dorsey's group.

By June, 1973, Gene was in the latter part of his career and teamed up with Benny , Teddy and Lionel for a reunion of the Quartet in New York. There was another appearance by the group the following week and a final concert in August at Saratoga Springs.

Just four months later, Gene died in his home in Yonkers, New York of leukemia. Two days after his death, his body was flown to Chicago for burial in his family plot.

Holy Cross Cemetery
801 Michigan City Road
Calumet City, Illinois
Directions: Take I-94 exit Sibley Road east turn south on Torrence Ave to Michigan City Road go east. Go to the Immaculate Section, park at the end of the section. Walk up until you see "P. SADOWSKI" Gene is directly behind that.

Buddy Rich
September 30, 1917 - April 2, 1987
Born into a vaudevillian family, show business was instilled in him at the early age of two. Then he started playing the drums and tap dancing for the Broadway show *"Pinwheel."* Buddy toured Australia at the age of six as *"Baby Traps -the Drum Wonder."*

By 11, Buddy played his first jazz gigs with Art Shapiro and Hot Lips Page, and two years later he moved into the big leagues of swing. By time he was 23, he had recorded with Harry James, Artie Shaw and Tommy Dorsey.

From 1939- 46, Buddy remained with the Tommy Dorsey Orchestra. At his best he pushed the band with flair and fire playing on several of Dorsey's 200 plus hits. At his worst he was brutally outspoken and made no effort to hid his intense dislike of Tommy and his choice of music.

In 1946, Frank Sinatra bankrolled the first of many Buddy Rich Big Bands, but it was a critical and financial failure. This failure was one of many things that dissolved their friendship.

Throughout the 50's and most of the 60's, Buddy teamed up with Harry James on many of his recordings and live performances. Rich's showmanship, flashy drumming, and talent for self promotion made him the group centerpiece. Aside from a two year hiatus due to a heart attack. Rich was now the highest paid orchestral musician at $1500 a gig.

Buddy left James for good in 1966 to reform his own group. Fronting a 16 piece big band. Buddy emphasized raw power. He was criticized by hard core jazz enthusiasts, for adding Beatles and Paul Simon tunes on his records.

Touring nine months out of the year, Buddy starred in his own TV variety show in 1968 and lent his name to a jazz club in LA. Rich trimmed his band down to a smaller combo for the early 70's, but then later reformed the full orchestra for the remainder of the decade.

Despite bypass surgery in 1985, Rich was back on the road and in the studio two weeks later. Rich's many appearances on TV talk shows and his flamboyant condemnation of certain types of music made him a controversial figure whose public personality often obscured his talent. But that didn't bother him, because he was still he was still popular. For the last 50 years of his career, he sold out every show he played.

Holy Cross Cemetery, Calumet City, Illinois

GENE B. KRUPA

1909 1973

SON

Buddy's active schedule came to a halt in the summer of 1987 when Buddy was diagnosed with brain cancer. The day before he died a new nurse came to his room and asked if he was allergic to anything. His reply was, "Only two things, Country and Western." He died on April 2nd, at the age of 70.

Westwood Memorial Park
1218 Glendon Avenue
Los Angeles, California
For directions to the cemetery see Marilyn Monroe in the Glamour Girls Chapter. As you enter the cemetery make a left and park. Walk to the Sanctuary of Tranquillity. As you enter the alcove, he is the second tomb on the bottom row.

Mel Torme
September 13, 1925 - June 5, 1999
This velvet voiced Melvin Howard Torme was born in Chicago to Russian Jewish immigrants. The family's name was originally "Torma," but it was changed by an immigration agent to Torme.

His parents who were poor immigrants urged him at an early age to pursue the American dream. The easiest way combined with his talent was undoubtedly show business. So they coaxed the 4 year old on stage, to sing with a restaurant band for $15 a session. By the time he hit 6, his career as an actor was booming, with steady work in vaudeville units and on the radio.

Torme left Chicago for Los Angeles in 1942 and attended Hollywood High School while singing with the Chico Marx Band. Later, Torme organized, led, composed and arranged for and sang with the Mel-Tunes, a group made up of students from the Los Angeles City College.

Newly on his own, he took the train to New York and was greeted by bobby-soxers waving signs that stated "Welcome Velvet Fog!. Somebody told me," he said in an interview with *The Times* in 1965, "that a local disc jockey named Freddie Robbins was playing my records 29 times a day and calling me the Velvet Fog or Mr Butterscotch or the one that really flipped me, "Gauze in His Jaws."

To his credit his success was not just in music, he acted in the musical motion pictures of the late 40's and 50's. He made his official debut in 1943 'Higher and Higher," starring another singer, Frank Sinatra. After that he would appear in five other films. He made many guest appearances on television programs, and his most memorable was a recurring role on "*Night Court*," which ran from 1984 - 92. The running joke on the show was that Torme was the musical idol of Harry Anderson's unhip character, Judge Harry T. Stone. Another television appearance was on sitcom, "*Seinfeld*," where he was cast in a cameo role where he serenaded a "retarded" Kramer.

His last performance was in Orange Grove, N.J., just prior to his stroke. He seemed to be in good spirits and health. In 1996, Mel suffered a stroke, which affected his speech and weakened him physically, forcing him to cancel his 20th annual appearance at the Hollywood Bowl, where he was customarily greeted by enthusiastic crowds.

On June 5, 1999, at 1 am, Mel began to experience difficulty breathing at his Beverly Hills home. He was rushed to UCLA Medical Center, where he later died from complications of the stroke he suffered in 1996. He was 73.

Westwood Memorial Park
1218 Glendon Avenue
Los Angeles, California
For directions to the cemetery see Marilyn Monroe in the Glamour Girls Chapter. As you enter the cemetery go left and park. To your left you will see a smaller patch of lawn with tombstones and some mausoleums. His is perhaps the largest tombstone there. It's maroon in color and easy to find.

Westwood Memorial Park, Los Angeles, California

BUDDY RICH
ONE OF A KIND
1917 — 1987

Westwood Memorial Park, Los Angeles, California

CARL PERKINS

APR. 9,
1932

JAN. 19,
1998

Chapter 18: The Day the Music Died....
Rock and Roll
1950's
Carl Perkins
April 9, 1932 - January 19, 1998

Carl was born the son of a poor Tennessee tenant farmer who wanted a better life for his son. Like most from that part of the country, music seemed to be the most easiest way to escape poverty. His father made Carl a guitar from a cigar box, a broomstick and bailing wire. At the age of 7, he started playing and perhaps was on his way to what would be a life long career. But before entering the music business full-time he was forced to support himself as a farmer, a bakery worker and then finally a disc jockey. No matter what profession he was in, he still continued to play, sing and write country songs.

After organizing a band, he got an audition with Sam Phillips of Sun Record Company. Coincidentally it was the same Memphis recording studio that spawned Presley and popularized rockabilly: a fusion of country rhythm, blues and rock music.

Perkins' first recording, *"Movie Magg,"* generated few sales, as did his second recording. His third recording, released on December 19, 1955, was *"Blue Suede Shoes."* This hit sold 2 million copies even before Presley did the song. It was the first ever to reach the top of the sales charts in all three major categories: pop, country, and rhythm and blues.

As bad luck would have it, a near fatal car accident prevented Perkins from performing his own song on both *"The Ed Sullivan Show"* and *"The Perry Como Show."* It was March, 1956, while on route to both shows that their car crashed near Dover, Delaware. The accident killed his brother and broke his neck. The wreck not only kept him from a once in a lifetime opportunity, but it also shattered his confidence in his musical ability. For many years after the accident, he stopped writing and singing. Instead Elvis introduced the world to rockabilly and made musical history, singing many hits, included Carl's *"Blue Suede Shoes."*

Although fame and a career of being a solo star eluded him, he still was recognized as a monumental song writer. Carl wrote for many popular stars including The Beatles, Patsy Cline, Dolly Parton, The Judds, George Strait, Johnny Cash, and many more.

He blamed the accident for his 15 year battle with the bottle, which he evenually overcame. Then when he was on the road to recovery and good health, he encountered a bout with throat and lung cancer. In November and December of 1997, Perkins suffered three strokes that left him weak. He never recovered from those strokes and in January he was taken to Jackson-Madison County General Hospital in Nashville, where he later died He was 65.

Ridgecrest Cemetery
200 Ridgecrest Road
Jackson, Tennessee

Directions: From I-40 get off at the 82B Highland Avenue South exit. The first light make a left and continue on Ridgecrest Road the cemetery is on your right. Go to the rear of the cemetery where the crypts are. He's in the second one from the top, 7th from left to right.

Elvis Presley
January 8, 1935 - August 16, 1977

After his 1973 divorce from his wife, Priscilla, Elvis' career began to wane. His finances were in a shambles and his rapid weight gain began to worry him. In an effort to regain his former image, he embarked on a regiment of pills and dieting to lose the weight rapidly.

In order for him to seriously lose the weight and at the same time maintain his health, he needed to change his life completely. This was something that he was not prepared to do. His lifestyle of staying up all night partying and then sleeping all day gave his life little structure, which only added to his health problems.

Graceland, Memphis, Tennessee

Although there were bad influences around him, there were also people who genuinely cared for him. Unfortunately those that cared were doomed to be witnesses to his self-destructive tendencies. If they were brave enough to attempt to "discreetly" counsel him on his habits and lifestyle, he would ignore them, and if they persisted, they were gone.

Inevitably it was this lifestyle that led to his early demise. On the morning of August 16, 1977, Elvis played a game of racquet ball and then retired to his living room where he played perhaps his last song, *"Unchained Melody."* After that, it is presumed that he went up to his bedroom where he was later found on the floor of his bathroom (the coroner's report states he was found on the floor of his dressing room) by then girlfriend, Ginger Alden. He had been laying there for about three hours before being discovered. Despite the length of time passed, and the early stages of rigor mortis setting in, all attempts were made to save "the King." Their efforts of course failed and he was pronounced dead at 3:30 am at a Memphis Hospital (now renamed Elvis Presley Memorial), by his personal physician George Nichopoulos.

The cause of death was announced as cardiac arrhythmia, an irregular heartbeat, which was brought on by "undetermined causes.' A more precise cause of death was due to drug dependency, obesity, high blood pressure and a weak heart.

An autopsy was ordered to find out the exact cause. One of the things the autopsy did find was that his death was attributed to clogged arteries. The most important thing that killed "The King" was the long list of "prescription" drugs that he ingested on a regular basis. Fourteen different drugs were detected in his blood stream by the autopsy, also included were toxic levels of methoqualone and ten times the normal dosage of codeine.

Elvis was taken from the hospital to the Memphis Funeral Home where he was prepared for viewing and burial. His final outfit was a white suit, white tie, and blue shirt. In order to fit Elvis' girth, a 900 pound steel lined copper coffin was specially ordered from Oklahoma. The next day, Elvis was brought back to Graceland for a public viewing.

Originally Elvis was buried in Forest Hill Cemetery at 1661 Elvis Presley Blvd. On October 3rd Vernon Presley, then applied for permits to have son and wife exhumed and brought to Graceland for burial. There were two reasons for this move, one, two guys attempted to steal "The King" one night so Vernon thought that Elvis would be safer in a more protected environment. Two, it would be financially advantageous to have Elvis buried in Graceland as an added attraction.

If you want to by pass the tours and just visit Elvis' grave you should arrive prior to 7:30am. The Graceland staff will allow you to walk to the grave and pay your respects. If you come later in the day (like I did), you will encounter long lines, the obligatory ride on the tour bus, complete with narrated tour by both Priscilla and Elvis, and of course the $12 fee.

Also never go on "The King's" birthday or the anniversary of his death (unless you are a hard core Elvis fan and don't mind crowds) or you will encounter a mob. I visited the day before his death's anniversary (dubbed Elvis week), and already there were Elvis impersonators camping out, preparing for the next day's festivities. Also there is a yearly ritual, (that has taken place since the first anniversary of his death) where thousands from around the world gather to pay tribute to "The King." At night, everyone is given candles as they line up in the world's longest line to walk up Graceland's drive-way and past Elvis' grave to pay their respects.

As you approach Graceland, you'll notice the onslaught of graffiti left by his adoring fans. Everything is covered with exception to the historical marker which is coated with wipeable plastic. Apparently this tradition began when Elvis first put up the wall a year after he purchased Graceland. Since then the tone of the graffiti has changed from love notes to notes of sympathy and tribute. After seeing many photos of Graceland, I was disappointed in it's size. Being that Elvis was such a mega star I expected to see "Tara" from *"Gone With the Wind,"* instead it seemed only like a large colonial house.

Recently Elvis' daughter, Lisa Marie had expressed her disgust on how her father's grave has turned into a side show attraction. She apparently is considering having him moved to a secret location. Perhaps she has forgotten that, had they not turned it into a tourist trap, Elvis' estate would have been forced to sell Graceland and her trust fund would have been quite barren. Elvis had a reputation for spending money faster than he made it, leaving him at the time of his death, with only $500,000 in liquid assets.

Forest Hill Cemetery, Elvis' prior place of interment, once kept the king's empty crypt on display as a tribute, and perhaps to attract people to visit their cemetery. But since overzealous fans were destroying the place, the cemetery has since thought it wise to remove Elvis' name and to put the crypt up for sale at an exorbitant price.

Forest Hill Cemetery
1661 S. Elvis Presley Blvd.
Memphis, Tennessee
Removed From Crypt C to
Graceland Mansion
3734 Elvis Presley Blvd.
Memphis, Tennessee

Directions: From I- 55 exit 5B. If you just want to see Elvis' grave and bypass the whole Graceland thing, follow the signs to the pool. There you will find them, Elvis, his father Vernon, his mother Gladys, and his grandmother. Tip: Be EXTREMELY respectful when there, most Elvis fans are very serious about their idol and will not hesitate to let you know if you are stepping out of line.

The Winter Dance Party

On January, 1959 all three musicians embarked on a trip to perform at the *"Winter Dance Party,"* a two month tour of the Midwest. While traveling from gig to gig the entertainers experienced the most horrendous conditions imaginable. There were no breaks in the schedule. The bus they chartered had no heat and repeatedly broke down leaving them constantly stranded in the harsh mid-western winter. There were no managers to arrange details at each show, so when they arrived at the show's venue, there would always be chaos.

Fed up with the road, Buddy chartered a private plane for himself and his two remaining band members, Waylon Jennings and Tommy Allsup.(Luckily for the third member, drummer Carl Bunch, he was in the hospital with frostbite). They arrived at the airport and met their 21 year old pilot, Roger Peterson and Jerry Dwyer who owned the plane at 12:40 am. It was a little before 1:00 am when the single engine aircraft took off. Peterson was not experienced to fly under conditions requiring navigation by instruments. It is also speculated that he also did not see the special advisories concerning poor visibility.

Most likely Peterson became confused during the flight as he attempting to read the unfamiliar gyroscope, thinking he was ascending. But instead they were descending causing the plane to crash only eight miles after take off. All three were thrown from the wreckage and killed. With exception to Peterson whose body was pinned in the crumpled plane. The wreckage was not spotted until 9:35 the next morning.

Despite the tragedy, *"The Winter Dance Party"* tour continued. A then unknown singer Bobby Vee was asked to open the concert in Moorhead, Minnesota. Two other new rockers, Fabian and Paul Anka were also added to replace the deceased singers.

IN LOVING MEMORY
OF OUR OWN

BUDDY HOLLEY

SEPTEMBER 7, 1936
FEBRUARY 3, 1959

City of Lubbock Cemetery, Lubbock, Texas

The crash took place on Albert Juhl's corn field that is now owned by the Nicholas family. The spring after the crash, when things began to thaw, Mr Juhl was planting hay in the field were the accident took place. There he found lots of plane parts, a few body parts and a few personal items. Everything was collected and put into an envelope to be stored at the county courthouse. In 1980, someone found the envelope that contained Buddy's glasses, four dice and a watch that belonged to the Big Bopper. These items were returned to the families..

Buddy Holly
September 7, 1936 - February 3, 1959

Born and raised in Lubbock, Texas, Buddy's musical beginnings were the result of the encouragement of both parents. As a child he played both the guitar and the piano. In high school, he formed *"Buddy and Bob."* They recorded a hit and opened for Elvis. After that, both Elvis and Buddy became good friends and were often seen together, cruising downtown Lubbock for girls. I guess that was before they invented groupies.

In 1955, he formed the group *"The Crickets,"* their first hit was *"That'll Be The Day."* In 1958, Buddy amicably split with *"The Crickets"* to record on his own. Around that same time Buddy, dropped his longtime manager and producer Norman Petty due to some unresolved financial misdealings. He spent most of his time writing songs at a feverish pace. In two short months he wrote and recorded in his apartment in Greenwich Village, New York, what would later be called *"The Basement Tapes."*

His former manager, Petty, froze Buddy's funds in New Mexico prevented him from getting any of his money. With no new jobs on the horizon, he was left little choice but to go on the ill fated *"Winter Dance Party."* The rest is Rock and Roll History....

Just seventeen feet from the wreckage lay Buddy in the frozen snow. Next to his leg was a large brown suitcase and his trademark glasses. Fine snow fell after the crash, partially covering his body. Some parts of his body was frozen due to the ten hours of exposure to the cold in temperatures that reached near 18 degrees that night.

Buddy's body was removed by acting coroner, Ralph E. Smiley. Upon examination it was determined that he died instantly from gross brain trauma. The coroner's report is as follows:

> The body of Charles H. Holley was clothed in an outer jacket of yellow leather, like material in which four seams in the back were split almost full length. The skull was was split medially in the forehead and this extended into the vertex region. Approx-imately half the brain tissue was absent. There was bleeding from both ears and the face showed multiple lacerations. The consistency of the chest was soft due to exten-sive crushing injury to the bony structure. The left forearm was fractured 1/3 the way up from the wrist and the right elbow was fractured. Both thighs and legs show-ed multiple fractures. There was a small laceration of the scrotum.

The fee for the coroner examination was $11.65, which was promptly deducted from the $193.00 found on Buddy's person.

Buddy was brought back to his hometown of Lubbock, Texas where his funeral was held at the Tabernacle Baptist Church. Over a thousand mourners attended the service, but his widow did not. Pregnant at the time of his death, she later lost the baby.

He is now interred in the City of Lubbock Cemetery. As you enter the gate there is a historical marker memorialize him. It ends by saying, "it is customary to place a guitar pick on the headstone so that the 'music lives on.'" He is buried along with his parents, Lawrence and Ella.

City of Lubbock Cemetery
201 East 34th Street
Lubbock, Texas
Section 44

IN LOVING MEMORY
JILES P. RICHARDSON, JR.
(THE BIG BOPPER)
OCT. 24, 1930 – FEB. 3, 1959

Forest Lawn Memorial Parks, Beaumont, Texas

Direction: From hwy 84 turn right on MLK Boulevard after you drive under the Loop 289 bridge at the south end of town. Drive north, past 50th Street, and over the bridge that goes over the railroad tracks, At the end of the bridge turn right onto 31st Street ans Teak Avenue you will see the cemetery. Drive through the gates and you will soon see the Holley plots located on the first row next to the road. This is a replacement tombstone, the original one was stolen.

J.P. Richardson - "The Big Bopper"
October 24, 1930 - February 3, 1959

The "Big Bopper," was born during the Great Depression in Sabine Pass, Texas. His mother was perhaps the only musical influence on him. She was an accomplished pianist and guitarist, who would entertain her sons for hours. J.P. fell in love with music and the idea of performing. His first job in the entertainment industry was in radio. He worked as a disc jockey playing popular hits which earned him the name, "The Big Bopper."

He then began to write his own songs which were gaining rapid popularity, especially with the teen market. When he was offered billing in *"The Winter Dance Party,"* he jumped at the opportunity. Little did he know this would be the worse decision he could have ever made...

Richardson's body was found lying forty feet from the wreckage, across the fence in a cornfield. Near him was a brown briefcase that was perfectly intact with all of it's contents.He was brought back to his hometown, Beaumont, Texas for burial. His wake was held in the Broussard's Funeral home. Elvis Presley and Colonel Tom Parker sent yellow roses to his funeral.

Beaumont is a small town located in southeast Texas. The day I arrived there it was pouring rain and the skies were dark gray. Not the best conditions for photography. I entered the office of the cemetery that he is buried in and met his cousin. She told me a few little stories that I had never heard before. She told me that Waylon Jennings had exchanged seats with J.P. Ever since that, Jennings has experienced extreme guilt for that decision.

Someday she would like to see a monument erected in his honor near the gravesite. The briefcase that was found at the crash site is now on display in the Janis Joplin Museum in Port Arthur, Texas.

Forest Lawn Memorial Park
4955 Pine Street
Beaumont, Texas

Directions: From Hwy 96 traveling south, drive past the Park Dale Mall on your right and take then next exit, Lucas Street. Turn left and drive about four miles to the end of the road. Cross Pine Street into the cemetery. Drive across the street from the office make the 1st left and park. On the left side of will be his grave, look for "Mitchell" in the second row, there are two together to the left of The Big Bopper. Lily Pool Garden Section

Richie Valens
May 13, 1941 - February 3, 1959

Richard Valenzuela was born in the San Fernando Valley of California. His family loved music and he was influenced by the sounds of the Mexican Mariachi bands. Despite his family's Mexican roots, Richie never learned to speak Spanish. It was his cousin who taught him how to pronounce the words to *"La Bamba,"* which later became a national hit.

In 1958, Bob Keane of Del-Fi Records, paid a visit to San Fernando to see a band called, *"The Silhouettes."* There he saw member Ritchie Valens for the first time. He signed Valens immediately and invited him to cut some demos. His first single was a hit and Ritchie became the first Latino singer to gain success in the pop music industry.

In January, 1959, Ritchie began that ill fated tour, *"The Winter Dance Party."* The trip was terrible and cold, but Ritchie's dedication to his fans kept him from canceling the tour. When he heard that Buddy Holly had chartered a plane for his band, Ritchie tried to persuade Tommy Allsup to give up his seat on the plane. Finally a coin toss would decide Ritchie's fate forever....

On Saturday, February 7th, Ritchie's body was taken from the Noble Chapel Funeral Home in the San Fernando Valley, to San Fernando Mission Cemetery by a copper colored hearse. He is interred in a medium sized cemetery that is host to several other stars. The cemetery is located in the San Fernando area, which is the area where he grew up. It is quiet and not as busy as the City of Los Angeles..

Concepción Reyes shares the same slate headstone as her son, Ritchie. Apparently the two were both musically inclined, due the references on the tombstones as pictured.

San Fernando Mission Cemetery

11160 Stranwood Avenue

San Fernando, California

For directions to the cemetery see Scott Beckett in The Little Rascals Chapter. As you drive through the gates, stay to the right and drive straight ahead just past the flower shop on the right. Park on the left where you see the number 247 on the curb. His black and silver stone is three rows off the road on the left.

1960's
Sonny Bono - "Sonny and Cher"
February 16, 1935 - January 5, 1998

He was born Salvatore Phillip Bono and began his musical career in the sixties His first hit was *"Needles and Pins,"* a song he composed in 1964. That same year he borrowed $175 to record *"Baby Don't Go,"* with his soon to be wife, Cherilyn LaPiere Sarkisian. The song landed the duo a recording contract, under the name *"Sonny and Cher."* From that point on they recorded such hits as *"I Got You, Babe"* and *"The Beat Goes On."*

In the 70's, things began to slow down for Sonny as his marriage to Cher fell apart. Trying to sustain his career without his wife was not going to work, so he abandoned the entertainment business to open a string of successful restaurants. But after running into some bureaucracy at city hall in Palm Springs, he decided to try yet another career, one in politics.

He was elected mayor of Palm Springs for a duration of 1988 to 1992. After that he ran for the Senate and lost, but two years later made a bid for Congress and won. In 1996, he was re-elected again, but announced that this would be the last time, he now wanted to now spend more time with his family.

While vacationing with his family in Lake Tahoe, Nevada, Sonny was killed in a skiing accident. According to the Douglas County, Sheriff's Department, Bono did not return from a skiing run at the end of the day. It was two hours after being reported missing, that his body was found. He reportedly died of head injuries after running head on, into a tree on an intermediate slope of the Heavenly Ski Resort. The accident was considered odd, because he was an experienced skier who had skied that same slope for more than twenty years.

Later it was revealed that Sonny was taking a large number of pain pills daily to cope with constant pain that he suffered in a prior accident. It is believed that he was mentally impaired when he hit the tree, due to the effects of the medication.

His funeral was a huge star studded affair complete with a teary Cher who eulogized him. Sonny is interred in the same city that he ruled as mayor: Palm Springs. The cemetery in which Sonny is interred is very receptive to visitors. In fact they have a little booklet made up with all their celebrity locations. They boast more about Sinatra than Sonny, which I thought was rather strange, especially since Bono was mayor.

VALENZUELA

BELOVED MOTHER & SISTER
CONCEPCION REYES
"CONCHA"

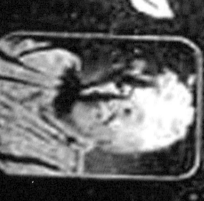

OCT. 6, 1915 — OCT. 18, 1987

"LA BAMBA"

BELOVED SON & BROTHER
RICHARD STEVEN
"RITCHIE VALENS"

MAY 13, 1941 — FEB. 3, 1959

"COME ON LET'S GO"

San Fernando Mission Cemetery, San Fernando, California

Sonny Bono

1935 - 1998

AND THE BEAT GOES ON

Desert Memorial Park, Cathedral City, California

Anyway, Sinatra and Bono are the only two with American flags on their graves so this makes them pretty easy to find.

Desert Memorial Park (Palm Springs Cemetery District)
69920 Ramon Road
Cathedral City, California
Directions: From I-10 get off at the Ramon Road exit, continue on Ramon Road and you will see the cemetery on your right. Go in and get a map or follow my directions and go directly to Sonny's grave. From the office, travel up the road until you see a fountain court waterfall, park there and walk to the left of it and then go straight ahead, Sonny is there. Grave location: B-35 #294

Carl Wilson "The Beach Boys"
December 21, 1946 - February 6, 1998

In 1961, Carl Dean Wilson along with brothers Dennis, Brian and cousin Mike Love formed the group *The Beach Boys*. Still only a teenagers, *The Beach Boys* had their first hit on the charts.

Most of the songs were about sun, surf and girls, the typical California lifestyle. However, the band's upbeat music had a dark side that started with an abusive father who managed the band with an iron hand. Also there was drug and alcohol abuses, a mental breakdown for Brian, and the drowning death of Dennis in 1983. In 1981, Carl left the band because he felt that their music had reached its potential and was now becoming too nostalgic. To avoid being though of as a has been, old man group he pursued a solo career for a short time. Later he rejoined what was left of The Beach Boys and performed up until his death.

At the age of 51, Carl died with his family at his side, of lung and brain cancer. Carl's now resting in good company, he shares a cemetery with many other famous people, including fellow contemporary musicians Roy Orbison and Frank Zappa. His grave marker is a simple marker that evokes a lot of love his family must have had for him. The words, " The world is a far lesser place without you," reminds me of one of their songs, called "God Only Knows What I'd Be Without You." Maybe this is weird but most tombstones I've seen, represent a feeling of something cold and dead. I didn't get that feeling from his, I felt kind of good. Who knows maybe I was getting "Good Vibrations" from him...sorry.

Westwood Cemetery
1218 Glendon Avenue
Los Angeles
For directions to the cemetery see Marilyn Monroe in the Glamour Girls Chapter. Once in the cemetery bear left and park. Walk complete around until you are almost to the chapel. Walk approximately two row in you should see his big tombstone.

1970's and 1980's
Karen Carpenter - "The Carpenters"
February 2, 1950 - February 4, 1983

When people were turning to hard rock in the 70's, The Carpenter's provided a breath of fresh air with their unique style of music. Their repertoire of love songs were rich with Richard's arrangements and Karen's vocals.

Karen was born in New Haven, Connecticut and grew up in a typically middle class environment. Later due to her father's health problems, her family moved west to California, while she and her brother were in their teens. It was her brother, Richard who had an ear for music and practiced everyday, while Karen pursued other interests. It wasn't until her late teens, that Karen followed in her brother's footsteps in music, as a drummer, not a vocalist.

The Heart and Voice of an Angel

♥ CARL DEAN WILSON ♥

DEC. 21, 1946 – FEB. 6, 1998

The World is a Far Lesser Place Without You

Westwood Memorial Park, Los Angeles, California

Their big break came as they performed and reached the finals of *"The Battle of the Bands, "* at the Hollywood Bowl. They were signed to a contract with RCA records as *"The Richard Carpenter Trio."* But nothing came of it.

After this initial disappointment Richard and new song writing partner John Bettis landed an unusual residency as a duo playing the *"Coke Corner"* on Main Street in Disneyland. After five months of faking banjo and standard Americana tunes, they were fired for being too radical. In the meantime, Karen tried out as drummer for Kenny Roger's First Edition, but was turned down.

Finally, in the Spring of 1969, their demo tape landed on the desk of Herb Albert, and they were instantly signed to a recording contract with A&M Records. Since Karen was only 19 she needed her mother's to sign for her. All was well as they enjoyed their successes. Four albums went gold, and every one of their concerts were sold out. Karen wanted more. She wanted to get married and settle down. Unfortunately, these things never happened for her.

As they toured into the eighties, Karen would tire easily. She lost weight and her appetite diminished; she was suffering from Anorexia Nervosa. Her weight dropped below 80 pounds, even at 5 foot 3, this is a very low weight to maintain.

Who knew that a stupid comment about her weight, would send her on an emotional tailspin that would kick off an uncontrollable eating disorder. She was now intent to do anything she could to keep her weight down, even if it meant starving herself to death.

After six years of battling this disease, Karen looked as though she was on the road to recovery. She gained fifteen pounds and she was proudly telling everyone. Unfortunately the ipecac syrup she took to induce vomiting and the thyroid medicine to increase her metabolism to burn calories, took its toll on her, permanently damaging her heart.

On Friday, February 4th Agnes, Karen's mom, woke up at 8:45 to prepare to go to the hairdresser. There was a noise in Karen's room, a rumbling. Agnes called out to Karen but received no response. Upon entering Karen's room, she found Karen lying in the closet, eyes rolled back in her head and no longer breathing. Agnes immediately called for both the paramedics and Karen's brother Richard, who lived around the block. It was too late, Karen was dead from heart failure. According to a coroners report she died of pulmonary edema (heart failure), anorexia, and cachexia (abnormally low birth weight).

Now because of the recent release of her autopsy report, there is a big controversy as to where she was really found. Now it is speculated that she was in the kitchen when she died. An ironic place for an Anorexic to die.

Four days after her death five hundred people filed into the Downey Methodist Church for her funeral. After the services, friend Herb Albert, led the pallbearers to Karen's marble crypt. The day before the funeral, Karen's ex-husband, Tom Burris threw his wedding ring into the coffin and disappeared forever.

Personally speaking when I heard that Karen Carpenter died I was really sad. I always thought that her music was so beautiful. So when I saw her final resting place I was really amazed on how equally beautiful her tomb is. A black and white photo does not do it justice. Once again, it is located in the cemetery-of-the-stars-but-stay-away, Forest Lawn, Cypress.

She is located in "The Ascension Mausoleum," in the 'Sanctuary of Compassion." As you walk in on your left you will see a stunning religious picture and below that, her crypt. She is buried with her mother and father. Next to her name is inscribed "1950-1983 A star on earth - a star in heaven." If I had been her family, I would have went the extra mile and had some of her music piped in for effect.

Forest Lawn Memorial Park
4471 Lincoln Avenue
Cypress, California
The Ascension Mausoleum, The Sanctuary of Compassion

Forest Lawn Memorial Park, Cypress, California

CARPENTER

KAREN 1950 – 1983 A STAR ON EARTH – A STAR IN HEAVEN

HAROLD 1908 – 1988 BELOVED HUSBAND, DAD AND GRANDAD

AGNES 1915 – 1996 BELOVED WIFE, MOM AND GRANDMOM

Directions: Take I-91 freeway south toward Orange County. Exit on Carmenita and turn right. Drive to Lincoln Avenue and turn right, continuing down about one mile. The cemetery on your right. Go through the gates and continue on the road, you'll see the Ascension Mausoleum on your right. Park anywhere and walk to the entrance on your left. As soon as you enter you'll see the Sanctuary of Compassion and there she is.

Andy Gibb
March 5, 1958 - March 10, 1988

Born in the Isle of Man, Great Britain, he was the youngest of the four handsome and talented Gibb brothers. While his brothers were enjoying international success in the early 70's as *The Bee Gees*, Andy was gaining attention as teen heartthrob in Australia, where he was raised.

By the late 1970's the BeeGees were considering whether to add their younger sibling to the group. But before a decision could be made, Andy hit the U.S. pop scene with his album, *'Flowing Rivers,"* produced by Barry. The first single from that album, *"I Just Want to Be Your Everything,"* hit number one on the charts in 1977. Andy was nominated for two Grammys that same year. His next two singles, *"Love is Thicker Than Water"* and *"Shadow Dancing"* also topped the charts, making Andy Gibb the first solo performer to have three consecutive "singles" hit number one. By the age of 21, Andy had sold over 15 million albums.

Most said that it was too much fame, too soon that led young Andy to develop a ferocious cocaine habit, but regardless of its origins his addiction was causing him serious problems by the early 80's . Although his pop-star/teen-idol status had diminished by that time, he was working as a host of the television dance program, *"Solid Gold"* and had been signed to star in the Broadway production of *"Joseph and the Amazing Technicolor Dreamcoats."* But despite his successes, Andy was unhappy and increasingly drug dependent. This drug problem interfered with his work and soon diminished his chances for employment.

As time went by, his unemployment problems contributed to many personal and financial problems. Eventually the once successful singer was forced into bankruptcy. His brothers encouraged him to seek help, but it wasn't until 1985 that Andy was admitted to the Betty Ford Clinic for the treatment of cocaine addiction.

Unfortunately for Andy, the damage had been done. Just five days after his 30th birthday, during the recording of an album for Island Records, Andy Gibb died. The death certificate listed the official cause of death as a viral-related heart inflammation. However at the time of his passing, rumors had been circulating that his addiction had caused permanent damage to his heart. His body was flown back to the United States to his final resting place at Forest Lawn, Hollywood Hills.

Forest Lawn Memorial Park -Hollywood Hills
6300 Forest Lawn Drive
Los Angeles, California

For directions to the cemetery see Bette Davis in the Glamour Girls Chapter. As you enter the cemetery get a cemetery map from the information booth, but do not ask for any directions to celebrity tombstones. Turn left at the Ascension Road which should lead you to the Courts of Remembrance. Walk up the path, you should see Bette Davis to your left, make a right. Andy's is an outside crypt, approximately 11 spaces from Ascension Road, second row from the bottom. The crypt number #2534, each crypt is numbered on the bottom base board.

ANDY GIBB

MARCH 5, 1958 - MARCH 10, 1988

"AN EVERLASTING LOVE"

Forest Lawn Memorial Park, Hollywood Hills, California

Terry Allan Kath - "Chicago
January 31 1946 - January 23, 1978

Born in Chicago he grew up in a musical household with plenty of opportunity for exposure to musical instruments. His brother played the drums and his mother played the banjo. By the ninth grade Terry had a guitar and amp of his own and spent his free time jamming with friends trying to duplicate the surf sounds of bands such as *"The Ventures."* By time he graduated high school he was an accomplished and self taught guitarist and bassist.

In 1966, Terry had formed a group with some friends called the *"Missing Links."* Before long they changed the name to *"Chicago Transit Authority"* (and later in 1970, shortened it to *"Chicago"*) and had taken their unique brand of jazz influenced rock on the road. The band quickly acquired a following, particulary in Los Angeles, where they were a favorite at the Whisky A-Go-Go.

Their first album, put out by Columbia in 1969, featured the hit single *"Does Anybody Really Know What Time It Is."* The early 70's were very successful years for the band as five consecutive Chicago albums topped the charts from 1972-75.

Unfortunately, the happiness was not destined to last. On January 23, 1978, Terry and his wife Camelia attended a party at the home of Don Johnson, a roadie for Chicago. Terry, an avid gun collector, brought along two guns, this was not unusual as he was frequently armed when he went out. After the party had broken up. Terry and Don were sitting around talking when Terry began playing with his guns, he spun the .38 revolver on his finger, put it to his head and snapped the trigger, the chamber was empty. Don nervously asked Terry to stop it. Terry then picked up the 9mm automatic pistol he had brought along, and in an effort to make his friend's feel more at ease, he said "Don't worry, it's not loaded." He then put the pistol to his head, and pulled the trigger. This time, he was wrong it was indeed loaded.

Terry died instantly, leaving his wife, one year old daughter and a legion of friends and family to mourn his passing. His funeral was attended by then- Governor Jerry Brown, Doc Severinsen and 400 other mourners.

Forest Lawn Memorial Park
1712 S. Glendale Avenue
Glendale, California

For directions to the cemetery see Jean Harlow in the Glamour Girls Chapter. After you enter the cemetery, get a map but don't ask for any directions. Follow the signs to the Freedom Court and head towards the Triumphant Faith Terraces. Stop and park at the Court of the Christus, you'll see a sign for this on your right hand side as you are coming from the direction of the Freedom Court. Walk up the steps to enter the court. At your immediate left is an entryway to the garden of Remembrance. Go into the garden and walk all the way through it into the second garden. At the second garden, turn right, then turn left, before the stairs, follow the path along the ten foot high wall. Walk several feet and on your right against the wall you'll find the Kath family plot.

Song Birds
Billie Holiday
April 7, 1915 - July 17, 1959

Billie Holiday was probably remembered more for the mishaps that happened in her life than for the musical endeavors she accomplished. She dated and married men who were abusive and would steal from her. Almost every penny she made went to alcohol and/or drugs. Her arrest record eclipsed her discography.

Eleanora Fagan was born in Baltimore, Maryland in 1915. Her mother was a housekeeper and her father a traveling guitarist. Her parents never married and with the news of Billie's impending birth, her father abandoned them. Still Billie adopted her father's last name at the start of her career.

Forest Lawn Memorial Park, Glendale, California

TERRY ALAN KATH

1946 — 1978

COMPOSER · GUITARIST · SINGER

THE MEMORIES OF LOVE HE LEFT ON

EARTH ALL THE WORLD HAS SHARED

ABLE AND GIFTED GENTLE MAN WHOSE

RICHES WERE A SYMPHONY OF EMOTION

YOUNG AND OLD BECAUSE HE CARED

♫ OUR LOVED ONE ♫

She her singing career in small Harlem nightclubs sometime around 1931. Later she toured for awhile with the Count Basie's and Artie Shaw's bands. Not much of her work with either of them is left as they were all signed to different labels. Some of her best jazz recordings, in which she was joined by many great artists such as pianist Teddy Wilson, were made between 1935 to 1942.

By 1950, Billie's life began its steady slide downward. Her voice was failing and she was troubled by unhappy relationships. Her heroin use and her drinking became excessive which caused a rapid deterioration of her health and career. Billie made her last album, *"Lady in Satin"* in 1958. She was barely able to choke out the words as she sang. At the age of 43, she sounded more like a woman of 73. She suffered from cirrhosis of the liver and a host of other ailment attributed to her abuses, yet her last performance was just two months before her death.

After years of abuse to her body she collapsed and fell into a coma on May 31, 1959. Her friend, Frankie Freedom, took her to the hospital by ambulance. Upon arrival to the emergency room, she was left to lay on a stretcher in the hallway, unattended by an overwhelmed hospital staff.

Then after she was admitted, she was beset with more than just health problems. On June 12th, the police raided her hospital room; and arrested her after finding a small amount of heroin. Since Billie was too sick to move, she was under house arrest. The police removed all of her personal belongings, fingerprinted her and took her mugs shots right in her hospital bed.

After suffering a kidney infection the following month, she had heart failure. On July 17th, at 3:10 am Billie Holiday died at the age of 44.

Billie Holiday is interred in St Raymond's Cemetery in the Bronx. She shares a headstone with her mother and the cemetery with Frankie Lymon minus his Teenagers. According to Billie Holiday's biography, her last husband Louis McKay, who was living large on her record royalties, took a long time in putting a marker on her grave. How's that for true love?

St. Raymond's Cemetery
2600 Lafayette Avenue
Bronx, New York
St. Paul's Section, Range 56, Plot 29, Grave 1 & 2
Directions: From the Cross Bronx Expressway (I-295) get off at Lafayette Avenue exit. You'll immediately see the cemetery. If you enter on the Lafayette Avenue entrance follow the road around St Joseph's and make a right at the St. Annes section, then make another immediate right and you should first see St Luke's on your left next to St. Paul's. Park there. Find the sign "Range 66" then count 6 paired rows up and then count 24 tombstones down. And there she is.

Mary Wells
May 13, 1943 - July 26, 1992
Born in Detroit she began signing at the age of 10 in clubs and talent contests. She approached the founder of Motown Records, Berry Gordy, hoping to sell a song and found herself signed as a performer. Wells became Motown's first big star.

Famous for her *"My Guy"* 60's hit, Mary brought a perky optimism to the pop and soul charts. Along with Smokey Robinson, the Supremes, the Temptations and the Four Tops, Wells was part a new sound of black music that found it's way onto the radio and record shelves of white America. It helped to break down the musical segregation of the time. For the first time teenagers of all races were enjoying the black sounds of dating and romance.

Despite the fact that she hit the Top 10 in the pop charts with several hits, she was broke. It was the old story, poor management and an ignorance for the business. Because of her financial dilemma she was forced to continue to perform in clubs and oldie revues, until she became ill with cancer.

HOLIDAY

DEAR MOTHER
SADIE
1896 — 1945

BELOVED WIFE
BILLIE
HOLIDAY
KNOWN AS
"LADY DAY"
BORN APR. 7, 1915
DIED JULY 17, 1959

St. Raymond's Cemetery, Bronx, New York

Mary who had been a heavy smoker for years was diagnosed with cancer. She lost her modest home in Los Angeles when she could not pay the rent. She had no medical insurance and was going broke from the all the bills she had incurred. Her friends came to her rescue, the Washington based Rhythm and Blues Foundation raised more than $50,000 to help pay her medical bills, the *very generous* Diana Ross donated only a mere $15,000 out her many millions, and several other performers also made donations.

Wells underwent surgery in 1990 to try to abate the cancer in her larynx. Afterwards, she embarked on chemotherapy and remained hospitalized for several months. Unfortunately in June 1991, doctors had discovered that the cancer had spread. The next step was an experimental drug regiment. After that failed she resumed the chemotherapy in late 1991.

In 1992, she finally died at the Kenneth Norris Jr. Cancer Center of the University of Southern California. She was 49.

Forest Lawn Memorial Park
1712 S. Glendale Avenue
Glendale, California

For directions to the cemetery see Jean Harlow in the Glamour Girls Chapter. Get a map if you'd like, but don't ask for any celebrity directions. Head to the Freedom Mausoleum. As you walk inside you'll see steps, go downstairs and look for the Columbarium of Patriots. If you face the columbarium, she would be on the right hand wall of niches.

Song Dudes
Nat King Cole
March 17, 1919 - February 15, 1965

He was born Nathaniel Adams Coles in Alabama. Later the family moved from Montgomery, Alabama to a ghetto in the South Side of Chicago. Nathaniel grew up in a home filled with music. His greatest influences were Earl "Fatha" Hines, Jimmie Noone and Art Tatum.

At the age of 12 he studied classical piano and learned to read and write music. Three years later he formed his own band the *"Nat Coles and His Royal Dukes."* They were paid a dollar a night for their efforts. By 1935, Nat was very popular with the jazz club scene. From there he began to play black night clubs earning him a big $16 dollars a night.

In 1938 he formed *"The Nat King Cole Trio;"* this worked out well because the big band sound was quickly becoming a thing of the past and their drumless sound was perfect for smaller clubs. They were able to find work every night for the next two years and their pay increased to $25 a week.

Nat began making a string of hits in 1944, like *"Straighten Up"* and *"Fly Right,"* which both sold a half million copies. The trio toured, were played on the radio and appeared in movies; all of which earned them more money that they could spend.

He kept up his busy schedule until his health began to fail. First he was plagued by bleeding ulcers that put him in the hospital. These attacks were so bad that Nat would throw up blackened blood. Finally surgery was ordered an attempt to correct the problem. Later in September of 1964, more health problems developed. Nat began to look worn out and tired. After a show, he would usually unwind by getting something to eat, having a drink, or catching a lounge act. Instead, exhausted, he would go straight to bed.

His weight became another issue as he grew thinner and thinner. Sparky who took care of Nat's clothes had to constantly take in his pants, or add another hole in his belt so his clothes would fit more snugly.

MARY E. WELLS

1943 - 1992

"OUR LOVING MOTHER"

Forest Lawn Memorial Park, Glendale, California

While on stage in Las Vegas, Nat experienced a burning pain that stabbed him in the chest, so hard that he was almost unable to sing. After the show, he headed for his room. On the way, he felt another agonizing pain. He pushed open the door and fell on the floor. Immediately he called a doctor.

The doctor told Nat that he would not be able to do any more shows for a while. Soon the pains were accompanied by a severe cough. Although Nat had recently had a physical, he did not get a chest x-ray. His doctor arranged for an x-ray right away. The results were bad, he had a tumor on his lung and was given only a couple of months to live. He was put on antibiotics and sent home.

Nat, who was a chain smoker, inhaled three packs of cigarettes a day. When the lung cancer was discovered; it was too late. He checked into St. John's Hospital in Santa Monica. His wife, Maria, was shocked as she walked into his sixth floor room, already he had tubes in his nose and throat.

By the fifth or sixth day, he began to experience horrible pain. The back pains were so strong that he could not hide the discomfort. At one point he began to scream, "Let me die!" His doctor was not there, so the nurses couldn't give Nat a shot without permission.

Nat's wife spoke to the doctor to find out what was going to be done about her husband's condition. He recommended surgery to remove the tumor. Instead Nat opted to go home for Christmas to be with his family, perhaps for the last time.

By time Christmas arrived, Nat was in no condition to leave the hospital. Instead the hospital staff allowed his family to do something it had never done before. They allowed his wife bring his children to the hospital to spend the day with their father. The Sisters at St John's fixed up a room for the family and prepared all the food. Unfortunately Nat was too ill to enjoy it.

On New Year's, Nat was feeling better and was able to come home for two days. Two nurses were assigned, one for the day and one for night. Nat spent most of the time sitting in his room in his rocking chair. Once he got up and walked out to the playhouse where his wife was sitting. He stood there for a few minutes; but he was so weak he could hardly hold his head up. That night he went back to the hospital.

Soon Nat began cobalt treatment for which he had to leave the hospital to go to a special laboratory. Newsmen were constantly taking photos of the emaciated Cole. By now his complexion greyed and his weight dropped from 170 to 120.The cobalt treatments failed to halt the spread of cancer, so the next step was surgery. Doctor's removed Nat's left lung in a three hour operation. Word spread that the surgery was a success.

Two weeks after surgery, doctors while tracing radioactive isotopes through his body, made a dreadful discovery; the cancer had spread to his liver. It had been his misfortune to have the virulent and rapid spreading type of cancer. He now had perhaps a week left to live. A few days later his condition worsened and he was put on the critical list.

Then one Saturday, in one of the inexplicable events that sometimes happen to terminal patients, he awoke and was rather cheerful and feeling much better. He even sat up on the side of the bed to have breakfast.

Sunday was Valentine's Day, and the weather was beautiful. Nat was feeling well enough to go for a ride down by the beach. The staff put Nat in his wife's car along with oxygen equipment and his nurse. They were gone for an hour and a half. Upon their return, the hospital staff was ready with a wheelchair, but Nat said "No, thank you, I can help myself." Finally Nat got in the chair and headed for his room.

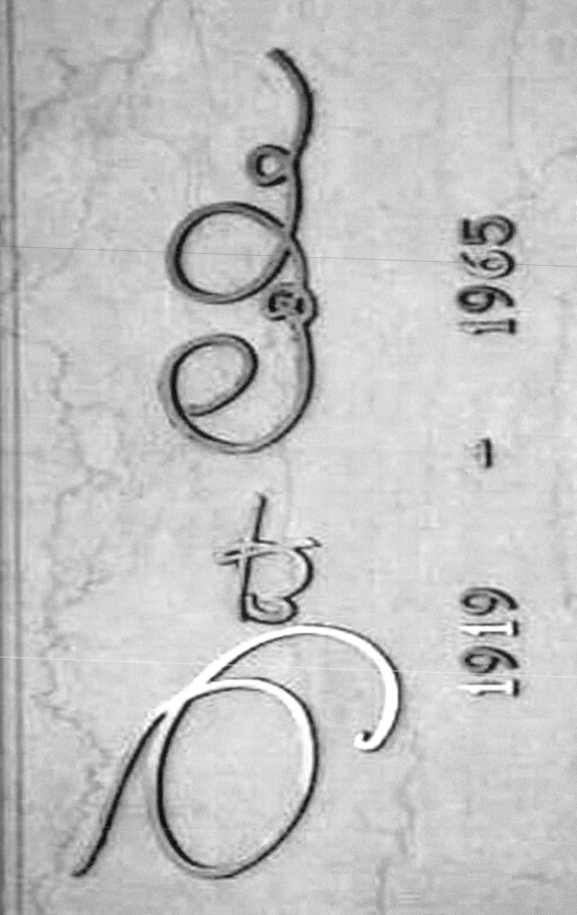

1965

1919

Forest Lawn Memorial Park, Glendale, California

A week later he began to weaken again. The cancer progressed so quickly that he rarely needed medication for the pain. He asked the nurse why he was feeling so weak and she, not wanted to alarm him, told him it was the "medication" and changed the subject. She thought about calling the doctor, but she knew that to call from the phone in his room would only scare him. Besides there was nothing anyone could do.

Nat lay back on the bed once more and began to repeat a name. Because of the lateness of her duty shift, Casey the nurse, had spent little time with Nat, so the name meant nothing to her. Nat said it several times. The name was "Skeez." Although the weakness had almost completely overcome him, Nat's voice, naturally soft, was nevertheless positive.

Realizing that Nat was still alert and lucid, Casey questioned him, "Who do you mean, Nat? I don't know anybody by that name."

"Maria," Nat said. He did not speak again.

He raised up, than lay back once more. Casey spoke to him, and then, believing he no longer understood her, she went to the phone and called the doctor. "I think you had better get over right now." Casey went back to Nat. He was lying on his back, but turned slightly on his right side, with his head facing the door. He drifted away at 5:30 in the morning. He died three months after the diagnosis.

Hundreds of people attended the services at St. James Episcopal Church in Beverly Hills to pay their last respects to Nat. Jack Benny delivered the eulogy.

Forest Lawn Cemetery - Glendale
1712 S. Glendale Avenue
Los Angeles, California
Freedom Mausoleum

For directions to the cemetery see Jean Harlow in the Glamour Girls Chapter.Get a map of the cemetery, but don't ask for any celebrity directions or you'll be asked to leave. Go up the hill on the main road past the Temple of Santa Sabina, stay toward the right onto Cathedral Drive. Turn right on Freedom Drive and continue straight to the end. There are also many signs that will guide you to the Freedom Mausoleum. Go into the mausoleum and turn right. Walk down the hallway and on your left you'll see the Sanctuary of Heritage. He's in the top crypt on the right wall.

Sam Cooke
January 22, 1931 - December 11, 1964

He was born in Clarksdale, Mississippi in 1931. Sam's father was the reverend in their local Baptist Church. So most of the family's time was spent in church, not in the bars or whorehouses that lined the streets of Clarksdale. According to Sam's father, he displayed his talent for singing as a young boy. He would sing to anything, sticks, rocks, or trees.

When the depression arrived the Cook family moved to Chicago where Rev. Cook continued his work with the church. The depression left the family very poor; so whatever cash they had, went to necessities. Sam would perform for commuters at the streetcar stop, for the extra change to help his family out.

Upon graduation from high school, Sam started his own singing group called the *QC's*. Eventually the group got a gig singing live for Chicago's WIND radio station. This gave him the opportunity to record three songs under his pseudonym Dale Cook. These records turned out to be mediocre hits. Finally, he got a big hit with *"You Send Me,"* which stayed on the charts for four months.

With everything looking great, his luck took a turn for the worse on one fateful night. Sam was sitting at the bar (at Martoni's Italian Restaurant in Los Angeles) drinking plenty of Martinis when Lisa Boyer was introduced to him. They had been talking for awhile by the time Sam went to pay the bill. When he opened his wallet, she was quick to notice that he had what looked like $2000 in cash.

As the people he was with headed for their table, Sam continued his conversation with Lisa at a nearby booth. After his friends left to go to a nightclub, Sam said he would meet them later. That would be the last time they would see their friend Sam, alive. Lisa and Sam left Martoni's about 2am, as it was closing. Both hopped into Sam's Ferrari and drove to a hotel in a bad part of town notorious for hookers and drugs.

The events that took place in that hotel room is only known to Sam and Lisa.

Lisa said that Sam brought her to the room against her will and once there he attempted to rape her. She claimed that she tricked Sam into letting her go to the bathroom where she gathered her clothes and ran down the street to call the police. Sam chased her only wearing a overcoat and one shoe. He ran to the manager's office and began to bang on her door, yelling for Lisa. When the manager, Bertha refused to open the door to the crazed man; he began to break it down.

After he gained entrance into the manager's small room he grabbed her wrists and demanded to know where the girl was. She broke free and grabbed a gun off the television and shot at Sam three times. One bullet entered his left armpit and tore through both lungs and pierced his heart. He died sitting upright against the blood splattered wall.

Sam sat unidentified in the morgue for more than six hours after the shooting. The police had no idea who he was. The police never did an initial investigation of the crime scene and simply took the statements of Bertha and Lisa at face value.

There were two funerals held for Sam; one in Chicago and one in Los Angeles which were packed with friends and relatives. In Los Angeles, Sam's widow arrived in Sam's Rolls Royce with his banker and her new boyfriend, Bobby Womack, by her side, who happened to be dressed in Sam's clothes.

Forest Lawn Cemetery - Glendale
1712 S. Glendale Ave
Los Angeles, California
Garden of Honor

For directions to the cemetery see Jean Harlow in the Glamour Girl Chapter.Once in the cemetery ask for a map, but not celebrity locations or you will be asked to leave. Follow the signs to the Freedom Mausoleum, park. To the right of the mausoleum you will see the south Garden of Honor. Sometimes the doors are unlocked or propped open. As you enter look for a large statue with DAVIS on it, that's Sammy Davis Jr. Sam Cooke is on the opposite side.

Harry Chapin
December 7, 1942 - July 16, 1981

Harry was born with music in his blood; his father was a swing band drummer for Tommy Dorsey and Woody Herman. At age 15, Harry started his own group with his other brothers. When the eldest dropped out, their father took his place.The trumpet was Harry's first instrument of choice, but later made the transition to the guitar.

After high school Harry joined the Air Force Academy to study architecture. Later he transferred to Cornell University to study philosophy. While all this was going on he put his music on hold. But when the rise of folk music took hold in Greenwich Village, he drifted back to his first love - music.

Forest Lawn Memorial Park, Glendale, California

His first album, *Chapin Music*, was recorded with his brother and father. The album made little impression on anyone. To get noticed they rented the Village Gate in New York City and played to fans and record executives. Soon their strategy worked and they received a record contract with Elektra.

Chapin's music was mostly folk music; this was at a time when the latest musical trend was ear shattering electric rock. Despite this, he reached his listener by telling stories of the common man. In 1972, he released his first hit single, *"Taxi."* That followed a string of commercially successful albums. His next big hit was *"Cat's in the Cradle."* This was the record that put him on the map, and made him financially secure. But this did not stop him, he embarked on a series of benefit concerts for a variety of causes. He ended up doing approximately 200+ concerts a year, over half of them were for benefits.

On the last day of his life Harry routinely did the things he usually did. When not on the road, his days mostly consisted of returning calls, organizing benefits, and driving into Manhattan to take care of business appointments. After a long day he headed back home to Huntington Bay, Long Island to get ready for a concert that night. He was scheduled to perform at a free outdoor music festival at the Lakeside Theater.

Not long after he entered the Long Island Expressway, he began to suffer severe chest pains. Fearing the worse he attempted to pull his car over. He slowed down to 15 mph and as he was trying to get to the side of the road he sideswiped a car. As he made another attempt, his blue Volkswagen Rabbit was hit from behind by a large truck. The impact sent his car flying down the highway and the sparks from the crushed car ignited the fuel tank. The car burst into flames and finally came to a rest.

The truck driver rushed over to the car to help get it's occupants out. Robert Eggleton, the truck driver suffered extensive burns as he removed Chapin from the burned wreckage. Harry was dead, not from the accident but from a heart attack.

His family and hundreds of fans mourned Harry at his funeral. Harry was then taken to his final resting place, the Huntington Rural Cemetery in Long Island. At another memorial service the week following his death he was eulogized by several state and world leaders. In Congress, nine senators and thirty congressmen, paid tribute to Chapin. His commitment to the many causes raised over five million dollars for the many charities he supported. A final tribute to Harry was the renaming of the Lakeside Theater to the Harry Chapin Lakeside Theater a week after his death.

Huntington Rural Cemetery
555 New York Avenue
Long Island, New York

Directions: Take the L.I.E. (I-495) to exit 49N and drive a good five to eight miles. The cemetery is on your left. As you enter the cemetery drive to the right just past the office. Drive around to the top of the cemetery. You'll see three sections, his rock/tombstone is in the middle section (section 6L) not far off the road.

Jim Croce
January 10, 1943 - September 20, 1973

Jim was born in Philadelphia, where he grew up in a musical household At age four, he would entertain his family for hours. Seeing young Jim's desire to perform, his parents gave him additional encouragement, by sending him to accordion lessons. After becoming proficient, five year old Jimmy took his show on the road; playing for friends and family, church functions and variety shows. At age 16, he opted for a "cooler" instrument, a guitar. So he got his brother's old clarinet, took it to a pawn shop and traded it for a guitar. Immediately, he took lessons on a regular basis.

HARRY CHAPIN
1942 — 1981

OH IF A MAN TRIED
TO TAKE HIS TIME ON EARTH
AND PROVE BEFORE HE DIED
WHAT ONE MAN'S LIFE COULD BE WORTH
I WONDER WHAT WOULD HAPPEN
TO THIS WORLD

Huntington Rural Cemetery, Huntington, New York

When Jim went off to College he was exposed to the talents of Woody Guthrie, Bob Dylan and Lenny Bruce. All of which changed his outlook on music and influenced his future style of performing. At Villanova, he met his wife, Ingrid, who would soon become his singing partner and worked many of the local clubs. Eventually, Jim when on to do solo gigs in Greenwich Village.

Jim got a long term gig at a rough bar called *"Riddle Paddock."* It was here where he was inspired to write many of his future hits. He told humorous stories in between songs to keep the crowd happy, which also kept the fighting down to a minimum. When a fight did break out he was quick to remove his guitar and avoid the punches that flew. That is why he gave up wearing a guitar strap.

In 1971, Jim sent a tape with *"Time In A Bottle," "You Don't Mess Around With Jim,"* and *"Operator"* to producer, Tom West. The producer liked what he heard and asked Jim to come to New York to record his first album, *"Don't Mess Around With Jim."* The album was a success. Jim had a Top ten hit with a single by the same name. Not only did this make Jim popular in clubs and concerts, it also provided an opportunity to make many appearances on the hit 70's television show, *"The Midnight Special."*

Along with fame came schedules and travel. One of Jim's pet peeves were the commercial airlines and their ability for losing luggage. After losing Jim's stuff one too many times, he vowed not to fly commercially anymore and that all his flying would be done by chartered planes.

On September, 1973, Jim and his band had just finished a concert for 2000 students at Norwestern University in Louisiana. As his private plane began to take off, something apparently went wrong, causing the plane to crash into a tree approximately 200 yards away from the runway, killing everyone on board.

Jim's body was brought back to Pennsylvania where he was buried in the Haym Salomon Memorial Park in Frazer.

Haym Salomon Memorial Park
200 Moores Road
Frazer, Pennsylvania
Directions: Take Rt 76 west toward Valley Forge and exit on 26B to Rt. 202 south towards West Chester. From Rt 202 take the first Frazer exit/Conestoga Rd. Go to Phoenixville Pike make a left that will take you to the cemetery. Drive into the cemetery's main entrance and stop at the last path on the right. Get out and walk to a large pine tree on left, just before some small hedges. He's under the tree.

Country and Western
Patsy Cline
September 8, 1932 - March 5, 1963
Born Virginia Hensley in Winchester, Virginia, she was left to grow up in a poor existence due to her father's early departure from the family. Her poverty is what fueled her desire to succeed in her singing career. Virginia's first exposure into show business was doing school plays, singing in church choirs and small beer joints. But this was not enough for the future Patsy, she had to find some way to promote herself.

The opportunity presented itself when Grand ole Opry star, *Wally Fowler and his Oak Ridge Quartet* performed in her town. Virginia bluffed her way backstage and got an audition. Although she received an offer from Roy Acuff, the money was not enough for her to quit her job at Gaunt's Drug Store. Virginia was forced to continued to perform locally and eventually married Gerald Cline. It was he who would later change her name to Patsy.

Finally in 1954, Patsy was asked to sing on the *"Town and Country Radio Show"* where she earned $50 and a million new fans. This was her opportunity to cut a single, *"It Wasn't God Who Made Honky Tonk Angels."* The next month she signed her first record contract.

JIM
CROCE
1943-1973

Haym Salomon Memorial Park, Frazer, Pennsylvania

Her next television stint was on the *Arthur Godfrey's Talent Scout Show*. It was there where she underwent an wardrobe transformation; she quickly exchanged the cowboy garb for evening gowns and cocktail dresses. She sang *"Walkin' After Midnight,"* which sold a mere 750,000 copies. This prompted the record execs to have her launch her first album, *"Patsy Cline."*

Patsy's career was climbing to great heights as she toured extensively. By the end of 1962, she had added two more record albums to her list of successes.

On March, 1963, Patsy had just completed a gig in Kansas City, to benefit the family of disc jockey Jack Call, who was killed in a car accident. Patsy mostly traveled with her manager, Randy Hughes, in his private plane. They intended to fly back to Nashville the next day, but storms postponed the trip for two days. Dottie West who was traveling by car, offered Patsy a ride; anxious to get to Nashville, she accepted. Finally as the weather improved, Patsy changed her mind and opted for the plane ride with her manager. Apparently the weather hadn't cleared, they were in the eye of the storm and the worse was yet to come.

As they flew the four person Piper Comanche plane they decided to stop in Dyersburg, Tennessee, to refuel and grab something to eat. Randy telephoned his wife in Nashville and she told him that the weather was fine. She too was unaware that they were in the eye of the storm and that they would be heading straight towards the worst of it.

The plane took off at 6:07 pm and within moments they were right in the middle of the storm. The Randy was not instrument trained, so when he lost all visibility he had no idea where they were heading. Somewhere above Camden, Tennessee, they started taking a nosedive. Investigators speculate that Hughes was trying to put the plane down on a nearby highway. Unfortunately he hit some trees and crashed in a hollow in a wooded area called Fatty Bottom, just west of Camden.

In an instant, the crash site was littered by broken guitars, boots, and Patsy's handmade dresses. Patsy's travel clock was found next to her; it stopped at 7:20pm at the moment of impact. They had only seventy miles to go, before they would have arrived at Nashville.

Patsy's body was brought back to her home for viewing in her living room. A prayer service for the victims was held on Thursday, March 7th at 5pm. Twenty five thousand people paid their respects. She was buried the Sunday after, in Winchester, Virginia on March 10th in Shenandoah, Memorial Park.

On July 6, 1996, a giant stone was placed at the crash site as a memorial to the victims. Despite all her success, Patsy seemed to have a black cloud hanging over her. She endured two serious auto accidents and finally a plane crash that claimed her life.

When I visited her grave, her tombstone was filled with a million pennies. It seems that despite her untimely departure thirty-seven years ago, she is still quite popular world wide. Along with the pennies there were flowers and gifts left by people in different languages and from different countries.

Shenandoah Memorial Park

Hwy 522

Winchester, Virginia

Directions: From Hwy 50 take 522 south. Drive about tow miles and before the light, make a right into first entrance into the cemetery. Turn right onto the first road and park. Look for the "Al hogan" memorial bench on your left. Her flat bronze marker is located about 10 feet from the road near the bench. Also there are always things left by fans, i.e., pennies, flowers, cards, balloons, etc. this alone will help you find her.

Dottie West
October 11, 1932 - September 4, 1991

Dottie's life had been a series of ups and downs, starting with a rape that was committed by her father as a young girl. She lived in abject poverty as she grew up, eating on lard lids and drinking out of tin cans. She quickly sang her way out of poverty and into stardom, even sharing billing with Patsy Cline on her last performance. In the 60's, Dottie became famous for her *"Country Sunshine"* song that she sang for a Coca-Cola commercial. She appeared on several television shows including roles on *"The Love Boat," "Hee Haw"* and *"Family Feud."*

In an *"Entertainment Tonight"* interview, she announced that she was broke. The I.R.S. was attempting to collect $1.3 million dollars from her. The bank foreclosed on her mansion, the one that appeared on *"The Lifestyles of the Rich and Famous,"* and evicted her. Dottie had become another star to fall victim of poor management.

In March, 1991, she was under investigation for non-disclosure of hidden property. The authorities arrested her, confiscated her possessions and sold them at an auction. In an attempt to salvage some of her possessions she bided on whatever she could afford. Some fans had bid on some of her expensive doll collections and upon winning them, gave them back to her.

On August 30, 1991, Dottie left her condo to perform at the Grand Ol Opry. Unlike most stars of her caliber she could not afford a limousine to get her to a performance. Her only mode of transportation was a three year old car that Kenny Rogers had given to her when her car was repossessed. When she got into the car to leave, it wouldn't start. A neighbor helped get it started and while en route it stalled. Wearing her stage costume, she flagged down a passing car for a ride. By chance it was the neighbor who had helped start her car earlier. He was passing that way and gave her a ride. As they sped to the show, her neighbor lost control of his car on the exit and the car sailed through the air for approximately 80 feet before hitting an embankment. They were rushed to Vanderbilt Medical Center. Her 81 year old good Samaritan made a full recovery and she eventually died. Her liver was extremely lacerated in which she needed 35 pints of blood to keep her alive. Later she endured two more operations, where on the second she died of heart failure. She was only 58

She was laid out at Woodlawn Cemetery where she received floral arrangements from virtually every country music star. Hundreds of mourners jammed Christ Church on Old Hickory Boulevard in Nashville.

Mountain View Cemetery
Spring Street
McMinnville, Tennessee
Directions: I-55 to Main Street to Spring Street all the way down the cemetery on your right. Go into the 1st cemetery gate, go to the fork in the road, stay straight look for the marker, "WARREN," "GILLIS" on your right hand side she is next to "Marsh."

Tammy Wynette
May 5, 1942 - April 6, 1998

A beautician turned country singer, she is remembered for the song *"Stand By Your Man,"* which took her only 20 minutes to write. Her last record that she recorded was *"One,"* a duet with her ex-husband George Jones. Her last performance was on March 5, 1998, in Plant City, Florida, where she was a last minute replacement for Loretta Lynn who had became ill.

Shenandoah Memorial Park, Winchester, Virginia

According to her husband, George Richey, she was sitting on the sofa with him when Tammy died. The coroner report states, however, that she was alone and discovered by her maid. Her body was taken to the Medical Examiner's office, and examined the next morning. Tammy's personal physician, Dr. Wallace Marsh flew in from Pennsylvania and contacted the Medical Examiner's office and related that he had been treating Tammy for several years for a variety of ailments, which included intestinal dysmotility with numerous complications, most serious of which were problems with adequate nutrition and blood clotting. His opinion was that she died of pulmonary embolus or a clot in the lung. The Examiner agreed and did not perform an autopsy.

One of her daughters, Jackie Daly, had stopped by to see Tammy at noon on April 6th, and found her asleep on the sofa. She stayed a few minutes and asked Richey to let her mother know that she had stopped by. Daly went out to dinner and returned home only to find a message on her machine saying that her mother had died. She went straight to her mother's house and at 9:30pm, found Tammy still on the sofa, covered and in a fetal position. "People were coming in and out, drinking coffee and smoking." she said.

A private funeral service was held early in the day of April 9th at Woodlawn Cemetery in Nashville. Tammy was laid out in one of her stage dresses, in the Dogwood Room at the funeral home. Her funeral was attended by many of country music's greats. A public service was held later that day at the former home of the Grand Ol Opry, The Ryman Auditorium in downtown Nashville, where Naomi Judd eulogized her.

In December, 1998 the Medical Examiner received letters from each of Tammy's three daughters expressing their concern over the cause of death of their mother and requested that she be exhumed and an autopsy performed. During a meeting at the coroner's office they expressed concerns about narcotics administered to their mother for control of pain and the sequence of events that transpired the day she passed away. The coroner contacted her personal physician who did not list the drugs she was administered, giving only a minimal amount of information concerning the possible causes that led to her death.

The daughter's filed a $50 million dollar wrongful death lawsuit against Tammy's husband and her doctor as well. Tammy's husband requested that her body be disinterred and an autopsy performed to quell any future allegations that the daughters might present. Exactly one year and eight days later Tammy was removed from her crypt and an autopsy was performed. The Medical Examiner found nothing suspicious, she had died of right-sided heart failure. He also stated that the relative contributions to her death were from the underlying natural diseases. The medications that might have been present in her body at the time of her death could not be ascertained, due to the embalming fluid's distortion of the test's results. The case was then closed and she was put back into her crypt.

As a result the daughters dropped their lawsuit against George Richey, but continued to sue Tammy's physician for prescribing too many drugs.

Woodland Memorial Park
660 Thompson Lane
Nashville, Tennessee
Directions: From I-65 exit at the Thompson Lane exit go east the cemetery will be on your left. Go to the mausoleum, it's open until 9pm. Walk into the mausoleum through the door by the phone. If you make each section, a section between two pillars, count 10 sections down on your right side passing a praying girl statue. And there is her crypt covered with mementos from loved ones.

DOROTHY MARIE MARSH
WEST

OCT. 11, 1932

SEPT. 4, 1991

OUR COUNTRY SUNSHINE

BELOVED DAUGHTER
WIFE AND MOTHER

MARSH

Mountain View Cemetery, McMinnville, Tennessee

Woodland Memorial Park, Nashville, Tennessee

JOHN CASSAVETES 1929 ~ 1989

Westwood Memorial Park, Los Angeles, California

Chapter 19: CUT! THAT'S A WRAP!
John Cassavettes
December 9, 1929 - February 3, 1989

Cassavetes was born in New York City, the son of Greek immigrants. As a youth he was a film buff and studied acting at the New York Academy of Dramatic Arts. He finally landed a bit part in the film "*Taxi*" and won the lead as a brooding young bullfighter in a dramatic vignette "*Omnibus,*" a television show.

After acting in films and television, he turned to directing. He started with the experimental "*Shadows*" in 1960, about a black girl living in New York with her two brothers. Shot on a shoestring, the film had no script and was improvised by a cast of Cassavetes' proteges.

Despite his many successful directing ventures he referred to himself as a professional actor and an amateur director. His last film, was Cassavetes' most commercial effort and the favorite of both him and his wife Gena Rowlands, its star. Cassavetes said that he had seen it 30 times and could not look at it any more because it was "too powerful an experience."

Cassavetes who was an extremely heavy drinker for many years destroyed his liver. For the last three years of his life he had been in poor health. He was admitted to Cedars-Sinai Medical Center where he died on February 3rd at 10:00 am of complications of cirrhosis of the liver. He was only 59. A private funeral was held at Westwood Memorial Park, where he was buried.

Westwood Memorial Park
1218 Glendon Avenue
Los Angeles, California

For directions to the cemetery see Marilyn Monroe in the Glamour Girls Chapter. As you enter the cemetery you'll see a little grassy section to your left with a couple of mausoleums. He's there in that area, not far from Mel Torme.

Cecil B. DeMille
August 12, 1881 - December 25, 1959

Cecil was born in the small town of Ashfield, Massachusetts, where his family was vacationing for the summer. His parents Henry Churchill and Beatrice DeMille were teachers who later wrote plays. When Cecil's father died, his mother supported the family by opening a school for girls and a theatrical company. This theatrical company later became a spring board for a career that would make Cecil very famous and very rich.

Too young to enlist in the Spanish-American War, he followed his brother William to the New York Academy of Dramatic Arts, making his stage debut in 1900. There he met the woman to whom he would be married to for sixty years. He had frequently told friends that he fell in love with her feet. This mild form of a foot fetish grew as he became older. It became common knowledge to any self respecting actress who required a role in one of his films, to make sure that at the very beginning of any casting, that he looked at her lovely feet.

For twelve years he was actor/manager of his mother's company. This gave him the background needed for his next venture. In 1913, he, Jesse.L.Lasky and Sam Goldwyn formed the Lasky film company, which later became Paramount. The next year, they produced the successful six reeler, "*The Squaw Man*" their first Hollywood film. He is also credited with championing the switch from shorts to feature length films. Some have also acknowledged the fact that he made Hollywood the motion picture capital of the world.

During his career he produced and directed seventy films and was involved in many more. His final picture was "*The Ten Commandments,* " it was there that he began to suffer heart problems. On December 9th, he suffered a heart attack which left him feeling very weak. Not letting a little thing like a heart attack interfere with his schedule, he continued to work until he was in great pain and unable to do so.While returning from a trip to New York he was in worse pain and felt very close to death. His speech was strangled as he sought breath.

Hollywood Forever Cemetery, Hollywood, California

Usually each Christmas Eve he would personally distribute checks to his employees. Despite his failing health he came into the office. For those who dropped by, he offered a glass of wine. He had a feeling that this was perhaps the last Christmas he would ever see.

At five, the next morning, Cecil had a final heart seizure which he did not survive. His wife, Constance, who had become somewhat senile, had not recognized him in the previous weeks, and was not informed of his death. Cecil was 77 years old.

The funeral was held on January 23th, at St Stephen's Episcopal Church. After the services he was interred next to his brother William at the Hollywood Forever Cemetery.

Hollywood Forever Cemetery
6000 Santa Monica Blvd.
Hollywood, California

For directions to the cemetery see Janet Gaynor in the Glamour Girls Chapter. Once you enter the cemetery make a left and travel to Section 8 the only section with a lake. As you reach the corner of section 8 and Midland Avenue, don't turn, but do park. His crypt is by the road, you can't miss it.

John Huston
August 5, 1906 - August 28, 1987

His loves were hunting, drinking, carousing and writing. He was an intense man, a "man's man" with a great attraction to women; after all he was married five times

Before arriving in Hollywood to become a script writer he was a newspaper reporter. And before that he had a few stints as a vaudeville entertainer. Huston later became a brilliant film maker. His "*Prizzi's Honor*" won Oscars for both his daughter, actress Angelica Huston, and his father, Walter Huston. John found his niche in directing classics such as "*The Maltese Falcon,*" "*The Treasure of the Sierra Madre,*" "*The African Queen*" and many more. An intellectual man, he produced several of these films from well known literary works.

He was a man of great charisma and occasional cruelty. The harder a film was to make and the more rugged the shooting conditions, the happier he seemed to be.

During his life Huston abused his body with tons of cigarettes and gallons of booze. He spent the later part of his life as a recluse living with a companion in some remote village in Mexico. Eventually he died of acute emphysema. He was 81.

His tombstone is most beautiful for a little marker. It is pink marble imported from Ireland and engraved in gold.

Hollywood Forever
6000 Santa Monica Blvd.
Hollywood, California

For directions to the cemetery see Janet Gaynor in the Glamour Girl chapter. As you enter the cemetery you can shell out $5 or just follow my directions. Make the first possible left onto Lakeview Avenue. When you get to section 8 (the only section with a lake) make a right at Midland Avenue and park. Get out and walk towards the mausoleum and you'll bump into him.

Hollywood Forever Cemetery, Hollywood, California

JOHN HUSTON
1906 – 1987

BELOVED MOTHER
RHEA HUSTON
1882 – 1938

David O. Selznick
May 10, 1902 - June 22, 1965

He was born into show business; his father was producer Lewis Selznick. David rose to the top on his own merit. His first film was based on a book his father had read to him as a child, *"Little Lord Fauntleroy"* (1936).

Selznick was used to having his own way and frequently ordered people around. It never failed to surprise him when people objected to his abusive treatment. Even his psychoanalyst, Dr May Romm, terminated him after a year of Selznick's sleeping through their sessions in her office. Often he would then show up at her door at midnight. His wife, Irene, daughter of Louis B. Mayer, sat up one night in bed and announced, "The jig's up," explaining that she was leaving him. Ingrid Bergman quit after their first meeting when he demanded she change her name and have her teeth and eyebrows fixed. The first thing he told her when meeting her for the first time was, "God! Take off your shoes!" making reference to her height of five feet, eight inches.

Many of his actors, however, did put up with his abuses because they knew that they would eventually end up in one of his many fine pictures. He had a knack for discovering many and making them into colossal stars. One of whom was Jennifer Jones, a star he later married in 1949. In order to further her career he needed to liquify some of his assets to purchase suitable vehicles for her. While at his attorney's office making the necessary transactions, he collapsed of a heart attack and died.

Forest Lawn Memorial Park
1712 South Glendale Avenue
Los Angeles, California

For direction to the cemetery see Jean Harlow in the Glamour Girls Chapter. As you enter the cemetery ask for a map but don't ask for any directions to celebrity graves. David O. Selznick is located in the Great Mausoleum which is open only to property owners and their guests. If you are invited go to the Sanctuary of Trust, he is located in his own alcove with SELZNICK located above the doorway.

Darryl F. Zanuck
September 5, 1902 - December 22, 1979

He was the only early movie mogul who did not escape Europe for a brighter future, he was born in Wahoo, Nebraska. Darryl's father was a roguish gambling man and his mother was too preoccupied with a string of lovers to give him a normal childhood. He was raised predominately by his grandfather who taught the young Zanuck horsemanship and how to hunt. He regaled the young boy with stories of his youth; when he was an engineer who helped build the Transcontinental Canadian Pacific railroad. While building the railroad, he fought off Indians receiving no less than 21 arrow wounds.

At the age of 14, he enlisted in the U.S. Army to fight in World War I. He was posted to France as a private in the 37th "Buckeye" Division from Ohio, an outfit that had taken many casualties in battle During that time, several of his letters that were sent home were published in his hometown paper by his grandfather.

Zanuck's talent was the ability to find stories that could be translated into motion pictures. He was also gifted as being a fine editor, which served him well in saving several films from disaster.

Forest Lawn Memorial Park, Glendale, California

His first writing attempts were that of a book with four stories. These stories were indicative of the talents Zanuck possessed. One was a Western adventure, another was a musical, "*Alexander's Ragtime Band,*" and the third concerned a mute Chinese man who witnesses a murder. All of these stories carried a common thread, they romanticized the struggles of life.. He was only 23 and on his way as a studio writer. But many of his stories went to "the dogs," for the films of his favorite dog, "Rin Tin Tin."

His last major movie was "*The Longest Day*" which was made in 1962 for 20th Century Fox. The budget was $8.5 million and the cast was just as huge with the likes of Wayne, Fonda, Eddie Albert, Mitchum, Robert Ryan, Peter Lawford, Fabian, Connery, Burton and many more.

Eventually Zanuck lost control of 20th Century Fox and suffered several strokes before his death in 1979. At his funeral, following his instructions, there were no death marches. Instead, the theme from his favorite movie, "The Longest Yard" was played over and over again.

Westwood Memorial Park
1218 Glendon Avenue
Los Angeles, California

For directions to the cemetery see Marilyn Monroe in the Glamour Girls Chapter.As you enter the cemetery make your first left and park. Walk to the north wall, his huge bronze plaque is 6 rows down towards the center. Near a large tree.

DARRYL FRANCIS ZANUCK

BORN - WAHOO, NEBRASKA, SEPTEMBER 5, 1902

PASSED ON - PALM SPRINGS, CALIFORNIA, DECEMBER 22, 1979

CO-FOUNDER, PRESIDENT AND PRODUCER OF 20TH CENTURY FOX STUDIO. DOCTOR OF HUMANITIES, UNIVERSITY OF NEBRASKA, LINCOLN, NEBRASKA. MADE SO FEW YEARS RECEIVING THE HIGHEST DEGREE IN HIS LIFETIME. RECEIVED SUCH A HOST OF DEGREES, DIPLOMAS AND AWARDS FROM ALL OVER THE WORLD, THAT IT IS IMPOSSIBLE TO STATE THEM ALL. PRIVATE WORLD WAR I OVERSEAS, 14 YEARS OLD. WORLD WAR II COLONEL, ACTIVE DUTY OVERSEAS, U.S. SIGNAL CORP, ALGIERS. LISTED BELOW ARE A FEW OF THE SERVICE RIBBONS AND DECORATIONS HE WAS PROUDLY AUTHORIZED TO WEAR: VICTORY MEDAL (WWI): MEDAL OF FRENCH LEGION OF HONOR WITH ROUGE ROSETTE (WWII): ASIATIC PACIFIC CAMPAIGN RIBBONS AND EUROPEAN-AFRICA-MIDDLE EASTERN CAMPAIGN RIBBONS.

A MAN WHO USED HIS IMAGINATIVE-CREATIVE GENIUS TO DELIVER INSPIRATION THROUGH HIS CELEBRATED MOTION PICTURES. HE IMPARTED A LIFETIME MESSAGE OF DECENCY, LOVE, PATRIOTISM, JUSTICE, EQUALITY AND HOPE THROUGHOUT THE NATION AND THE WORLD. BELOVED HUSBAND, FATHER, GRANDFATHER AND GREAT-GRANDFATHER. I LOVE YOU, DADDY - YOU WILL NEVER BE FORGOTTEN.

- DARRYLYN

Westwood Memorial Park, Los Angeles, California

About the Author

Elaine McCarthy was born and raised in New York and then later lived in various parts of the country. She attended and graduated from Florida Atlantic University where she earned a Bachelor's of Fine Arts with a minor in English. After graduation, she returned to her native New York were she taught High School English in the South Bronx. There she published the school newspaper and yearbook, creating a yearbook class with a curriculum that she incorporated as an English requirement.

Although this is her first book, it is not the first time she has had something published. At age 7, she sent in an idea for a comic to Dale Hale who draws the "Figments" cartoons. He liked it so much that he had it published.

She now lives in California with her husband, three daughters, and their Doberman. When she is not hunting for new graves, she does freelance writing for various publications. She is already working on her next book, "Morbid Curiosity: Celebrity Tombstones Across America, Volume 2." Eventually she would like to write a European version.

Acknowledgments

Special thanks to friends Regina and John who lent me the use of their garage to print up my photos and store my stuff while we traveled. Thanks to all those who helped me on the road, you know who you are, if not check the corresponding stories and you'll find your name. Thanks to friends Anne and Gail for help on some grave locations, after I misplaced some of my notes. Thanks to the San Luis Obispo Arroyo Grande Library for their help and resources for some of the research that went into this book and for not always adhering to their "no two hours back-to-back" policy for the internet.

Bibliography

A variety of obituaries from the New York Times and Los Angeles Times

Bette Davis : An Intimate Memoir / Roy Moseley. New York : D.I. Fine, c1990.Joan Crawford : A Biography. /Thomas, Bob, Simon and Schuster, c1978.If This Was Happiness : A Biography of Rita Hayworth / Barbara Leaming. New York : Viking, c1989.Jayne Mansfield : a biography, /Mann, May Drake Publishers, c1973.Crypt 33 : The Saga of Marilyn Monroe-- The Final Word / Milo Speriglio and Adela Gregory. Secaucus, N.J. : Carol Pub. Group, c1993.Platinum Girl : The Life and Legends of Jean Harlow / Eve Golden. New York : Abbeville Press, c1991.Sal Mineo : His Life, Murder, and Mystery / H. Paul Jeffers. EDITION 1st ed. New York : Carrol & Graf, c2000

Moe Howard and the Three Stooges : The Pictorial Biography of the Wildest Trio in the History of American Entertainment / by Moe Howard. Secaucus (N.J.) : Citadel Press, c1977

Peter Lawford : The Man Who Kept The Secrets / James Spada. New York : Bantam Books, c1991.Everybody Loves Somebody Sometime (Especially Himself) : The Story of Dean Martin and Jerry Lewis. Hawthorn Books, 1974.All The Way : A Biography of Frank Sinatra / Michael Freedland. London : Weidenfeld and Nicolson, c1997.Erma Bombeck : A Life In Humor / Susan Edwards. EDITION 1st ed.New York : Avon Books, c1997.Lost Friendships : A Memoir of Truman Capote, Tennessee Williams,and others / Donald Windham.New York : Morrow, c1987

By Force Of Will : The Life and Art of Ernest Hemingway / Scott Donaldson.Viking Press, c1977

Southern Daughter : The Life of Margaret Mitchell / Darden Asbury Pyron.New York : Oxford University Press, c1991

America's Queen : A Life of Jacqueline Kennedy Onassis / by Sarah Bradford,.New York : Viking, 2000.The Estate of Jacqueline Kennedy Onassis : April 23-26, 1996. New York : Sotheby's, [1996]Jacqueline Kennedy Onassis : A Portrait of Her Private Years / Lester David.IMPRINT Secaucus : Carol Pub. Group, c1994.Love Affair : A Memoir of Jackson Pollack [i.e. Pollock].Kligman, Ruth.IMPRINT New York : Morrow, c1974

Andy Warhol : Heaven and Hell Are Just One Breath Away! late paintings and related works, 1984-1986 / essay by Charles Stuckey ; foreword by Vincent Fremont ; afterword by John Richardson.IMPRINT New York : Gagosian Gallery : Rizzoli, 1992.Andy Warhol, 1928-1987 : Commerce Into Art / Klaus Honnef. IMPRINT Koln, West Germany : Benedikt Taschen Verlag, c1990.Forever Lucy : The Life of Lucille Ball / by Joe Morella and Edward Z. Epstein.IMPRINT Secaucus, N.J. : L. Stuart, c1986

The Great One : The Life and Legend of Jackie Gleason / William A. Henry III.IMPRINT New York : Doubleday, c1992.How Sweet It Is : the Jackie Gleason Story / by James Bacon. IMPRINT New York : St. Martin's Press, c1985

Jackie Gleason : An Intimate Portrait of the Great One / W.J. Weatherby.IMPRINT New York : Pharos Books, 1992.Fred Allen : His Life and Wit / Robert Taylor. IMPRINT Boston : Little, Brown, c1989.This Laugh Is On Me : The Phil Silvers Story / Phil Silvers, with Robert Saffron.Prentice-Hall, c1973.Bogie : The Biography of Humphrey Bogart / Introduction by Lauren Bacall. New American Library, 1966

James Cagney : A Celebration / by Richard Schickel. Boston : Little, Brown, c1985

Capone : The Life and World of Al Capone / by John Kobler. 1st Da Capo Press ed.The Legacy of Al Capone : Portraits and Annals of Chicago's Public Enemies. Putnam, 1975

The Don : The Life and Death of Sam Giancana / William Brashler. Harper & Row, c1977.Little

Man : Meyer Lansky and The Gangster Life / Robert Lacey.Boston : Little, Brown, c1991.The Last Testament of Lucky Luciano / Charles "Lucky" Luciano, Martin A. Gosch and Richard Hammer. Little, Brown, 1975.Case Closed : Lee Harvey Oswald and The Assassination of JFK / Gerald L. Posner.EDITION 1st ed. New York : Random House, c1993.Lee : A Portrait of Lee Harvey Oswald / by his brother, Robert L.Oswald, with Myrick and Barbara Land. Coward-McCann, 1967

Legend : The Secret World of Lee Harvey Oswald / Edward Jay Epstein.[New York] : Reader's Digest Press, c1978.Dallas Justice : The Real Story of Jack Ruby and His Trial / by Melvin M. Belli and Maurice C. Carroll.McKay, 1964.Trial of Jack Ruby / by John Kaplan and Jon R. Waltz.Macmillan, 1965.Montgomery Clift : A Biography / Patricia Bosworth. New York : Harcourt, Brace, Jovanovich, c1978.Ladd, The Life, The Legend, The Legacy of Alan Ladd : A Biography/ by Beverly Linet.New York : Arbor House, c1979.

The Answer Is God : The Inspiring Personal Story of Dale Evans and Roy Rogers.McGraw-Hill, 1955.Abbott and Costello in Hollywood / Bob Furmanek and Ron Palumbo.New York : Perigee Books, c1991.The Abbott & Costello Story /Cox, Stephen Cumberland Press 1997

George Burns : In His Own Words / compiled and edited by Herb Fagen.New York : Carroll & Graf Publishers, 1996

George Burns and The Hundred-Year Dash / Martin Gottfried.,New York : Simon And Schuster, c1996.Clark Gable : A Personal Portrait / by Kathleen Gable.Englewood Cliffs, N.J. : Prentice-Hall, c1961

Clark Gable : A Biography / by Warren Harris. New York : Harmony Books, 2002.The Clark Gable and Carole Lombard Murder Case / George Baxt. EDITION 1st ed.IMPRINT New York : St. Martin's Press, 1997

Hollywood's Golden Era, Leading Ladies [videorecording (VHS)] / MPI Home Video.IMPRINT [S.l.] : Maljack Productions, c1988.The Boss : J. Edgar Hoover and the Great American Inquisition / Athan G. Theoharis and John Stuart Cox. Philadelphia : Temple University Press, c1988.From the Secret Files of J. Edgar Hoover / edited with commentaryby Athan Theoharis.IMPRINT Chicago : I.R. Dee, c1991.J. Edgar Hoover, Sex, and Crime : An Historical Antidote / Athan Theoharis. Chicago : Ivan R. Dee, 1995.Charles Boyer : The Reluctant Lover / Larry Swindell. Garden City, N.Y. : Doubleday, c1983.Bing Crosby : The Hollow Man / by Donald Shepherd and Robert F. Slatzer.New York : St. Martin's Press, 1981.Bing Crosby : The Illustrated Biography / Michael Freedland. London : Chameleon Books, 1998.Brother Sam : The Short Spectacular Life of Sam Kinison / Bill Kinison with Steve Delsohn.EDITION 1st ed.IMPRINT New York : Morrow, c1994.Escape King : The Story of Harry Houdini / John Ernst and Stefan Martin.Prentice-Hall, c1975.The Life and Many Deaths of Harry Houdini / Ruth Brandon.EDITION 1st U.S. ed.IMPRINT New York : Random House, c1993

Kovacsland : A Biography of Ernie Kovacs / by Diana Rico.San Diego : Harcourt Brace Jovanovich, c1990

Nothing In Moderation : A Biography of Ernie Kovacs. Drake Publishers, 1975.Liberace : An Autobiography.New York : Putnam, 1973.Liberace : The True Story / by Bob Thomas. New York : St. Martin's Press, c1987

Finch, Bloody Finch : A Life of Peter Finch / by Elaine Dundy.New York : Holt, Rinehart, and Winston, 1980

Peter Finch : A Biography / by Trader Faulkner; foreword by Liv Ullmann. Taplinger Pub. Co., 1979.An Affair To Remember : The Remarkable Love Story of Katharine Hepburn and Spencer Tracy / Christopher Andersen.EDITION 1st ed. New York : William Morrow and Co., c1997.Damned in Paradise : The Life of John Barrymore / John Kobler.New York : Atheneum,

1977.Doug and Mary : A Biography of Douglas Fairbanks and Mary Pickford / by Gary Carey.IMPRINT New York : E. P. Dutton, c1977

Errol Flynn : A Memoir / by Earl Conrad. New York : Dodd, Mead, c1978.Errol Flynn : The Untold Story / Charles Higham. Doubleday, 1980.Mary Pickford, America's Sweetheart / by Scott Eyman. New York, N.Y. : D.I. Fine, c1990.Mary Pickford and Douglas Fairbanks : The Most Popular Couple TheWorld Has Ever Known / by Booton Herndon.Norton, c1977.The Secret Life of Tyrone Power / by Hector Arce. New York : Morrow, 1979.Tyrone Power : The Last Idol / by Fred Lawrence Guiles.Garden City, N.Y. : Doubleday, c1979

Duet in Diamonds : The Flamboyant Saga of Lillian Russell and Diamond Jim Brady in America's Gilded Age. Putnam, 1972.Magic of Rudolph Valentino / Mackenzie, Norman A., with a foreword by S. George Ullman.London : Research Pub. Co., 1974.Traps, The Drum Wonder : The Life of Buddy Rich / Mel Torme.New York : Oxford University Press, c1991.

All shook up! : The Life and Death of Elvis Presley / by Barry Denenberg.EDITION 1st ed.New York : Scholastic Press, 2001.Don't Ask Forever : My Love Affair With Elvis : A Washington Woman's Secret Years With Elvis Presley / as told by Joyce Bovato William Conrad Nowels.New York : Kensington Books, c1994

Buddy Holly : A Biography / Ellis Amburn.EDITION 1st ed.New York : St. Martin's Press, 1995.Billie Holiday / Bud Kliment.New York : Chelsea House Publishers, c1990The Legendary Ladies of Rock & Roll [videorecording (VHS)]New York : Home Box Office, c1987.You Send Me : The Life and Times of Sam Cooke / Daniel Wolff with S.R. Crain ... [et al.].EDITION 1st ed.New York : W. Morrow, c1995.Jim Croce : The Feeling Lives On / by Linda Jacobs.St. Paul : EMC Corp., 1976.I Fall To Pieces : The Music and The Life of Patsy Cline / Mark Bego. EDITION 1st ed.IMPRINT Holbrook, Mass. : Adams Pub., c1995

Tammy Wynette : A Daughter Recalls Her Mother's Tragic Life and Death / Jackie Daly with Tom Carter., New York : G.P. Putnam's, c2000.